Reconsidering Shakespeare's 'Lateness'

Reconsidering Shakespeare's 'Lateness'

Studies in the Last Plays

By

Xing Chen

Cambridge
Scholars
Publishing

Reconsidering Shakespeare's 'Lateness': Studies in the Last Plays

By Xing Chen

This book first published 2015

Cambridge Scholars Publishing

Lady Stephenson Library, Newcastle upon Tyne, NE6 2PA, UK

British Library Cataloguing in Publication Data
A catalogue record for this book is available from the British Library

ISBN (10): 1-4438-7236-9
ISBN (13): 978-1-4438-7236-2

For my parents

CONTENTS

ACKNOWLEDGEMENTS

I would like to express my deepest gratitude to Greg Walker, whose invaluable advice guided me through my research and writing process. Through discussions with him on the subject of Renaissance drama and Shakespeare in general and this book in particular, I have gained a better understanding of my research topic as well as further insight into academic research. I cannot thank Greg enough for all the kind help and encouragement he has given me.

I am grateful to David Salter and Peter Smith, who read an earlier draft of this book and gave me valuable feedback. For various acts of friendship and intellectual stimulation, I am indebted to Xi Zhao, Xin Shen, Yan Wang, and Chunbao Liu; and for unfailing moral support, my parents. I should also like to express my thanks to Cambridge Scholars Publishing for accepting and publishing this book.

And finally, of course, thank you Master Shakespeare for your genius. Thank you for producing these plays which, in addition to being a joy to watch and to read through, present a wealth of research possibilities for a student of English Literature today.

X. C.

INTRODUCTION

Towards the end of his career, Shakespeare wrote a series of plays which modern scholarship tends to consider as a distinctive group. C. L. Barber and Richard Wheeler, surveying his career, observe that

> [i]n all of Shakespeare's development, there is no change in dramatic style so striking as that between the final tragedies and the late romances. (298)

This striking change in dramatic style is manifested in noticeable differences in the plays' generic affiliation, thematic concerns and dramatic style from those of the playwright's previous works. These last plays apparently share a thematic interest in separation and reunion, loss and restoration, and repentance and forgiveness. Their plots all head towards tragedy but end, at least in form, happily. Yet their characterisation seems to show "not greater artistic maturity, but less" (Edwards 1). Their verse style is often considered "too difficult, too knotty, and for some too self-indulgent on Shakespeare's part" (Shapiro 286). That these manifestly different plays were produced in succession during Shakespeare's last active years as a playwright adds to the sense of their standing apart from the other works in the canon.

This striking degree of apparent homogeneity in composition, especially when taken in conjunction with the plays' seemingly sudden departure from the mode and style of the great tragedies, has long aroused scholarly interest in how these works came about. Speculation and theories are many and varied on why Shakespeare switched from tragedy to a genre which, for want of a better tag, is now vaguely referred to as "romance" or "tragicomedy"; why he concentrated in these plays on the idea of family, with an emphasis on the qualities of forgiveness and reconciliation; why he returned to the "archaic" sources of his earliest comedies to produce these, in Ben Jonson's words, "mouldy tales"; and why he developed a style that is marked by its "verbal obscurity" and "poetic difficulty" (McDonald, *Late* 32). In short, considerable research has gone into unravelling why, late in his career, Shakespeare wrote these plays, a question, as Philip Edwards has pointed out, "inextricably intertwined with the question, 'What is the significance of these plays?'"(1).

Because the plays were written at the very end of Shakespeare's career, attempts to answer these questions are often underlined by theories about his "lateness". In other words, analyses are frequently built on assumptions about the relationship between Shakespeare's last years and the plays' distinct differentness. It is usually assumed that the two are cause and effect. But exactly which aspects of the former were the "cause", or how that cause brought about the effect, is not, and probably will not be, agreed on. It has been suggested that the plays are a reflection of the playwright's personal experience and emotional struggle in his last years; or that they reveal his boredom, depression, or deterioration of dramatic technique; or that they demonstrate, as many late works of great artists are believed to, a serene reconciliation with life and reality, or an irreconcilable struggle against them; or that they are the crowning glory in the development of his dramaturgy—his last bow, as it were.

This book attempts to come up with its own answers to some of the puzzles surrounding the composition of these plays: the possible causes for the playwright's turn from the tragic mode to the form and subject of the last plays, the relationship between their linguistic style and their thematic concerns, the extent to which considerations other than literary or artistic ones were involved in their making, the connection between Shakespeare's last period and his last plays, and the influence—if any—of collaboration on the playwright. In short, this book hopes to come to terms with the idea of Shakespeare's lateness through exploring in detail the last plays and the circumstances under which they were produced.

By the end of this book, I hope to have convincingly demonstrated that Shakespeare's lateness is marked by sustained professional energy and continuing artistic development. The apparent significant changes in the style, dramaturgy, theme, and genre of the last plays are, at the same time, manifestations of the playwright's unchanging professional approach to his art. Shakespeare in his lateness, as he had been in his youth and maturity, was exploring the possibilities of language and theatricality, reacting to his own previous achievements, absorbing and responding to influences from other playwrights and literary sources, and trying to maximise dramatic effect with the company resources available to him. Thus, in a manner of speaking, this "lateness", rather than the fulfilment or the dwindling-off of a career, was part of Shakespeare's ongoing exploration of the power, effect and possibilities of the medium of his livelihood.

To support this argument, I shall offer my readings of *Pericles, Cymbeline, The Winter's Tale, The Tempest, Henry VIII (All Is True)* and

The Two Noble Kinsmen.[1] A major point of inquiry which runs through the chapters—and strings them together—is art and language in the plays, not only in terms of the works' linguistic and dramatic style, but, more importantly, of their treatment and presentation of art and language as a topic of discussion. As we shall see, Shakespeare in the last plays engages himself in the examination and exploration of the effect of language and the power of dramatic art, developing his argument from play to play. His presentation of the power and possibilities of language and theatrical performance changes from the negative portrayal in the tragedies to positive dramatisation in the first three of the last plays and eventually to a more sceptical approach in the final three. In charting his concern with language and performance, I will also be examining the relationship between Shakespeare's distinctive late verse style, the thematic emphases of the plays, and the audience's and readers' linguistic, dramatic and metadramatic experience in watching and reading them.

The reading of each play will be given a separate chapter, in which, in addition to the underlying concern with language and art, the play's individual features and the special circumstances surrounding its composition will be analysed. The chapter on *Pericles* examines its relationship to previous tragedies and how the personal experience of the co-author may have influenced Shakespeare's style and interest. *Cymbeline* is approached through its peculiar resistance to generic classification, which leads to an analysis of its exactingly balanced treatment of contemporary political topics and generic elements, which results from (and reinforces) the play's interest in the process of communication and interpretation. Cued by Polixenes and Perdita's debate, the chapter on *The Winter's Tale* focuses on the play's treatment of the relationship between art and nature, and on how its "realistic" language reveals about its dramatic structure. Analysis of *The Tempest* starts from an examination of the method and effect of Prospero's project and ends on the playwright's "double perspective" in the play, his transcendence of fiction and reality, and the play's endeavours at presenting "the whole picture". The chapter on *Henry VIII* discusses its presentation of the workings and the re-presentation of history, while that on *The Two Noble Kinsmen* concentrates on the characters' bondage by established form and the playwrights' attempts at breaking it. These two chapters also take up once more the subject of collaboration, but rather than approaching it from

---

[1] Unless stated otherwise, all quotations from Shakespeare's plays are drawn from the Norton edition of the complete plays of Shakespeare (Greenblatt, Stephen et al., eds. *The Norton Shakespeare.* 2nd ed. London and New York: W. W. Norton & Company, Inc., 2008. Print).

the co-author's special knowledge in one subject or genre, they look at how John Fletcher's characteristic linguistic style is incorporated in the scenes to complement the theme of the plays.

CHAPTER ONE

PERICLES

George Wilkins

Pericles, frequently considered to be Shakespeare's first late play, is probably a collaboration; and the collaborator was probably George Wilkins.

It is on grounds of stylistic disparity between the first two acts (or the first nine scenes in editions that follow the First Quarto in not dividing the play into acts) and the last three (or the last thirteen scenes) that the theory of collaboration is put forward, despite the fact that only Shakespeare's name appeared on the title page of the First Quarto. The differences between the two parts are clearly noticeable, even to untrained ears. In an often-quoted passage, Jonathan Bate recalls his first encounter with the play:

> I remember when I first read *Pericles* as a teenager, ignorant of authenticity disputes and putative collaborations. I couldn't put my finger on what it was, but something wasn't quite right about the language of the first two acts. Then the storm broke at the beginning of Act Three—"The god of this great vast, rebuke these surges, / Which wash both heaven and hell"—and suddenly the verse was humming, and I knew I was reading Shakespeare. By the time I reached the reunion of Pericles and his daughter in Act Five, I knew that it was not just Shakespeare, but Shakespeare at his greatest. ("Writ" 3)

A series of linguistic and stylistic tests have substantiated this impression and lent support to the theory of collaboration. These tests, while confirming that Acts 1 and 2 of *Pericles* demonstrate little kinship to Shakespeare's own writings at any period of his career, have also revealed that the un-Shakespearean features tend to link them with the surviving works of George Wilkins.[1]

---

[1] For a detailed survey of these tests, of the evidences and arguments for and against the theory of collaboration, and of the case for and against Wilkins's

Although the theory of collaboration is by no means accepted by all, before any irrefutable evidence of Shakespeare's single authorship surfaces, I will consider *Pericles* as a collaboration between Shakespeare and Wilkins, for it seems hard to overturn internal evidence accumulated by a century's rigorous attributive studies. Besides, there seems to be circumstantial evidence that may suggest why Shakespeare chose to collaborate at this point. He collaborated with Wilkins because as the chief dramatist of the King's Men and a share-holder of the company, he had a professional as well as financial interest in identifying new playwrights. Meanwhile 1607 had been a particularly trying year for Shakespeare. The marriage of a daughter and the funerals of a brother and a nephew, all occurring within close proximity to one another, must have demanded a good deal of his time, not to mention whatever unknown psychological effects they might have had on him. It would, then, not be too surprising that he should have opted for a collaboration at this point—and Wilkins, whose *The Miseries of Enforced Marriage* had recently been produced by the King's Men, seemed to be an adequate choice. On the other hand, it is also possible that the initiator of the collaboration was Wilkins himself. Suzanne Gossett, for example, envisions a scenario in which Wilkins, having enjoyed a taste of the theatre business, "prodd[ed] Shakespeare to consider a collaboration" (57). Wilkins's poetic talents were certainly well below Shakespeare's, but his "recent success for the King's Men and his collaborations for other companies" (59) seemed to indicate that his prose and poetry at least passed muster with the Jacobean audiences, which appeared to be enough reason to induce Shakespeare into collaboration, for, as Northrop Frye reminds us: "[Shakespeare's] chief motive in writing…was to make money, which is the best motive for writing yet discovered" (*Natural* 38).

Doreen DelVecchio and Antony Hammond, editors of the New Cambridge edition of *Pericles*, dismiss the whole authorship debate as "something that wrongfully and frivolously turns the reader's attention away from the text to non-textual side issues" and declare that

> [w]e as editors don't really care who wrote *Pericles* (though we do believe it to be the product of a single creative imagination): we really care that it is, in the Oxford editors' words, "a masterpiece". (15)

---

involvement in the composition of *Pericles*, see Vickers, Brian. *Shakespeare, Co-Author: A Historical Study of Five Collaborative Plays*. Oxford: Oxford University Press, 2004. 291-332. Print., and/or Jackson, MacDonald P. *Defining Shakespeare: Pericles as Test Case*. Oxford: Oxford University Press, 2003. Print.

Insofar as the value of *Pericles* as a text for literary comprehension and appreciation should not be and is not affected by knowledge of single or dual or even multiple authorship, DelVecchio and Hammond are right in treating authorship as a side issue. However, when standing from the viewpoint of understanding Shakespeare's lateness, knowledge of authorship, instead of being a dismissible triviality, can be one vital as well as interesting clue to his development as a dramatist and poet. Individual studies accumulated over the years on why Shakespeare took his "sudden" switch from tragedy to the genre of romance suggest that this was not simply the result of his internal artistic development as a playwright, but that external factors such as the trend of popular taste, the prospect of the acquisition of the Blackfriars theatre, and events in his personal life must also have had their influence on the playwright in his choice of source stories for the last plays. The knowledge that *Pericles* may have been a collaboration now adds another possible source of influence, however slight, to that list of external factors: the man George Wilkins.

Wilkins had a brief but prolific literary career. Most of the literary output that can be associated with him was produced between the years 1606 and 1608: a translation from Latin *The History of Justine* (c.1606), a single-authored pamphlet *Three Miseries of Barbary* (c.1607) and a co-authored one with Thomas Dekker *Jests to Make You Merry* (1607), an independent play *The Miseries of Enforced Marriage* (1607) and some scenes in *The Travels of Three English Brothers* (1607), the first two acts of *Pericles* (c.1607) and a pamphlet *The Painful Adventures of Pericles Prince of Tyre* (1608). After 1608 his literary career suddenly ended. The cause of this abrupt termination remains to be determined.

Compared with his brief appearance on the London literary scene, Wilkins's presence in the records of the Middlesex Sessions of the Peace was more "enduring". From 1610 to 1618 there was a steady stream of cases in which Wilkins was accused of committing theft, felony or violence against women. The session records also frequently connect him with bawds, prostitutes and men who had "unlawfullye begotton" girls "with child" (qtd. in Nicholl 201). This and the fact that Wilkins, who was most often specified as a "victualler", appeared to have set his establishment at the junction of Cow Cross Street and Turnbull Street, the latter an "area…notorious as the haunt of whores and thieves" (Prior 141), seem to point to his being a "pimp", a brothel-keeper, the kind into whose hands Marina falls in Mytilene.

This knowledge, though hardly a boost for Wilkins's reputation, might be helpful in disclosing what initially drew Shakespeare or the King's Men's attention to him. Between the years 1604 and 1605 there was a "particular concentration of interest in prostitution on the stage" (Nicholl 214), exemplified by John Marston's *The Dutch Courtesan* and Thomas Dekker's *The Honest Whore*. Shakespeare's own *Measure for Measure* of 1604 may partly have been an attempt at accommodating the popular taste for "city comedies". *Measure for Measure*, however, though no doubt a masterpiece of subtlety and intellectual power, was probably not a business success, for before the publication of the First Folio no one appeared to have thought it worthwhile to have the script published in any form. Thus the *louche* Wilkins, who had "intimations of literary talent" and, more importantly, "[knew] this seedy brothel world from the inside" and "live[d] this world which the other writers only look[ed] on" (220), may have struck Shakespeare and/or the company's other shareholders as a solution to their problem. If what the theatre-going public wanted at the moment was more "honest whores" and "Dutch courtesans", this could be the man to satisfy them and bring in the money. That there is an extended brothel scene in *Pericles* and that the events in the brothel are directly presented on stage (their counterparts in *Measure for Measure* are only reported) seem a further indicator that Wilkins was involved in the composition, though one cannot be sure whether it is because there is a brothel episode in the story of Apollonius of Tyre that Wilkins was called on to join in the production, or because Wilkins joined the production that the play ended up with an extended brothel scene.

Wilkins's only unaided play, *The Miseries of Enforced Marriage*, is a "tragicomedy" of some sort in that it has, appended to an otherwise unhappy story, a rather awkward happy ending, in which the main character, William Scarborrow, sufferer as well as contributor to the "miseries" of the "enforced marriage" in the title, all of a sudden acknowledges the wrongs he has done. Scarcely twenty lines before his sudden repentance, however, he was reacting to his wife's plea of "Husband" and children's "Father" by vehemently calling the former "a strumpet" and the latter "bastards" and cursing the world in general. The entry of his uncle, brothers, and sister and her husband is greeted by Scarborrow's "Iniurious villen that preuentst me still" (2805). His sudden conversion is thus rendered almost inconceivable.

Part of the reason for the awkwardness of this dénouement lies in the fact that the original story on which it is based is a thorough tragedy, which Wilkins's limited dramatic skills have failed to twist into a convincing comedy. The source story is the Calverley case: Walter

Calverley of Yorkshire murdered two of his three sons and brutally wounded his wife. Calverley himself was executed on 5 August 1605. The case was something of a national topic in 1605 and inspired not only Wilkins's "tragicomic" adaptation, but also *A Yorkshire Tragedy*, which, as the title demonstrates, has kept the tragic ending. The title page of the 1608 published version of *A Yorkshire Tragedy* refers to it as "All's one, or, one of the foure plaies in one, called A York-shire Tragedy as it was plaid by the Kings Maiesties Plaiers" and attributes its authorship to "W. Shakspeare". The last part of the attribution has since been proven false. The former claim that the play was staged by the King's Men, however, "may well be correct" (Jackson 33). In that case it would mean that during the short period between 1606 and 1607 when the theatre was not closed down by plague, Shakespeare's company staged two versions—one tragic and one "tragicomic"—of essentially the same story, possibly in close succession so as to "lure in" potential theatregoers when the murder was still a topic.

Whether Shakespeare was directly involved in the composition of *A Yorkshire Tragedy* or whether his company produced the play, he must have been aware that in the London theatres there were two productions based on the Calverley case going on, one with a tragic ending and the other a happy one. Thus, at least two years before Beaumont and Fletcher's *Philaster* (c.1608-10), considered by some to be the herald of Jacobean tragicomedies, Wilkins's alternative rendition in 1606 of the tragic story of the Calverley case in a "comic" form and the audience's apparent acceptance of it[2] may have first directed Shakespeare's serious attention, up to this point wholly immersed in the world of tragedy, to the dramatic possibilities of this hybrid genre, still more or less in its primitive form. It could have been Wilkins who, at the outset of their collaboration, persuaded Shakespeare to give their new play a happy ending. Or it might even be possible that the younger playwright's crude attempt in *The Miseries of Enforced Marriage* at twisting a tragedy into a comedy reminded Shakespeare of his former failure—in terms of popularity with theatregoers—with *Measure for Measure* and thus provoked in him an urge to "re-test" his own skills, so that when he started to draft a new play in late 1607, he decided to make it a "tragicomedy". It may have been during the composition process that Shakespeare realised that this new form of "romance/tragicomedy" could be the ideal medium to present his "conflicted and developing opinions about the stage and about his own professional status" (McDonald, *Late* 42). And the resulting production,

---

[2] "It was popular enough to merit three quartos, the second shortly after the first" (Gossett 57).

Pericles, turned out to be such a success[3] that he was encouraged to go on pursuing this new genre in three more successive plays before "changing his mind again" (254) by the time of his collaboration with Fletcher on *Henry VIII* and *The Two Noble Kinsmen*.

It is in the company of Wilkins that one finds Shakespeare at the outset of his last phase, and in the company of Wilkins that he started his voyage into the world of romance/tragicomedy. Although obviously one should not over-read into this collaboration and magnify the impact Wilkins had on him, there is little doubt that Shakespeare, who could "pick up stylistic hints from any source and work them into major techniques" (Wright 184), was to a certain degree influenced by his collaborator. Although Wilkins himself soon afterwards deteriorated into a thief and abuser of women, he had nevertheless left his mark on the London literary scene with his one unaided play, two pamphlets and a number of collaborative works. But the more significant mark he left was probably on London's leading playwright. His contribution to the composition of *Pericles* has made Wilkins, in MacDonald Jackson's words, the "part-author of a masterpiece" (9) and one who "deserves credit for stimulating the far greater dramatist to undertake" (xii) scenes which eventually display great theatrical power. Moreover, more than a contributor to the making of one masterpiece, the possible influence he may have unconsciously had over Shakespeare's artistic development might mean that Wilkins, poet, victualler, brothel-keeper, thief and abuser of women as he was, could be seen, albeit in an indirect way, as a contributor to five or six more masterpieces.

Late Style

Pericles demonstrates an unmistakable kinship to Shakespeare's last plays not only in its genre and preoccupation with the themes of familial loss and return, but also by the verse style in the Shakespearean half of the play. The "humming" verse in Acts 3 to 5 that finally pacifies Bate's anxiety that "something wasn't quite right" with the first two acts is marked by a style that is obscure and difficult, but at the same time rich and melodious, creating a kind of "jagged music" peculiar to the last plays.

Certain adjectives recur in discussions of Shakespeare's late linguistic style: elliptical, convoluted, repetitive, irregular, abrupt, digressive. "Elliptical"

---

[3] "Certainly it [*Pericles*] was successful. All the quartos—there were six from the first publication in 1609 to its adoption into the second issue of the Third Folio in 1664—call it a 'much-admired play'; it crowded the Globe; it was carried to court more than once, and lived on into the Restoration" (Tompkins 315).

summarises his late habit of omitting standard components of word or sentence structure from his lines. Syllables and phonetic units are frequently elided. Connectives between clauses of a sentence are often left out. Yet economy of utterance is not what he is striving for. Having made room, as it were, in his lines, he crams the space with repetitive units of sounds, words, phrases and rhythms. Alliteration and assonance, which somewhat faded out from his mature verse, now return. Also present in the verses are metaphors which "[gleam] momentarily, and [are] rarely extensive enough to be catalogued and analysed" (Kermode, Introduction lxxix); ideas closed in dashes, commas and brackets[4] that digress from the main argument at hand; and streams of prepositional phrases tagged to the main body of the sentence. Partly as a result of this almost fevered unleashing of poetic talent into the limited space of his lines, Shakespeare in his last plays has produced an abundance of "aggressively irregular" (McDonald, *Late* 33) blank verse in which "enjambments, light or weak endings, frequent stops or shifts of direction, and other threats to the integrity of the line" (ibid.) consistently appear. These elements of irregularity also contribute greatly to the "convoluted syntax" characteristic of his late style, where he takes liberty in writing deformed phrases, abruptly changing the drift of his argument and altogether forming intricately structured sentences that present quite a challenge to the audience's process of comprehension.

A look at a passage chosen at random from his last plays can yield ample examples of features of the late Shakespearean verse mentioned above. Here, for instance, is Pericles' greeting to his new-born daughter in the first scene of Act 3:

---

[4] It has often been noted that it was probably not Shakespeare himself who was responsible for the sudden increase in the numbers of hyphens and parentheses in the texts of *Cymbeline*, *The Winter's Tale* and *The Tempest*. Rather, it was probably the scribe Ralph Crane, whose fair copies of the three plays were used in the preparation of the First Folio, who first introduced these punctuation marks into the plays. Jackson remarks that Crane is known to have had a "passion for parentheses, apostrophes and hyphens" (qtd. in McDonald, *Late* 110). Nevertheless, that Crane could indulge his passion for inserting phrases and sentences in round brackets or between dashes when preparing the texts seems a fair indicator of the abrupt and digressive style of Shakespeare's last plays. In other words, Crane's can be looked upon as a typical reader response to the frequent abrupt changes of direction or introductions of less-than-relevant information apparent in the verse of the last plays. But whereas the ordinary reader could only add in the parentheses, apostrophes and hyphens in their mind's eye, Crane had the opportunity to record and publish his impression/interpretation in print.

27   Now, mild may be thy life!
28 For a more blusterous birth had never babe;
29 Quiet and gentle thy conditions, for
30 Thou art the rudeliest welcome to this world
31 That ever was prince's child. Happy what follows!
32 Thou hast as chiding a nativity
33 As fire, air, water, earth and heaven can make
34 To herald thee from the womb.
35 Even at the first thy loss is more than can
36 Thy portage quit, with all thou canst find here.
37 Now the good gods throw their best eyes upon't!

                                    (3.1.27-37)[5]

Examining the passage from the level of sound and words, one is first struck by a noticeable repetition of sound in the first five lines, /ai/ in line 27, /b/ in 28, and /w/ in 30 to 31. Such repetition of sound units will eventually become one of the dominant linguistic features of the recognition scene in Act 5, where even a single line like "**My name is Marina / O, I am mocked**" (5.1.133) is packed with echoes of the same sound, giving an uncanny musicality to the scene, even before Pericles himself becomes aware of the "music of the spheres".

Accompanying this sound repetition are instances of elided syllables, one of which can be found in the "upon't" in line 37. Depending on the edition one is consulting, there might be more examples of syllabic elision in this passage. The Norton edition, for example, shows that the "blusterous" in line 28 is elided into "blust'rous", "ever" in 31 "e'er", "heaven" in 33 "heav'n", "the womb" in 34 "th'womb", and "even" in 35 "ev'n". The editor of the latest Arden edition, whose version is quoted above, has chosen not to elide the syllables in these words, thus resulting in a display of pentameter lines with extra syllables. It is an arrangement also consistent with Shakespeare's stylistic habits in the last plays.

Which brings one to the examination on the level of sentences. What is immediately noticeable is that of these eleven lines, lines 29, 30, 32, 33 and 35 are enjambed, their full intention not revealed until at least the next line. Indeed, line 32 goes so far as to run on to line 34 before yielding its full meaning. Closer examination reveals that line 34 is only half a pentameter. Line 31 has a feminine ending.[6] Apart from the elision of

---

[5] As the Norton *Pericles* follows the First Quarto in not dividing the play into acts, for ease of reference, I am using instead the Arden Third Series edition.

[6] The Norton *Pericles* elides the word "even" in line 31, in which case the line becomes a pentameter with a weak ending rather than one ending with an extra unstressed syllable (a feminine ending). Norton editors have also chosen to restore

syllables, there are also instances of omission of larger linguistic units in the ten lines. Line 29 and 31 are elliptical sentences where the verb "be" is missing—"Quiet and gentle [be] thy conditions" and "Happy [be] what follows". Although technically such ellipsis is perfectly grammatical (its syntactic principle the same as the one guiding the sentence "I love you and you me"), the fact that "Quiet and gentle thy conditions" and "Happy what follows" are separated from where the important verb first appears ("Now, mild may be thy life") by one line and three and a half respectively means that extra effort at comprehension is required of the audience and even readers. The line that stands between "Now, mild may be thy life" and "Quiet and gentle thy conditions", line 28, is itself rather syntactically convoluted, presenting a case of late Shakespeare's freedom with handling mobile grammatical components, in this case a reversal of subject and verb order, the much more accepted sequence being "For a babe never had a more blusterous birth" or possibly "For a more blusterous birth a babe never had". The preceding line, line 27, can also be said to be an instance of inverted word order. "May thy life be mild" or "Mild may thy life be" might be the more normal versions, though it should be noted that Shakespeare's choice of word order here could in fact have been deliberate, using the sound of "may be" to cast a shadow of doubt over the child's future and hint at the trials and tribulations that Marina is going to face when she grows up.

On the level of comprehensibility, the much-observed obscurity of meaning of Shakespeare's late verse is also manifested in this eleven-line greeting to baby Marina. As we have seen, a portion of the interpretive difficulty in this short speech is caused by ellipsis and inverted sentence structure. Another factor that makes the meaning of the late verse uncertain is ambiguity of reference. Lines 35 to 36 present such a case: "Even at the first thy loss is more than can / Thy portage quit, with all thou canst find here". The key to the interpretation of these two lines hinges on the reference of "thy portage". The primary meaning of "portage" in *The Oxford English Dictionary* is

> [a]n amount of space or weight on board a ship allowed to a mariner for his own cargo in lieu of wages, enabling him to make a personal profit through

---

the pentameter of line 34 by adding in the phrase "poor inch of nature"—taken from Wilkins's account of the same scene in the pamphlet *The Painful Adventures of Pericles Prince of Tyre*—after "To herald thee from the womb". The editor of the Arden Third edition, however, claims that "there is no evidence that it was originally present" (Gossett, qtd. in *Pericles* 281, note to l.34).

trade; cargo carried under these terms…Hence in later use: a mariner's
wages. ("Portage n.1", Def. 1)

3.1.35-6 from *Pericles* is in fact quoted in the *OED* as an example
illustrating this definition. Viewed in this light, "thy portage" is a
metaphor referring to Marina's hereditary felicity—as opposed to worldly
prosperity, reflected by the phrase "all thou canst find here" in the same
line—the idea being that all the natural endowments which Marina has
brought (or "carried") with her from birth and worldly comfort that she
will gain cannot make up for the child's initial loss of her mother.
Considering that Pericles' daughter is born at sea and will be named
Marina, the association of portage—"a mariner's wages/cargo"—with the
new-born babe is rather a neat one. However, "portage" can also suggest
the "action or work of carrying or transporting goods, letters" ("Portage
n.1", Def. 2a), in which case "thy portage" could be referring to the act of
"carrying" and "transporting" the infant, in other words Thaisa's
pregnancy and Marina's birth. Interpretation of lines 35-6 thus becomes
"The fact that you were nurtured in your mother's womb and born (i.e.
you have gained life) cannot compensate for your losing your mother."
That Pericles' emphasis here should fall on Thaisa and the act of child-
bearing is not inappropriate when one takes into account the larger context
of the speech: the news of Marina's birth is accompanied by that of the
"death" of Thaisa, whose travails arrested the whole of Pericles' attention
only moments ago. In accordance with this interpretation, the reference of
"all that thou canst find here" becomes "your experience in life/your future
prospects". The whole meaning of the two lines thus becomes something
along the lines of "Your gaining life, with all your future prospects before
you, cannot make up for your loss of your mother", which seems equally
appropriate in the context of the speech.

Apart from lines 35 and 36, this speech also contains another instance
of lines that may cause confusion of comprehension, in lines 30 to 31:
"Thou art the rudeliest welcome to the world / That ever was prince's
child". Upon first glance, what Pericles seems to be saying is that Marina
is the rudest welcome to the world, which is strange, for it seems illogical
that a babe should be compared to an act of welcome. An alternative
interpretation could be that the "welcome" here, rather than implying its
modern meaning of "greeting", takes on its original meaning of "one
whose coming is pleasing or desirable; an acceptable person or thing"
("Welcome, n.1, adj., and int.", Def. A). Thus "rudeliest welcome"
becomes a powerfully oxymoronic reference, presenting a paradoxical
situation in which the birth of Marina is at once pleasing and desirable and
"rude", for in a way it is her birth that has brought about Thaisa's death.

This interpretation appears to be supported by the previous line "Quiet and gentle thy conditions", which is connected to line 30 with the word "for", signalling a loose cause and effect relationship between them. The "conditions" in line 29 may be interpreted to mean "[p]ersonal qualities; manners, morals, ways; behaviour, temper" ("Condition, n.", Def. 11b). And Pericles' logic here appears to be that, "because with your birth you have displayed a 'rude' disposition, my wish for you is that you will grow up to be someone gentle and quiet". The main problem with this interpretation, however, is that according to the *OED*, it is only in Old English around the ninth century that this usage of the word "welcome" is employed. Even if Shakespeare himself was capable of looking a long way back to Old English to, as it were, dig out the original meaning of "welcome", it is doubtful whether his early-seventeenth century audience could all catch the reference. Moreover, if the meaning of "conditions" here, instead of referring to personal qualities, implies, as the note in the Third Arden edition points out, "circumstances" and "mode of life" (Gossett, qtd. in *Pericles* 281, note to l.29), then Pericles' logic would instead be that because immediately at birth Marina has been accosted by "unquiet and ungentle conditions", he is hoping that her future circumstances shall henceforth be quiet and gentle. This interpretation seems equally possible and applicable. Considered in this context, the "the rudeliest welcome to the world" in line 30 seems no longer to refer to Marina, but rather to the kind of welcome that the infant has received upon birth: the loss of her mother, the roaring tempest and the tossing "great vast" (3.1.1). The adjective "blusterous" in line 28 describing the circumstances of Marina's birth seems to lend support to this interpretation. Lines 30-31 thus come to mean that, greeted by the storm at sea, Marina has met with the rudest welcome to the world that has ever been presented to a prince's child. Yet this interpretation would imply that the "thou" in line 30 has temporarily shifted from referring to baby Marina, whom Pericles has been addressing, to the surging waves and thunderous storm. If so, this would be a particularly confusing move, for not only is the change of addressee sudden and abrupt, it is also incompatible with the clause "that ever was prince's child", unless one assumes that the playwright has omitted an important verb here—"that ever was [presented to][a] prince's child"—which seems a bit extreme even for the elliptical Shakespeare of the last plays. "Thou art the rudeliest welcome to the world / That ever was prince's child" thus turn out to be among those late Shakespearean lines that seem to resist close grammatical analysis and only yield a vague sense of what is being said.

The uncertainty of interpretation of lines 35-36 and 30-31 presents a typical instance of one's experience with the late Shakespearean verse, where although one is able to grasp the drift or gist of a character's utterance—in the first case "the birth of Marina cannot make up for the death of Thaisa" and the second "the circumstances of Marin's birth are rough"—one either fails to locate the exact references of unexplained metaphors or has trouble discerning the precise connections between parts of the sentence. As a result, there is a prevailing feeling of uncertainty accompanying the reading/listening of the last plays as well as an impression that an utterance in fact contains more than it actually says, which is intensified not only by the quick succession of multi-layered metaphors, but also by the almost incantatory repetition of syllables and words.

Certain other linguistic features of Shakespeare's late verse, though not apparent in this particular speech, are to be frequently met with in other parts of the play. Lines like "'Tis most strange / Nature should be so conversant with pain" (3.2.24-5) and, immediately following it, "I hold it ever / Virtue and cunning were endowments greater" (3.2.26-7), where the relative pronoun "that" ("most strange [that] nature…"; "hold it ever [that] virtue…") is omitted, are instances of Shakespeare's removal of grammatical elements that normally tighten the relationship between parts of a sentence. A further manifestation of this late practice of omission is the increased usage of asyndetic structure, an example of which can be found in Pericles' "O Helicanus, strike me, honoured sir, / Give me a gash, put me to present pain" (5.1.180-1). This dropping out of conjunctions between parts of the sentence is a feature that will become even more frequent in plays produced after *Pericles*. *Cymbeline*, for example, contains

> seventy-eight instances of asyndetic construction, nearly twice as many as *King Lear* and *Antony and Cleopatra*, which themselves have more than the earlier tragedies. (McDonald, *Late* 90)

At the opposite end of the practice of omission is his late habit of piling up appositional or elaborative phrases in the space of a single sentence. In *Pericles*, Lord Cerimon's speech about his medical knowledge, for instance, offers a glimpse of this "additive impulse":

> 'Tis known I ever
> Have studied physic, through which secret art,
> By turning o'er authorities, I have,
> Together with my practice, made familiar

To me and to my aid the blest infusions
That dwells in vegetives, in metals, in stones,
And I can speak of the disturbances
That nature works and of her cures, which doth give me
A more content and cause of true delight
Than to be thirsty after tottering honour,
Or tie my pleasure up in silken bags
To please the fool and death. (3.2.31-42)

Grammatically, this long speech amounts to only a single sentence built up gradually by relative clauses ("through which…", "that dwells…", "that", "which"), prepositional phrases ("together with…"), infinitives ("to please…"), alternatives ("or tie…") and predicates introduced in mid-sentence ("and I can…").

Even in shorter exchanges Shakespeare seems frequently unable to shake off the impulse to insert a bit of elaboration into the main sentence, as is the case with Dionyza's instruction to the hired assassin Leonine that he should not hesitate about killing Marina:

Let not conscience,
Which is but cold, inflame love in thy bosom,
Nor let pity, which even women have cast off,
Melt thee, but be a soldier to thy purpose. (4.1.4-7)

The "which is but cold" tagged on after the imperative "let not conscience" prevents, for a fleeting second, the movement of the sentence from reaching its main verbal phrase "inflame love in thy bosom". And "which even women have cast off" does the same for the second imperative sentence. Together these two inserted relative clauses postpone the main point in the instruction: "be a soldier to thy purpose". In later plays the manifestation of this digressive style will become more obvious in a visual way, where the speaker's abrupt change of direction in speech is often marked out by the presence of (possibly Crane's) colons, semi-colons, commas, dashes, hyphens or parentheses. The style contributes to the sense that speakers in the last plays often wander off, however briefly, from the main course of their argument, though in the end they manage to return to their initial point. The presence of piled-up elaborative clauses, however, delays both the speakers' and the listeners' arrival at the designated conclusion of their argument, thus holding the latter in no little suspense.

This, then, is the linguistic style in which Shakespeare composed the last plays: elliptical, additive, rich and obscure. One of its major effects on readers and audience, as the above analyses of sample speeches have hopefully revealed, is instilling in them a sense of uncertainty. Complex or convoluted syntax, ambiguous references and rich metaphors (multi-layered but not fully articulated) in quick succession bring about an uncertainty about the exact meaning of a line or lines as well as about the speaker's true intention in employing such expressions. The absence of certain conventional connectives between parts of speech or clauses of a sentence generates uncertainty about the relationship between the components of a sentence or argument. The piling up of appositional or elaborative phrases creates uncertainty about where a sentence or speech is going, when it is going to end, and whether its argument can be brought around to the designated point of conclusion.

To comprehend and enjoy this poetry, a certain amount of patience as well as faith is thus helpful. It helps if one believes that the knotty sentences are in the playwright's control and will eventually be sorted out and that patience will be rewarded with a final explanation. And indeed, quite paradoxically it would seem, hidden in the "uncertain" language itself are signs of assurance that all will in time become clear. The repetition of vowels or consonances, syllables, words and images, apart from contributing to the musicality of the plays, also helps to establish a sense of familiarity with the surrounding linguistic "environment". Ambiguous references may result in confusion of comprehension on matters of detail, but the general gist of the sentence can always more or less be grasped, especially when one gives up "fussing about" details of grammatical connections between parts of speech. Although arguments digress as a result of accumulating elaborations, at the same time the ellipses within the sentences or phrases that make up the argument quicken the pace of the speech towards its final conclusion.

"A sense of uncertainty", "loss of logical connections", "the importance of patience and faith", "all in control"—these are also descriptions of qualities, features or morals frequently found in analyses of the drama of the last plays. The experience the audience have with the language of these plays appears to be strikingly similar to that of witnessing plot events. It would seem that towards the end of his career, the playwright who earlier in his career had recommended that an actor should "suit the action to the word, the word to the action" (*Hamlet* 3.2.16-7) had himself achieved a unity between the words and the dramatic actions in his plays. Indeed, one of the main arguments Russ McDonald has put forward in his *Shakespeare's Late Style*, to which study this present analysis is greatly indebted, is that Shakespeare's late language style is a linguistic echo of the larger dramatic structure of the last plays:

> As Shakespeare adapts his source materials to the task of telling stories on stage, his arrangement of his dramatic materials corresponds, in shape and effect, to his ordering of the poetic constituents. (38)

As a result, "[t]hroughout the late verse, particularly in the most difficult passages, the sentence itself becomes a kind of miniature romance narrative" (169).

Another manifestation of how Shakespeare's late style in the last plays reinforces concerns of the larger dramatic unit can be seen from his severing, or at least weakening, of the relationship between speaker and style. According to Northrop Frye, the genre of romance, as one form of New Comedy, is "a structure [in which] the characters are essentially functions of the plot" ("Masque" 11). Thus, in signalling the centrality of plot in his new working genre, Shakespeare

> has adjusted his language and dramatic art to the demands of a new mode, one in which plot, on the whole, has become more vivid and emotionally charged than character. (Barton, "Leontes" 149)

From the Shakespearean part of *Pericles* onwards, the connection between character individuality and linguistic style is gradually weakened. Although in certain speeches the language still seems to adhere to the specific mood of the character at the moment of speaking—Leontes' lexical repetition after he begins to suspect Hermione of infidelity, for example, serves to illustrate his brooding madness—most of the time in the last plays, it is difficult to discern the traits of a character through his or her language. The innocent and sweet Miranda is capable of bitter harshness when addressing Caliban, while the latter, though a born savage, is allotted possibly one of the most beautifully musical and moving speeches in *The Tempest* (3.2.130-8 "The isle is full of noises..."). The buffoon Cloten in *Cymbeline* has his moments of eloquence. And his mother the degenerate Queen, when refusing the continuation of Britain's annual tribute to Rome, describes the kingdom in a way that reminds one of John of Gaunt and his "This England" speech. In other words, specific linguistic features are no longer to be considered as markers of Pericles' or Innogen's or Prospero's personal style, but rather as manifestations of Shakespeare's own late style.

The separation of speaker and speech demonstrates a reversal in artistic development in late Shakespeare. Before the romances, Shakespeare's artistry with his language was usually exerted with the aim of suiting a character's speech to his or her personality or specific state of mind. In other words, not every character speaks in roughly the same style:

> [t]hat Shakespeare learned, as he reached professional maturity in the mid-1590s, to make his speakers sound like themselves is one of the triumphs of his craft, one of the talents for which he is celebrated and by which he is differentiated from lesser dramatists. (McDonald, *Late* 34)

Now, however, he weakens the link between language and their speaker as well as between utterances and the context of their utterance, replacing individual character style with an overriding style that is unmistakably the playwright's.

This appears to suggest that in the last plays, one of Shakespeare's concerns seems to have been to introduce the figure of the playwright into the narrative. Indeed, both on a linguistic and dramatic level, the audience are being made continually aware of the presence of the playwright. Linguistically, the flurry of repeated vowels, consonances and syllables, rapid outbursts of multi-layered metaphors which frequently result in wordplays and double ironies, complex syntax caused by reversal of word order, insertion of digressive information and the piling up of additional clauses all disclose a poet aware of his own virtuosity and taking a self-conscious delight in his performance. Moreover, because this language is often clotted, jaggedly musical and difficult to understand, it calls attention to itself and consequently to its creator by diverting part of the audience's mental focus from the task of keeping up with the plot to the task of comprehending what is really being said. The poet's own voice is further enhanced by the separation of speech from character, for, naturally, when all the characters speak in roughly the same linguistic style, that style will more readily be associated with the playwright who writes in it than with the individual who speaks in it. Dramatically, solution to problems through divine intervention and suppression of logical motives for behaviours—in short, the choice of the genre of romance itself—mean that the plays are patently unrealistic. The hands of the playwright, previously hidden behind the dramatisation of events which are brought about by human agency and more or less conform to the logic of cause and effect and the laws of nature, are now unashamedly evident.

Indeed, in the last plays, Shakespeare goes a step further to impress upon the audience how much a poet or artist figure is in control of the actions on stage. In *Pericles*, episodes are stitched together by the poet

Gower, whose presence continually reminds the spectators that what they are witnessing is essentially a poet relating a story. In *The Winter's Tale*, the statue scene, where Hermione puts on a dumb show (or a sort of wordless masque) of resurrection—complete with curtain and background music—staged by Paulina, serves to remind the audience that the reunion is pre-arranged by a playwright and/or director. And in *The Tempest*, all the events of the play dance around the magic staff of Prospero. Indeed, Prospero's ultimate identity as "the man who has staged the events of *The Tempest*" is so successfully reinforced by the plot that he has subsequently been associated with Shakespeare himself and his adieu to the audience seen as Shakespeare's farewell to the stage, which, of course, it is not. These examples demonstrate how art and the artist are foregrounded in these plays.

This particular direction of development in Shakespeare's last plays, like that of the severing of linguistic style from speaker and situation, appears to demonstrate another reversal of his achievement in the tragedies. Prior to the composition of the romances, Shakespeare's general direction of development in both poetic and dramatic arrangement tended towards artlessness in presentation both of language and of dramatic actions. In terms of the development of his metrical art, "the movement during Shakespeare's early life is unmistakeably toward a verse with…an increasing speechlike line-flow" (Wright 96). In other words, before the last plays, he was striving for a poetic effect natural in its resemblance to everyday speech and unostentatious in its display of artistry. On the level of dramatic narrative, development was equally towards a more realistic and thus "artless" presentation of characters and events. The turn of events became less the result of chance than that of cause and effect. Characters, too, steadily moved away from their identity as stock figures towards becoming self-subsisting human beings whose behaviours and actions, though still ultimately controlled by the decision of the author, at least appeared to be directed by logical motives that observe the contours of human psychology instead of frankly revealing the artist's manipulation. Now in the last plays, however, Shakespeare appears to have reversed all his previous achievement in this respect and reinstalled the figure of the all-controlling playwright into the narrative. In a way, this deliberate foregrounding of artistic control directs the audience's attention to art and the use of art. And as we shall see, the subject becomes a major concern in these plays.

Another reversal of artistic development concerns the portrayal of the effect and power of language. In the first three romances at least, Shakespeare's treatment of language is much more balanced and positive overall than that of the tragedies. There appears to be a renewed trust in its power, manifested, besides in his own frank display of artistry, in a significant decrease in representations of language's destructive effect. Of course, its damaging power is still occasionally portrayed, as is seen in Dionyza's persuasions or Caliban's curses. But generally in the last plays, language does not have its predecessor's ruinous effect in the tragedies. Indeed, in some cases, spoken language is shown to have revitalising power. Pericles is gradually roused from his torpid state by Marina's words. All the confusions and misunderstandings in *Cymbeline* are finally resolved in the last scene, when a succession of characters step forth to relate their stories. It is also worth noticing that even in *The Tempest*, *Henry VIII* and *The Two Noble Kinsmen*, where language and communication are portrayed as problematic, their effect never reach the malign extent evident in the tragedies.[7]

The last plays present these subjects in a way which is almost in defiance of their roles in the tragedies. Together, these reversals in artistic treatment seem to bespeak a reversal, or at least a change, in Shakespeare's perception of language, art and life. He seems to have passed from suspicion of the power of language and theatre and despair of human experience in general to a renewed faith in them, at least for the duration of the first three romances.

This reversal in opinion concerning theatre and language appears to be part of a general movement of "looking back" in which Shakespeare became fully engaged towards the end of his career. He looks backward in order to look forward and uses old methods to achieve new effects. This is manifested in the dramatic motifs and thematic concerns of his last plays as well as in the language in which these plays are written.

On the level of drama, with his turn to romance, Shakespeare seems to be reviewing and revising works produced in his relative youth. He re-engages himself with happy endings, returns to source stories explored

---

[7] It can be argued that the immediate cause of the fall of almost all the late tragic heroes lies in language. King Lear is beguiled by Goneril and Regan's elaborate declaration of filial love. Macbeth's ambition of supplanting Duncan is first kindled by the witches' prophecy. And it is Lady Macbeth's powerful persuasion that goads him on to overcome his hesitation and commit regicide. Coriolanus' tragedy starts when he bows to his mother's wish that he run for consul. Facing opposition, he says rather more than he should and is eventually declared a traitor and banished from Rome for his words. And the downfall of Antony is set when he is seduced by Cleopatra's charm, to which her way with words contributes a great part.

before and re-elaborates on dramatic motifs of his earlier plays. The story of *Pericles*, for example, is derived from that of Apollonius of Tyre, which is also one of the principal sources for *The Comedy of Errors*, an early play. The story of father and daughter separated and reunited can be found in *As You Like It*. The sea motif, where family members are sundered by tempests at sea, had appeared earlier in *The Comedy of Errors* and *Twelfth Night*. Indeed, in *The Tempest*, he resorts to opening the play with a scene of shipwreck, which he did before in *Twelfth Night*. The intervention of supernatural power in human affairs is previously dramatised in *A Midsummer Night's Dream* and *As You Like It*. Even one of the key motifs of the romances, the rediscovery of the kin whom one has never, or almost never, met, can be seen as a variation of the reunion between lost twins in *The Comedy of Errors*. The list can go on, but these few examples will suffice. They reflect a Shakespeare building new scenarios from old motifs, offering alternative solutions to old problems and presenting other answers to old philosophical questions. It should be noted that even at the time when they appeared in the earlier plays, many of the dramatic motifs and arrangements were not Shakespeare's original inventions but old stock borrowed from existent stories and plays. If the comedies were Shakespeare's first experiment with them, the last plays may be his latest attempt at revising both others' and his own previous treatment of them. And out of these old motifs he has turned out plays markedly different from what he wrote previously, so much so that later scholars would feel the need to set up a category within the canon especially for them.

This "using old methods to achieve new effects" is equally evident in Shakespeare's late linguistic development. Many of the old techniques which he gradually left out in his development towards the mature style of the mid-1590s are now picked up once more and used with rather a fervour. Furthermore, in certain aspects of verse formation, he appears to have achieved a radical reversal of linguistic effect by following his old path of language development. George T. Wright remarks that the movement of Shakespeare's poetic development in his early life has been towards "a verse with diminished rhyme, a less blatant meter and an increasingly speechlike line-flow" (96). This description seems equally applicable to his latest development in poesy. The late verse is indeed seldom rhymed. The abundance of metrical variety in the pentameter, achieved through an increase of short lines, lines with extra syllables and weak or feminine endings, breaks the monopoly of regular iambic pentameter and does make the meter "less blatant". And the frequent enjambed lines are at least a superficial imitation of everyday speech, where speakers rarely manage to constrain their ideas into one end-stopped line. However, the effect these "artistic movements" produce, when they are combined together in the last plays, is certainly not one of natural speech-like smoothness, but rather one jaggedly musical and frankly artificial.

It is this apparent practice, linguistically and dramatically, of both looking back and looking forward in the last plays that has led scholars to the designation of a late style to Shakespeare, as it seems to correspond to recognised features of late-style writing:

> There is…in late work, a broad and radical perspective, that of an artistic achievement which sweeps both back to the distant past and forward to a perhaps equally distant future. Late work celebrates and summarises (or, perhaps, in Adorno's terms, offers a critique of) what precedes it, offering a glimpse of a future that is always paradoxically in fact a past. (McMullan, *Idea* 44)

In the sense that "lateness" is, in Gordon McMullan's term, "a commemoration" of a chosen artist, "imposed by critics as a product of hindsight" (62), Shakespeare's linguistic and dramatic style in the last plays certainly fits its description. Chronologically, it is the last, or almost the last, fully developed style of Shakespeare, who would be dead in 1616, about two years after the production of *The Two Noble Kinsmen*. In effect it lives up to the expectation of the "format" of late style: "a looseness and a detachment, a dreamlike quality" (44) and "a kind of self-imposed exile from what is generally acceptable, coming after it, and surviving beyond it" (Said 16).

However, "late writing" also implies a deliberate or intuitive summary of a life's work or a "swan song" inspired by a conscious or unconscious cognisance of a finality to a career. In this respect Shakespeare's style in the last plays is not late, for it is most certainly not the end. As we shall see, *Henry VIII* and *The Two Noble Kinsmen* are evidence that he was still developing his art and striving for new departures.

Moreover, although the last plays do fit the idea that late work "celebrates and summarises what precedes it", it should be noted that this is a feature of almost every play in the Shakespearean canon. The list of reused motifs in the last plays is indeed impressive. But if one sifts through, say, the dramatic motifs of the tragedies, one can discover equally striking parallels between them and those of the histories, comedies and problem plays. The tragedy *Romeo and Juliet* and the comedy *A Midsummer Night's Dream*, for example, composed one after the other (though it is uncertain which came first), appear to have been written "out of some very similar materials" (Greenblatt, "*Romeo*" 897). *Macbeth* shares a theme of usurpation with *Richard II*. The ill-treatment of father by daughter in *King Lear* can be said to have its less foul (though equally condemnable) precedence in Jessica's treatment of Shylock in *The Merchant of Venice*. In short, most of Shakespeare's works contain materials used in other plays and can be looked on as reactions to what went before them. Thus his tragedies are a reaction to preceding comedies and histories, as are his romances to his mature tragedies. *The Two Noble Kinsmen*, marked by the "bleakness of a medieval romance that goes wrong" (Cooper 375) and thus "sometimes viewed as an antiromance" (Cohen 3204), might have been the start of a new round of "reactions", this time to romances. Shakespeare engages himself with "retrospective evaluation of his earlier work" (McDonald, *Late* 220) throughout his whole career: "It is a commonplace that Shakespeare often borrows from himself, although he never repeats himself exactly" (ibid.). Therefore the "summarising", "celebrating" and "revising" of former works evident in the last plays are no isolated artistic practices confined to the last period of his career.

Although it is indeed in the last plays that this "exercise of revaluation", as it were, becomes rigorous, rather than attributing it to Shakespeare's unconscious or conscious urge to summarise his life's career, there may be a more solid explanation. In turning to romance, he was taking up a

> popular and primitive form of drama…full of violent action, whether melodramatic or farcical…dancing and singing, ribald dialogue, and picturesque settings. (Frye, *Natural* 55)

It is a form which comedy accommodates better than tragedy. [8] Shakespeare's artistic skills ensure that his romances are distinctly different from his comedies, but it is inevitable that because of an inherent closeness between the two genres, his romances and comedies should display a similarity in the selection of dramatic motifs, most of which are stock dramatic arrangements anyway. And as his comedies were written in a relatively early period in his career, this sharing of dramatic motifs subsequently makes it look as if he was consciously revisiting the dramatic output of his rather "distant" youth, which in turn provokes a sense of nostalgia frequently associated with "late style" but which may have been wholly unintended on the part of the playwright.

Wright, surveying the development of Shakespeare's verse, observes that "[a]s a man of the theater, Shakespeare appears to have realized quite

---

[8] "Comedy preserves this primitive form better than tragedy" (Frye, *Natural* 55).

early the value of change, which works at different levels" (236). Every period of significant development both in his dramaturgy and in his verse is thus an attempt at bringing a change to the presentation of "the root situation of drama—two persons in dispute" (240). The audacious, difficult, jaggedly musical and rich style of the last plays is his most recent attempt at this. Had he lived a few more years, there might have been at least another, and possibly even more.

From Tragedy to Romance

The many and repeated appearances of familiar motifs from Shakespeare's earlier works in his last plays are partly responsible for generating the idea that these plays are examples of his late style. And in turn, the recognition of the plays as late-style works, or the attribution of a late style to the playwright and these plays, reinforces the idea that these motifs and arrangements are signs of a deliberate or instinctive re-engagement with the past. It is a view that heightens a sense of rejuvenation, as if the playwright has leaped back over the "tragic period" to revisit scenes of his youth. As a result, when discussing Shakespeare's last plays today, one tends to talk of him "switching" from tragedy to romance and call it his "post-tragic turn". The verb "switch" and the noun "turn" connote a sense of abruptness: a sudden whim, an attack of nostalgia or an unaccountable return of optimism—or possibly a swift adaptation of dramatic mode in order to make full use of the company's newly acquired indoor theatre, or a hurried change of dramatic direction to keep up with the trend of popular taste. Accompanying that sense of abruptness is also the suggestion of a break from and a rejection of the tragedies that went before. The words "switch" and "turn" thus leave one with the impression of the playwright suddenly turning his back on what he has achieved in the tragedies to embrace the "new" genre of romance. This impression of abruptness and break marks the effect the last plays have on readers of Shakespeare, especially if they follow the chronology when exploring the canon, moving from the tragedies to the last plays, for the happy finale of reunion and upcoming marriage in *Pericles* does seem suddenly to burst upon one after the deaths, downfalls and despair of the tragedies.

But "switch" and "turn", with their implications of suddenness and break, can be misleading. They cannot be said to be a precise reflection of how Shakespeare advanced from the tragedies to the last plays. For one thing, he did not turn his back on the tragedies entirely. He may have, for the present, departed from tragic endings, but in no way was he finished with the thematic concerns of the late tragedies. Indeed, one only needs to remember that other term frequently associated with the last plays—tragicomedy—to see that "tragedy" is still there, which, moreover, will come back with renewed force in *The Two Noble Kinsmen*, as Chapter 6 shall demonstrate.

But more importantly, it is in fact possible to detect in the late tragedies Shakespeare's gradual development towards his late linguistic style and the thematic conclusions of the last plays. That the culmination of this development should come around 1608 in the shape of *Pericles* does perhaps have a touch of the accidental in it, prompted as it must have been by a series of outside circumstances which to different degrees influenced his composition. But internal evidence suggests that this was a move that he was going to make sooner or later. Indeed, elements and features of this new development were already beginning to manifest in the late tragedies. In other words, the last plays are more the inevitable result of gradual development in his artistic view and style than a sudden and unexpected switch.

A good indicator of Shakespeare's progression from the late tragedies to the last plays is, again, linguistic style. A number of the key components of the "last-plays style" had in fact already emerged in the late tragedies. The sudden darting from one underdeveloped metaphor to another resulting in difficulty of comprehension, for instance, is a striking feature of *Macbeth*. A famous example is Macbeth's rather trying simile

> pity, like a naked new-born babe,
> Striding the blast, or heaven's cherubin, horsed
> Upon the sightless couriers of the air. (1.7.21-3)

Macbeth also sees an abundance of unremitting repetition, not only of words, but also of consonants and vowels, rhythmic configurations, phrases, and images "reiterated, not just immediately but memorably, across several scenes" (McDonald, *Late* 47). This obsessive repetition is also an important marker of certain scenes in *Coriolanus*. Indeed, as soon as the first act opens, the audience are accosted by an act of repetition, with the Roman citizens chanting "speak, speak", "resolved, resolved", "We know't, we know't", and "away, away" (1.1.2, 4, 7, 10).

But the most prominent feature of the language of *Coriolanus* is its protagonist's habitual employment of asyndetic constructions where the transition from one sentence to another is achieved "by force" (McDonald, *Late* 57). Coriolanus, for instance, is in the habit of using a series of imperatives without any conjunction to signal interdependence between sentences: "Nay, let them follow. / The Volsces have much corn. Take these rats thither" (1.1.239-40); "Look to't. Come on…Follow" (1.5.11, 13); "He used me kindly. / He cried to me; I saw him prisoner" (1.10.82-3). This asyndetic structure is also a noticeable linguistic feature of *Antony and Cleopatra*, which "ha[s] more [asyndetic constructions] than the earlier tragedies" (McDonald, *Late* 90).

Asyndetons create a feeling of characters speaking in short bursts, an impression reinforced further by Shakespeare's increased usage of short sentences, which becomes "[o]ne of [the] determining properties" (69) of *Antony and Cleopatra*. Lines are "broken into several segments, shaped and combined in a great variety of ways" (Wright 220). Furthermore, this frequent usage of short or disrupted sentences, together with the employment of inversion of word order and weak or feminine endings, contributes to a growing metrical irregularity in *Antony and Cleopatra*. As a result, "the dramatic verse of the tragedy is copious, unruly, showing, and demanding" (McDonald, *Late* 70), a description already sounding very much like that of Shakespeare's last-plays style.

It is also in these tragedies that the function of linguistic style begins to move towards that in the last plays. While rhetorical devices in the former still largely hold the office of giving individuality to a character or illustrating a particular state of mind, they are beginning to be used more and more to reflect larger concerns of the plays and their structure. In *Macbeth*, the use of unremitting repetition helps to create the sense of hypnotic and obsessive madness shrouding this play. In a way, it also reinforces the idea that assassination, as Macbeth has foreseen, is politically untenable. Just as a sound, a word or an image once picked up will continually reassert itself into speeches, a murder once committed will entail more killing. On the level of speech, repetition in *Macbeth* eventually comes to symbolise a mind that has snapped, as in Lady Macbeth's

> To bed, to bed. There's knocking at the gate. Come, come, come, come, give me your hand. What's done cannot be undone. To bed, to bed, to bed.
> (5.1.56-8)

In parallel, on the level of plot, repeated murders in the play signify a political situation getting out of control, which in turn reveals that Macbeth's reign, like Lady Macbeth's sanity, will not and cannot sustain. It is also worth noting that it is with *Macbeth* that Shakespeare begins his severing of style from characters. "The separation between speaker and verse begins to emerge noticeably in *Macbeth*" (*Late* 47), observes McDonald. And Nicholas Brooke cites the First Murderer's lyrical evocation of the evening,

The west yet glimmers with some streaks of day.
Now spurs the lated traveller apace
To gain the timely inn, (3.3.5-7)

as an example of poetry suited to the play rather than the speaker.
In *Coriolanus*, the protagonist's preference for speaking in short
imperatives and omitting conjunctions between sentences and ideas, apart
from revealing the nature of a man of action who is impatient with words
and desirous of ridding himself of any kind of bonds to

> Stand
> As if a man were author of himself
> And knew no other kin, (5.3.35-7)

is a linguistic recapitulation of the dramatic message of *Coriolanus* that
members of a community are interdependent, their relationship impossible
to deny. Superficially, asyndetic structure denies the relationship between
clauses or sentences by suppressing the use of conjunctions. But the fact
that asyndetic constructions, however fragmented, are still comprehensible
reveals that the removal of signs of logical connection does not and cannot
suppress the semantic or grammatical connections between clauses or
sentences, without which communication will break down. The same can
be said of social and political relationships in the plot. Although
Coriolanus and the Roman populace have both refused to recognise their
dependence on each other, that dependence is nonetheless there. Any
attempt at breaking it will result in tragedy, as it indeed does. Coriolanus,
in threatening to annihilate the community that bore him, dies an
ignominious death as a traitor; and Rome, in "imaging it can dispense with
him and what he represents...comes close to bringing destruction on its
head" (Maus 2798).

The frequent usage of short sentences in *Antony and Cleopatra*
presents brief but recurring outbursts which "challenge the sovereignty of
the pentameter line" (McDonald, *Late* 69). In a similar fashion, the
abundance of weak or feminine endings upsets the regular iambic rhythm
of the verses. And together with the tendency of "sense [to run] over...into
the next line" (Wright 222), such metrical irregularity creates "a verse-
style that is closer to prose than in almost any of the earlier works"
(McDonald, *Late* 70). The challenge posed by short sentences and weak
and feminine endings to the authority of the iambic pentameter which
represents poetic stability is the stylistic equivalent of the threat, in the
shape of the pleasure-seeking and female-dominant world of Egypt, to the
rule of the practical and patriarchal Rome. Similarly, the obscured

boundary between verse and prose recapitulates the transcendence of barriers operating at different levels in the play: the melting of the distinction between truth and fiction presented in the shape of Cleopatra's imaginative re-creation of the "idea" of Antony after his death, a recuperation of image that "out-imagines the imagination, out-dreams dream" (Tanner 630); the bridging of the barrier between the masculine and the feminine as well as that between the Attic and the Asiatic signalled by the union of Antony and Cleopatra; and, perhaps most importantly, the transcendence of the boundary between tragedy and romance implied by Cleopatra's staging of her own death. The heat of the Egyptian sun and the charm of Cleopatra melt everything, from rhythmic and syntactic regularity to distinctions of verse and prose to boundaries between men and women, East and West, imagination and reality, transcience and eternity, tragedy and romance.

Although *Antony and Cleopatra* is a tragedy, Shakespeare's portrayal of the death of Cleopatra is not tragic but triumphant. Furthermore, a large part of that triumph should be attributed to the imaginative exploitation of language, which is the medium through which Cleopatra achieves her and Antony's immortality. Had she said nothing but simply taken her own life, she would still have scored one over Caesar politically by thwarting the latter's plan to parade her in Rome as spoils of war. But the gesture of suicide in itself, even if heroic, lacks that almost exhilarating sense of triumph generated by Cleopatra's elaborate re-imaging of Antony and staging of her own death. With the help of the power of language, Cleopatra is able to defy "the downward turn of Fortune" (Tanner 635) by taking the presentation of the story of her life into her own hands. Her poetry, spoken "with an overflowing superabundance of language" (629) which anticipates the richness of the last plays' linguistic style, "completely transforms her desolate state…inverting it into the occasion of her own triumph of the imagination" (ibid.). History and tragedy are thus turned into romance by the intensity of her self-validating poetry. Death metamorphoses into a spectacular play.

It is interesting to remember that Cleopatra is inspired to stage her own death partly by her horror and scorn at the prospect of someone else staging and contorting the story of Antony and Cleopatra:

> The quick comedians
> Extemporally will stage us, and present
> Our Alexandrian revels. Antony
> Shall be brought drunken forth, and I shall see
> Some squeaking Cleopatra boy my greatness
> I'th'posture of a whore. (5.2.212-7)

So rather than subjecting herself to that treatment, she puts on her own play, "on her own stage, with her own costume, speeches and gestures" (Tanner 636), counterbalancing the power of language and theatricality with the power of language and theatricality. The situation is made doubly significant when one jumps out of the plot to see that on stage in Shakespeare's time, these lines and other speeches of royal magniloquence in this scene were in fact delivered by a "Cleopatra boy"—possibly "squeaking"—in a dramatic production that could hardly be taken as a faithful representation of history. However, despite these "defects", the language and drama of this last scene make *Antony and Cleopatra* "*the* play that will take her [Cleopatra] into Eternity" (638) and etch the image of Cleopatra and Antony on the human imagination as tragic but triumphant lovers.

The triumphantly positive role language plays in the last scene of *Antony and Cleopatra* somewhat balances the presentation of language in other parts of the play, where it has hitherto been shown as the instrument of corruption, idleness and devious political manoeuvres, the last usage most manifestly in the mouth of Caesar, as Cleopatra comments on his tricks and strategems: "He words me, girls, he words me, that I should not / Be noble to myself" (5.2.187-8). Cleopatra's suicide is the first major occasion in the late tragedies in which language plays a non-negative, if not altogether positive, role. Up until this scene, language has been more or less the tool of deception and the cause of misfortune. Evil characters exploit it in order to confuse, to deceive, or to egg the indecisive on to crime, while the virtuous characters remain askance of rhetoric, speaking with an economy, the effect of which is equally disastrous. Cordelia and Coriolanus are examples which immediately spring to mind, though perhaps Coriolanus is better described as "not evil" than virtuous. Neither can heave their hearts into their mouths and so bring on misfortune through their inability to engage rhetorically with their worlds. The linguistic richness of Cleopatra's triumphant suicide arrangements breaks the late tragedies' deep suspicion of the power of style, rhetoric and theatricality to move towards a more balanced understanding of language.

It is tempting to conclude that Cleopatra's triumphant suicide, with its poetic richness and imaginative power, heralds the birth of the romances, plays written with an unprecedented profusion of imagination and linguistic style and where tragic situations have a satisfying resolution. It is unfortunate, however, that there is no hard evidence to prove that *Antony and Cleopatra* is Shakespeare's very last tragedy written before the last plays. But it seems not illogical to speculate that having experimented with the poesy of Cleopatra's final self-apotheosis, he would wish to push it further in the plays which followed, exploring the positive connotations of a rhetorical "something" rather than the limited potential of the poetics of "nothing". The argument would of course be less neat if *Coriolanus* was in fact written after *Antony and Cleopatra*, but it is nonetheless possible to claim that towards the end of the great tragedies, around the time of the composition of *Antony and Cleopatra*, the stylistic as well as ideological ground for the transition from the late tragedies to the last plays has been fully laid. *Pericles* and the other last plays were just one or two steps away.

The scene of Cleopatra's suicide offers the audience only a brief glimpse of the positive power of language and storytelling. Its successor *Pericles*, however, can be said to have been built upon a full acknowledgement of that power. The importance of storytelling is given special emphasis by the presence of the poet Gower as Chorus, who strings the episodes of the story together. And storytelling and rhetoric are key devices in *Pericles* for the bringing about of the final reunions.

Pericles opens with ancient Gower arising from "ashes" to "sing a song that old was sung" (1.0.2, 1). The story of Apollonius of Tyre, on which *Pericles* is based, is an ancient one, "probably first told to eastern Greeks by a romance written no later than the third century A. D." (Welsh 89). Its survival no doubt owes as much to its containing some "old and abiding truths" (Tanner 697) as to the pleasure afforded by witnessing Pericles' eventful but ultimately rewarding travels. Gower summarises the quality of the tale as "restorative". It is a story, he assures the audience, that has been sung on various occasions and read by generations "for restoratives" (1.0.8). Thus the old tale manages to survive through the ages, passed down from generation to generation through the agency of spoken and written language, its survival and enduring popularity a testament to the recuperative power of language and its triumph over time.

Not only is the story of *Pericles* as a whole, according to Gower, a restorative old tale, within the story itself key episodes, especially that of the last three acts, demonstrate the restorative power of language as well. One such episode concerns Marina's experience in the Myteline brothel in Act 4. By preaching divinity there, she not only protects her own virginity, but also succeeds in reforming the brothel-goers. Two of them, after hearing her speak, vow that "I am for no more bawdy houses" and "I'll do anything now that is virtuous, but I am out of the road of rutting for ever" (4.5.6-7, 8-9) before going off together to "hear the vestal sing" (4.5.7). Marina's act of speaking is in effect medication to the "rotting" disease rampant in the brothel, which the Bawd, Pander and Bolt were discussing shortly before the pirates bring in Marina. Rather than treating the symptoms, however, her words go directly to the root of the disease, a treatment much more efficacious and possibly relapse-resistant. Later, it is also through her rhetorical power that she succeeds both in resisting Bolt's advance and in persuading him to remove her from the brothel and restore her "amongst honest women" (4.5.197).

If language in the brothel is a defence and medication against lust, on board Pericles' ship it becomes a dose of hope against despair. Having failed to arouse the grief-stricken Pericles' responsiveness through music, Marina finally manages to awaken him through the act of speaking. She tells him her own life story. Pericles' restoration is marked by a return of his old skill with riddles: "O, come hither, / Thou that beget'st him that did thee beget" (5.1.184-5). Having refused to speak for three months, Pericles is now actively re-engaging with language. Moreover, by calling Marina "[t]hou that beget'st him that did thee beget", he recalls and corrects the incestuous relationship between father and daughter that opens the play. Antiochus' relationship with his daughter effectively terminates his own future. But Pericles' riddle "marks the restoration of a healthy father-daughter relationship in which he can do what Antiochus could not do: give away his daughter to a husband" (Welsh 101), which would ensure the succession of his line and which he almost immediately negotiates with Lycimachus. Thus in this climatic scene of the play, language and rhetoric are not only antidotes to despair, but mark the evaporation of despair as well.

But Pericles' riddle reacts to more than just Antiochus' incestuous relationship with his daughter, for the latter is not the only malformed parent-child relationship in the play. There is also Dionyza, whose love for her child has driven her to murderous jealousy of the accomplished Marina. Her attempt on Marina's life will eventually cause the angry people of Tarsus to burn the whole family in their palace. Then there are also the parents of Tarsus, who literally eat up their children during the great famine. Pericles' riddle therefore can be said to react to them all. Seen from this perspective, the power that language and rhetoric have of driving away despair thus operates on two levels. It operates on a personal level in the revival of the catatonic Pericles. It also works on a social level, for Pericles' riddle announces the restoration of proper familial relationship and the promise of a future, which finally ends the sense of hopelessness permeating the play, a hopelessness resulting partly from the portrayal of a succession of contorted family relationships in which the action of the parent destroys their own future by devouring the child.

It is perhaps worth noting here that in its power to reform brothel-goers and revive Pericles from his lethargy, language becomes a weapon against some of the capital sins. In the first instance it overcomes the sin of lust. The case with Pericles, however, is less straightforward. It has often been observed that Pericles is an example of a hero more sinned against than sinning, a sort of pagan Job who has been trifled with by a capricious Fortune before he is restored to her favour. However, while for the most part of the play he seems to have been an example of virtue, his desperate grief upon learning about the "death" of Marina, manifested in a state that can only be termed "living death", may be said to be one form of sin. According to Andrew Welsh, depending on different perspectives, Pericles' sin could be that of excessive sorrow, or *tristitia*, "an eighth capital sin" in "a tradition [which] persist[ed] in England up until the twelfth century" (105); or of *acedia*, spiritual as well as physical sloth in the scheme of the seven capital sins; or—and this is probably the best description of his state, which is almost a spiritual suicide—of despair, which, apart from being incorporated in the scheme of the seven capital sins as another form of *acedia*,

> belonged to another tradition, a group of sins known as the "unforgivable" sins against the Holy Spirit, "unforgivable" because these were sins that by their very nature put obstacles in the way of forgiveness. (106)

In short, Pericles has committed the sin of shutting away hope and refusing to seek grace. And it is Marina's language that is finally able to penetrate the thick wall which he has built around himself, reviving as well as reforming him.

From Pericles' reunion with Marina onwards, language maintains its positive power through to the end of the play. Pericles' reunion with Thaisa, like that between him and Marina, is again achieved with the help of language. The party's travel to the temple of Diana in Ephesus, where Thaisa turns out to be, is undertaken upon the instructions of the goddess herself, who appears in Pericles' dream and actually speaks to him. Once in the temple, it is by the act of relating his life story—"call / And give them repetition to the life" (5.1.232-3)—that the recognition between Pericles and Thaisa is achieved. The happy reunion of Pericles' family is followed by Cerimon inviting the company to his house to hear him tell the story about how the "dead" Thaisa was revived and preserved. "Lord Cerimon, we do our longing stay / To hear the rest untold. Sir, lead's the way" (5.3.84-5), requests Pericles. And thus the main action of the story ends with the promise of another storytelling session, one which will no doubt clear up mysteries and raise more wonder, joy and gratitude.

On that note, Gower, the representative, so to speak, of all storytellers in the play, comes up the stage once more to summarise the morals of the story. The ancient poet assures the audience that while Pericles, his daughter and queen are finally "crowned with joy", Cleon and Dionyza are severely and justly punished for their evil deeds: "Virtue preserved from fell destruction's blast, / Led on by heaven and crowned with joy at last" (Epilogue 5-6) and "[t]he gods for murder seemèd so content / To punish, although not done, but meant" (14-5). Gower's tone here highlights the didactic function of storytelling. Later, as he says farewell, he compliments the audience on their patience and wishes them joy: "So on your patience evermore attending, / New joy wait on you" (16-7). "*New* joy" here implies that the audience have already experienced one form of joy in hearing the story about Pericles, a reminder that the story has given pleasure as well as been educative. In short, the story has been pleasantly restorative.

To a certain extent, then, *Pericles* can be seen as a play written with the restorative power of language about the restorative power of language. In terms of the dramatic context of the play, within the narrative there are episodes in which righteousness is rekindled in the wicked and hope in the hopeless, a lost child restored to the bosom of the family, and divine intervention revealed to mortals through the agency of language. On a metadramatic level, the tale of Pericles of Tyre itself is an early-modern English revival of a text that has survived more than a dozen centuries and passed from Greek to Latin to Old English and various other vernacular languages of Europe. Ancient Gower, the poet who lived two centuries before this play, is also revived on stage through the agency of language. Speaking for the playwrights who remain behind the scene, the revived poet offers the revived tale in a performance presented mainly through spoken words as a restorative to members of the audience. Thus language, especially in the form of storytelling (which is of course Shakespeare's own line of business), triumphs over time, space and despair both within and outside the plot of *Pericles*.

Of course it needs to be said that the function of language is not always pleasant in the play. *Pericles* has its share of dangerous language, used to conceal, deceive and to instigate crime. Antiochus seeks to conceal incest by a riddle, both failure and success in solving which mean death. Dionyza uses her rhetoric to persuade Leonine against the influence of conscience or pity and to reconcile Cleon to the plan of getting rid of Marina. And of course the false cause of Marina's "death" is passed on to Pericles through language, supported by the fake epitaph on her fake monument.

Each of these negative images of the function of language, however, has within the play a positive counterpart that triumphs in the end. Antiochus and his daughter use riddles to conceal. But Marina, who is also skilled with riddles (Gower informs the audience in the fifth chorus that she outwits the city's scholars with riddles they cannot answer), uses it to reveal, as "Shakespeare…made Marina's riddles an integral part of the recognition scene" (Welsh 99). Marina's preaching of divinity, itself a form of persuasion, contrasts with Dionyza's murderous persuasive power. Dionyza's instructions to Leonine on the assassination of Marina are counterbalanced by Diana's instructions to Pericles, which help him to recover his wife. And finally, the false information of Marina's "death" fed to Pericles has its positive counterpart in Cerimon's promised explanation of Thaisa's survival. Thus, just as Pericles' sufferings will eventually be replaced by felicity, the portrayal of the power of language and stories, though sometimes negative, ends on a triumphant and positive note.

This generally positive presentation of the power of language not only brings to mind its inheritance from Cleopatra's spectacular suicide scene, but also recalls the almost antagonistic attitude towards this medium of communication demonstrated in the other late tragedies. Such an attitude is particularly evident in *Coriolanus*. Coriolanus has no patience for, indeed detests, language. He is also desirous, as has been mentioned, of standing "[a]s if a man were author of himself / And knew no other kin". Coriolanus' attitude sets him in sharp contrast to Pericles, who not only has a way with language (as his skills with riddles demonstrate), but also displays an eagerness for words in the recognition scene. "What say you?" (*Pericles*, 5.1.89); "Prithee speak" (5.1.110); "Report" (5.1.120); "Tell thy story" (5.1.125); "Speak on" (5.1.145), demands Pericles as he gradually awakens to the presence of Marina. Also present in the scene is a sense of Pericles' thrill in the knowledge of regained kinship (this is, after all, a recognition scene). Pericles is aroused from his state of living death by Marina's tale, a tale about her life and parentage. Indeed, it is the word "parentage" that first penetrates his torpidity and draws from him his first non-monosyllabic verbal response: "My fortunes—parentage—good parentage— / To equal mine. Was it not thus? What say you?" (5.1.88-9). Language will eventually prove Coriolanus' nemesis, beaten as he is by a political process founded on verbal rather than physical competence. And when he severs his relationship with Rome—an act of denying his kinship with the community that bore him—he is destined for ruination. For Pericles, however, language and kinship are the miraculous tonic that cures and revitalises.

However, a closer look at the comparison between Coriolanus and Pericles will yield some interestingly ironic points. Of the two, it is really Pericles who has effectively shunned language and human relationship, becoming "[a] man who for this three months hath not spoken / To anyone" (5.1.20-1). Coriolanus, for all his distrust and disgust for language, in fact "speaks one quarter of the play's 3200 lines, a part longer than any in the tragedies except for Hamlet, Iago, and Othello" (McDonald, *Late* 52). Although he professes an inadequacy of rhetorical skills and an unwillingness "[t]o brag unto them [the people] 'Thus I did, and thus'" (*Coriolanus* 2.2.144), his speeches—especially the "Your voices" passage (2.3.115-21)—in the marketplace are forceful enough to win him the consulship. Similarly, despite his desire to rid himself of kin, he remains, "ineradicably, a *mother's-boy*" (Tanner 600). And it is by bowing to his mother's wishes that Coriolanus enters the arena of politics for which he is so ill-fitted. Yet of the two it is Pericles, who has decidedly rejected language and human relationship for a while, who is ultimately saved by them. In both plays, then, the power of language is portrayed as clearly overwhelming. But while in *Coriolanus* that power is shown to be altogether negative, in *Pericles* it is its positive effects that have ultimately been emphasised.

Language and storytelling in *Pericles* can have positive effects because they provide the missing link between the present and the past and are thus able to put things back into their proper place to make possible the engendering of a future. In other words, the power of language in *Pericles*, as well as in the ensuing *Cymbeline* and *The Winter's Tale* at least, is ultimately the power of bringing back the ability to hope and to look forward to the future. That this ability is deemed an important and admirable quality in *Pericles* is revealed early in the play, during the tournament in Pentapolis. Of all the six knights competing for the hand of Thaisa, Pericles is the only one whose motto on the shield, "*In hac spe vivo*" (2.2.43), pronounces a dependence on the power of hope. And it is Pericles who wins the heart of Thaisa and the approval of Simonides. Later, after he has lost his wife and daughter, Pericles temporarily abandons hope; but then he is revived by Marina, "his future, the fruit of his past hope" (Welsh 111), whose story reawakens hope in him and promises him the future which he thought was denied him.

Language has no such restorative function in the tragedies because the element of hope is exactly what is denied both the characters in the plays and the audience watching them. In the tragedies hope is either illusory or transitory, raised only to be dashed. And it is man's desperate and failed attempts at realising and retaining that hope that give the endings of tragedies their pathos. Language, which is already potentially unreliable because of

> the futility and inadequacy of speech, particularly compared to deeds; the unreliability of the verbal sign and its consequent vulnerability to manipulation; and finally—the negative side of one of its principal virtues—its guilty role in the stimulation of dangerous illusion, (McDonald, *Arts* 181)

is thus determined by the genre to have a disastrous effect in the tragedies, as it is the main medium through which hope is communicated and denied.

Pericles and the ultimate triumph of hope, then, appear to signal a more favourable and optimistic view of the world in general. The positive portrayal of language is one manifestation of that changed view. It is also revealed in a series of episodes in the play whose setups have extremely similar counterparts in the late tragedies, but whose results are significantly different from their tragic predecessors. It is almost as if Shakespeare is deliberately revising outcomes of dramatic situations already explored in the late tragedies to call attention to this improved opinion of the workings of the world.

The painful adventures of Pericles are started by a dilemma between the choices of speech and silence, one which is arguably more pressing and intractable than that which Cordelia faces near the beginning of *King Lear*. Both can be said to have chosen silence, or rather a refusal to word their responses according to the expectation of the questioner, Cordelia in refusing to describe her love for Lear in elaborate terms, Pericles by not stating plainly whether he knows the answer to the riddle. Cordelia's response results in her departure from her native land. It is also in a way responsible for Lear's wandering in the wilderness. Pericles' answer causes him to flee from his own country to embark on a journey which can more or less be described as peregrination—wandering. Cordelia gains temporary facility from her initial choice of "silence" by inspiring respect, love and an offer of marriage from the King of France. Pericles' hedging answer eventually brings him to Pentapolis where he weds the fair and virtuous Thaisa. Cordelia's happiness does not endure. After a brief reunion with Lear in which she nurses her deranged father back into sanity, she is captured by Edmund and hanged, with Lear dying almost immediately afterwards of a broken heart. Pericles' domestic facility does not sustain either. He loses his wife in a storm at sea and eventually hears about the death of his daughter. But Pericles' story does not end there, for death is ultimately replaced by revival, and separation by reunion. Thus, while the concatenation of circumstances in the wake of Cordelia's choice of "silence" ends in death and despair, in the case of Pericles, they, although equally trying in process, culminate in resurrection and hope.

Of the two major "resurrections" in *Pericles*, one, the spiritual resurrection of Pericles himself by Marina, is achieved through language, as has already been discussed at some length. The other, the physical resurrection of the apparently dead Thaisa by Cerimon, is supposedly achieved by medical treatment, though it is strongly suggested that magical power has been employed, as "it is apparently the music which finally revives Thaisa" (Gossett, qtd. in *Pericles* 301, note to 1.90). Music and the "blest infusions / That dwells in vegetive, in metals, stones" (3.2.35-6) have their gruesome counterparts in *Macbeth*, in the scene where the Weird Sisters enter, throwing ingredients such as "[e]ye of newt and toe of frog / Wool of bat and tongue of dog" (4.1.14-5) into a boiling cauldron while speaking verse which, as the quoted lines show, has an undeniably sing-song quality to it. The rhyme-speaking witches, with their magical power of interpreting nature, precipitate the Macbeths into their descent into destruction. Cerimon, on the other hand, equally "magical" with his knowledge of "disturbances / That nature works and of her cures" (*Pericles* 3.2.37-8) and use of music, is instrumental in bringing about the eventual reunion of husband and wife.

Husband and wife also owe their reunion to the help of Diana, who descends into Pericles' dream and gives out precise instructions as to where he should go and what he should do:

> My temple stands in Ephesus. Hie thee thither,
> And do upon mine altar sacrifice.
> There when my maiden priests are met together,
> [
>   ] before the people all,
> Reveal how thou at sea didst lose thy wife.
> To mourn thy crosses with thy daughter's, call
> And give them repetition to the life.
> Perform my bidding, or thou liv'st in woe;
> Do it and happy, by my silver bow. (5.1.227-35)

Thus ordered, as well as promised, the goddess. Although she does not plainly reveal the outcome of Pericles' performance of these orders, the instruction themselves are clearly stated and unambiguous. The articulate Diana is a great step forward from the silent (or almost silent) gods in *Lear*, whose usual answer to Lear's appeal is

silence. When they do speak at all, they do so in the form of thunder: an
undistinguishable blur of sound which will not resolve itself into words, let
alone into doctrine. (Barton, "Limits" 27)

Diana is also different from the forces of divine justice in *Macbeth*, who,
although ultimately just, operate "deviously" (Cohen 3204) as they give
out cryptic prophecies through the agency of the witches, which can be
said to have initiated all the tragic events in *Macbeth*.

Other parallel situations that end differently include Marina's
successful revival of her father, a feat which Cordelia has ultimately failed
to achieve; and the "almost talismanic quality" (Tanner 720) of names in
the play (the retention and recognition of which confirm kinship and
promise happiness), which brings to mind the contrasting effort of
Coriolanus "to reject or leave behind his names" (671). These variations
not only reveal a playwright deeply aware of, as Wright has pointed out,
the value of change, but also one who seems to have adopted a more
benevolent attitude towards the world and its inhabitants, at least for now.

One is tempted to imagine that the playwright was inspired and even
moved by the enduring vitality of the source story on which he was
working. The undying popularity, reaffirmed once more by the
commercial success of his own version of it, of the story about sufferings
rewarded ultimately by helpful gods may have instilled in Shakespeare a
respect, if not an awe, for "the human imagination labouring in faith and
hope and love to engender a future" (Welsh 112).

Shakespeare's own imagination had indeed engendered a sort of a
future in his playwriting career. *Pericles* announces the arrival of his new
post-tragic period. In some ways, it is an extension of the imaginative
power of Cleopatra's suicide scene, completing the gradual transition from
despair to spiritual triumph, tragedy to romance, as well as reality to
imagination. It is the first play in the latter part of the canon in which
features of the late Shakespearean style, used more or less individually in
the previous few tragedies, are employed collectively as the universal style
of the play. It is also in *Pericles* that speech, speaker and occasion become
fully separated and that style serves to recapitulate the greater structure of
the drama. Stylistically, then, *Pericles* represents the culmination of
linguistic developments accumulated in the late tragedies. In terms of plot,
the play contains a great collection of dramatic episodes and scenarios
already explored in the tragedies, but which have alternative outcomes
from their tragic counterparts. Style and plot together may imply a
Shakespeare with an improved opinion of the world, manifested in an
altogether more balanced and positive representation of language, which in

the play has the power of generating hope and the future. These are the themes and style with which he will continue to work in at least *Cymbeline*, *The Winter's Tale* and, to a certain extent, *The Tempest*. *Pericles*, then, might be seen as standing in the position of a "thesis statement" in which the last plays' stylistic and thematic continuities from the late tragedies are summarised, and by which Shakespeare announces the style and theme which he is going to explore and the power of hope which he is to emphasise in the next plays.

CHAPTER TWO

CYMBELINE

Peculiarities

Wilson Knight, in his chapter on *Cymbeline* in *The Crown of Life*, regularly uses the adverb "peculiarly" to modify descriptions of the play.[1] The word seems particularly, or, as Knight himself would put it, peculiarly, to have been on his mind when he was examining *Cymbeline*. I have counted a total of twenty-two "peculiarly"s in the whole of *The Crown of Life*, of which eleven appear in the chapter on *Cymbeline*, while the rest are divided among the other last plays. In most cases Knight uses it as a synonym for "particularly, especially" rather than the adverb form of "peculiar" meaning "oddly or strangely", though in a number of instances the latter seems also implied. It is more than probable that the relative high frequency of it in the chapter merely points to an idiosyncratic fondness— and perhaps a passing one—for the word. Yet one cannot resist the speculation that the sudden increase of the use of "peculiarly" in the chapter may well have been a manifestation of his perhaps subconscious evaluation of the play as a peculiar piece of work among Shakespeare's last plays, particular as well as strange, or rather, particular in its strangeness.

Cymbeline is indeed a rather peculiar play, standing out even in Shakespeare's "peculiar" group of last plays. But it is only fair to Knight to point out here that he never states out loud that *Cymbeline* is peculiar. He does, however, remark fairly early in the chapter that "[t]he play is not...easy of approach" and that it is a "peculiarly studied work" (129). And one of the implications of the "peculiar studiedness" of *Cymbeline*, according to Knight, is that "[i]t is, indeed, to be regarded mainly as an historical play" (ibid.).

---

[1] For example, "*Cymbeline* strikes one as a peculiarly studied work" (129); "Iachimo is peculiarly well done" (142); "In this guise she is felt as peculiarly, pathetically, attractive" (155); "in this peculiarly Roman play" (185); and "something peculiarly indefinable and invisible" (199).

In that last statement, in fact, lies one of the major peculiarities of *Cymbeline*: the play appears to be one of those literary works which defy classification. Although *Cymbeline* has an un-tragic ending, with families reunited, forgiveness distributed and peace declared, it has been labelled a tragedy, and this by none other than the first authority on the printed text of Shakespeare, the compositors of the First Folio. On the other hand, although the play contains ample romance elements, it has frequently been looked on as more of a history than a romance or a comedy. The earliest surviving audience account of the play reports the impressions created by a (probably) 1611 production, recorded in the private memorandum book of Simon Forman. He began his entry with

> Remember also the storii of Cymbalin king of England in Lucius tyme, howe Lucius Cam from Octauus Cesar for Tribut, and being denied, after sent Lucius with a greate Arme of Souldiars who landed at Milford hauen, and Afftere wer vanquished by Cimbalin, and Lucius taken prisoner, (qtd. in Chambers 338-9)

which seems to suggest that his immediate impression of the play was as a history. In any case, the written record appears to reveal that the historical framework of the story left a deep impression on at least one member of the audience in Shakespeare's day. Nowadays, a number of scholars seem to have taken their cue from Forman's recollection and embraced the idea that it might be worthwhile to shift their focus from the romance of the story to its historical setting. Knight, as mentioned above, believed it to be mainly a carefully studied "historical play". More recently, J. Clinton Crumley, for example, contended that *Cymbeline* should be looked on "as a kind of history play, a play that has something to say about history and historiography" (298). Besides being categorised as a romance (or tragicomedy), a history or a tragedy, it has also at times been included in discussions on Shakespeare's "problem comedies". William Lawrence, for example, in his *Shakespeare's Problem Comedies*, groups it with *Measure for Measure* and *All's Well That Ends Well* on the grounds that its earlier scenes present "a perplexing and distressing complication in human life…in a spirit of high seriousness" (156). In the light of all these different impressions, it is perhaps Tony Tanner's playful, "Polonisian" identification of it as "this extraordinary play, classifiable, if at all, rather helplessly as a tragical-comical-historical-pastoral-political romance" (721) that can best sum up *Cymbeline*'s peculiar genre.

Part of the reason for the uncertainty must lie with its peculiar dramatic arrangements. The narrative begins like a conventional romance, with the exile of the hero and the forced separation of lovers. It develops, however, in the "spirit of high seriousness" of a tragedy or a problem play by the disturbing and distressing wager plot and its disastrous consequences on the one hand, and in the manner of a history play with the dramatisation of the dispute between Britain and Rome over tribute on the other. Yet the plot ends in the shape of romance with the descent of Jupiter, the reunion between family members and the prospect of a peaceful relationship between two states. Thus tragedy, romance, history and comedy all make an appearance in this many-branched storyline. Moreover, Shakespeare appears to have given equal weight to elements of these genres in the narrative. The tragedy and brutality of the consequence of the wager plot are balanced with Posthumus' voluntary repentance and the love and joy of the final reunion. The "reality" of the historical framework concerning ancient Rome and Britain is counterweighted by the fictionality of the Posthumus-Innogen story. In short, not one generic characteristic stands out as the dominating mode of the play, thereby raising confusion over its exact generic status.

Into that generically-obscure and many-branched storyline, Shakespeare has inserted dramatic elements which are equally defiant of easy classification. In terms of the setting, ancient Rome and Renaissance Italy apparently co-exist, the former represented by the fine qualities of Caius Lucius, the latter by the Machiavellian villainy of Giacomo. In terms of characterisation, there is a hero who is mostly absent and whose actions, in the few scenes which feature him, apparently deviate considerably from what is expected of a man "most prais'd, most lov'd" (1.1.47), which is how he is presented to the audience at the very beginning of the play. Plotting against the hero and heroine is the wicked Queen, who, oddly enough, is allotted one of the most patriotic and invigorating speeches in the whole play. And of the title character Cymbeline, it can only be said that he is more of a dramatic device than a dramatic personality. As plot machinery he is of some importance, for he functions as a centre of tension in the play, linking the main- and sub-plots together by his status as King of Britain, husband of the Queen, and father to Innogen and the lost princes. But as a king he seems to demonstrate few leadership qualities, and as a man, "there is little to say [of him]" (Knight 130). In other words, where the title makes one expect a play *about* Cymbeline in the way that *Othello*, *Macbeth* or *Hamlet* are about their respective title characters, dramatic arrangements here frustrate that expectation. In terms of plot, the battle between Rome and Britain ends rather peculiarly, for, having defeated the Romans, Cymbeline

>   submit[s] to Caesar
>   And to the Roman empire, promising
>   To pay our wonted tribute. (5.6.460-2)

And there is of course the final scene, which for some is a powerful example of dramatic *tour de force* while for others a hurried and clumsy stitching-up of loose ends, where no fewer than twenty-two plot complications are untied in fewer than five hundred lines.[2] Together, these peculiar dramatic arrangement have earned Dr. Johnson's scorn:

> To remark the folly of the fiction, the absurdity of the conduct, the confusion of the names, and manners of different times, and the impossibility of the events in any system of life, were to waste criticism upon unresisting imbecility, upon faults too evident for detection, and too gross for aggravation. (183)

While Johnson in the eighteenth century did not hesitate to call Shakespeare's dramatic manoeuvres in *Cymbeline* "unresisting imbecility", later critics who feel uncomfortable with the play, rather than blaming its peculiarities on the playwright's sudden attack of imbecility, sometimes attribute the blemishes to the possible existence of a collaborator. Although this theory is now generally dismissed, the fact that suspicions about the authenticity of certain sections existed at one point in the history of Shakespearean research points to the difficulties of coming immediately to terms with certain aspects of the play. This, in turn, reflects the peculiarities of the dramatic arrangements of *Cymbeline*.

Coming to terms these peculiarities in the composition of *Cymbeline*—genre, characterisation, stagecraft, style, dramatic purpose—then, will be the main purpose of this chapter, in the process of which some insight into the sources of influence on the composition of this play in particular and Shakespeare's last plays in general will hopefully be gained.

---

[2] The number varies somewhat depending on how one counts (whether the Queen's three deathbed confessions should be considered as one revelation or three, or whether the account of the Queen's death and how she dies should be looked on as one piece of news or two, for example). It fluctuates slightly around twenty-five. I have counted twenty-two; Tony Tanner counted "no less than twenty-five" (722); while Roger Warren found "some twenty-four revelations" (57). In any case, whatever the exact number, the effect is the same: the number of knots untied in a space of a single, approximately 490-line scene is overwhelming.

Topics

Of the three likeliest years for the composition of *Cymbeline*, 1609, 1610 and 1611, 1610 appears to have the most support from researchers. This is unsurprising, as 1610 witnessed an important political event which, among other things, may have partly contributed to Shakespeare's choice of Milford Haven as a central geographic location in the plot. The event was Prince Henry's investiture as Prince of Wales on 5 June 1610. This particular investiture probably appeared doubly significant to Jacobean England, for Henry was the first crown prince to be invested as Prince of Wales in nearly a century. As a result, the event "put the political symbolism of Wales at a premium" (Butler 5). Among the entertainments eventually presented at court during the celebrations was the masque *Tethys' Festival* by Samuel Daniel, in which Milford Haven was given special emphasis as "[t]he happy court of union, which gave way / to that great hero Henry and his fleet" (qtd. in Warren 64). The special attention paid to Milford in *Tethys' Festival* provides an example of the particular significance attached to the port in the Jacobean court, especially around the time of Henry's investiture.

Celebratory preparations for the event started as early as Christmas. Presumably, as James's own "men", Shakespeare and his company would have been called on to make a contribution. It is not impossible that the company should have offered a new play by its chief playwright. *Cymbeline*, with its story partly built upon the history of ancient Britain and its inclusion of Milford and the Welsh mountains in the plot's geography, could have been the new play. But even if it was not prepared for the celebration, or indeed, written in 1610 at all, it is still not too unreasonable to suppose that Shakespeare was to a certain extent influenced by this topical event. After all, from late 1609 to late 1610, or possibly even early 1611, Henry's investiture could well have been the talk of the town, first as an exciting upcoming event and then as an important past event. Discussions of kingship, succession, the country's future and Wales' symbolism were probably popular.[3] Shakespeare,

---

[3] Prince's Henry's investiture triggered discussion as early as in 1608, for the fact that it was so long since England had a Prince of Wales meant that there were a series of important questions which required extensive research. As a result, before the event could even be considered, a great "range and quantity of historical research [was] commissioned between 1608 and 1610" (Croft 183).

The year of the investiture, 1610, very much "belonged to Prince Henry" (Bergeron, "Creating" 434). "The celebrations was set for June, and court life moved toward it" (Wilson 78). Starting on the last day of the old year, there were a

whether or not purposely catering to the interest of his audience, might have seen in them materials and ideas worth dramatising. Of course, without the support of written records, all this is only surmise. Still, it is hard to overlook the fact that both in the entertainments that *were* offered at the investiture celebrations and in *Cymbeline*, Wales in general and Milford in particular were given special emphasis, almost becoming a motif. Martin Butler writes:

> It cannot be claimed that Shakespeare was reacting to Henry's investiture, nor that the play would necessarily have been any different had it not taken place. Nonetheless, the coincidence between the play's geography and the summer's political symbolism is very striking. (5)

1610 was also, in terms of international relations, a surprisingly peaceful year for Europe. It was, as Emrys Jones points out, in fact "the only year, of this period, in which all the European States were at peace" (96). Roger Warren believes this to be a "further contributory crumb" (67)

---

series of festivities in anticipation of the event. A challenge to all knights of Great Britain was delivered in the presence chamber by Henry on 31 December. "Thereafter until January 6 Henry kept open table at St. James's" (78-9). On the 6th the barriers took place, in which the prince participated. Ben Jonson was called on to provide a masque for the occasion. On St. George's day "the loyal and loving citizens of Chester" put up a "great 'triumph'" to "[show] their devotion to their prince" (80). On 31 May the prince enjoyed a water pageant on the Thames. And on 4 June, a day before the investiture, he witnessed the creation of twenty-five Knights of Bath in his honour.

The investiture associated the prince with a tradition which could be traced back to Henry III, thus emphasising "the continuity of English kingship" and underscoring "the legitimacy of the new Stuart line" (Croft 184). It was also a rite signalling that "the agonizing worries about the succession that had plagued Elizabethan Englishmen" (ibid.) could be put to rest. The message of stability and futurity was enhanced by the figure of Henry himself. The prince was well loved by his subjects—"Henry was probably the only popular Scot in England" (185)—and had conscientiously cast himself and his circle as the "youthful symbol of reconciliation" (ibid.). He was also considered by many to "offer the possibility of a new era for an England fully engaged with Continental Protestantism" (McMullan, Introduction 64).

Taking into consideration the novelty of the investiture, the prolonged investigation into precedent cases, the amount of celebration in anticipation of the event, the political message of the installation of a Prince of Wales , and Henry's personal popularity, it seems reasonable to suppose that between 1608 and 1611, discussions on topics of investiture, kingship and the country's future were popular both at court and, perhaps to a slightly lesser degree, among the commoners.

to the hypothesis that *Cymbeline* was written in 1610. But whether or not *Cymbeline* was written in the peaceful year of 1610, peace is indeed a main theme of the play. The action of the story shows how strife and war are resolved into harmony and cordiality between states. And the play emphasises this by ending with the word "peace": "Never was a war did cease, / Ere bloody hands were washed, with such a peace" (5.6.484-5). It is also of interest to note that in Holinshed, Cymbeline's reign was "in fact a time of peace" (Jones 88). It is probable that the play's original audience would have been alerted to its concern with peace both by its narrative and its historical setting.

Many modern Shakespeareans believe that the original audience might also have been reminded by the play that

> the reign of King Cymbeline spanned the time of universal peace—the *pax Romana*—during which Jesus Christ was born in Bethlehem, and that their current king, James I, who liked to be known as Jacobus Pacificus, prided himself especially on his achievements as a peacemaker who had brought about the union of the British isles. (Wells, qtd. in Warren 62)

This hypothesis is not impossible, for the play does contain possible references to the king as well as his peace-making policies, which Shakespeare's contemporaries might easily have identified. There is, of course, Milford, symbolically important not only because it is in Wales, but more so because it was where Henry Tudor landed in 1458 to begin his fight for the crown of England. The port can therefore, in a way, be looked on as the birthplace of the Tudor Dynasty, to which James was keen to present himself as a "natural successor" (Warren 62). He also sought to establish himself as the inheritor of Henry VII's symbolic role as unifier and pacifier. At his entry to London in 1604, he was compared to Augustus, who laid the foundation for that period of comparative universal tranquillity known as the *pax Romana*, and who shared one feature with the historical Cymbeline, for it was also during Augustus' reign that Christ was born. One of James's first achievements upon ascending the English throne was speedily ending England's war with Spain in 1604. In 1609, by the mediation of England and France, Spain and the Netherlands declared a twelve years' truce. In 1610 James's peace-making credentials were again strong, for he was once more acting as mediator between Spain and the Netherlands in the Julich-Cleves Crisis which threatened to collapse the previous year's truce. Taking these together, it would seem that *Cymbeline*, dating between 1609 and 1611, with its choice of Milford as a geographic centre and with its dramatic action moving from war to peace, may indeed contain references to the king and his strenuous peace policies.

Indeed, Jones insists that "[i]t is in the context of the political use made by James of the Tudor-British myth that the relevance of Milford Haven in *Cymbeline* is to be understood" (93).

Scholars have also discovered other, apparently more substantial ties between *Cymbeline* and King James. Towards the end of the play, the Roman Soothsayer refers to the British king as "the radiant Cymbeline, / Which shines here in the west" (5.6.475-6). Jones points out that "monarch of the west" was one "panegyric imagery...frequently applied to James in the early years of his reign" (92). James himself also actively participated in this Jacobean tradition—or maybe it was he who started it. At any rate, in 1609, he published *A Premonition to All Most Mightie Monarches, Kings, Free Princes and States of Christendom*, in which he referred to himself as "a Westerne King".

The Soothsayer also at one point describes Cymbeline as "the majestic cedar...whose issue / Promises Britain peace and plenty" (5.6.457-8). The cedar is an emblem of patriarchal sovereignty. In the Bible it is associated with the generation of a prosperous and stable future:

> it shall bring forth boughs, and bear fruit, and be a goodly cedar; and under it shall dwell all fowl of every wing; in the shadow of the branches thereof shall they dwell. (*King James Bible*, Ezekiel 17.23)

Thus it is possible to read in the Soothsayer's mention of the cedar a reference to James, who, like Cymbeline and unlike Elizabeth I, was parent to heirs who promised comparative smoothness and stability of succession, the investiture of Henry as Prince of Wales in a way an elaborate display and assurance of the fact. Therefore the original audience of *Cymbeline*, watching the play when the nation was either awaiting the celebration of the investiture or talking about it as a recent event, probably would have seen in this description of Cymbeline an allusion to their own king. Butler suggests that

> [w]hen Cymbeline announces "My peace we will begin"...Jacobean audiences would have taken the possessive pronoun as echoing their own monarch's pride in the stable empire that he alone guaranteed. (40-1)

Cymbeline's position as the King of *Britain* also possibly connects him with James, who preferred to style himself as "King of Great Britain and Ireland", despite the fact that union between England and Scotland was never legalised during his lifetime. The Soothsayer's reference to the cedar also seems to consolidate this association, as the image of the king as a cedar was used in promoting the Union of England and Scotland. The two kingdoms were compared to two branches and the king the central trunk. The union was an important component of James' peace schemes. He believed that at home

> [the] vnion [would be] an eternall agreement and reconciliation of many long bloody warres that ha[d] beene betweene these two ancient Kingdomes, ("Speach" 163)

and hoped that externally across Europe "his status as monarch of several peoples would give him weight as a political arbiter" (Butler 40). While a united Britain was a constant theme throughout the early years of the king's reign in England, it is possible that around 1610 it was particularly brought to the foreground in public attention by Henry's investiture, an occasion which the king may have hoped would warm Parliament and the English people to the idea of the union. Ros King suggests that Prince Henry's investiture "was…an opportunity for the Crown to make political capital" (47). Besides, the prince himself

> since 1603 had promoted in his circle the notion of "Cambro-Britains" or "Scoto-Britains", the rising generation who would embody the union of England and Scotland. (Croft 184-5)

Cymbeline, written around this time, with its choice of ancient Britain as setting, may thus have contained a reference to James's political vision.

To summarise: Wales, Britain and peace are three key concepts apparently shared by the fictional world of *Cymbeline* and the real world of Jacobean England around 1610. In the former they are manifested in the geographic importance of the port Milford Haven in the plot, the setting of the narrative in ancient Britain, and the play's theme of peace, while in the latter the event of Prince Henry's investiture probably occasioned much discussion about them. This, together with the play's inclusion of expressions or imagery associated with King James in Jacobean culture, appears to suggest that the composition of *Cymbeline* was indeed informed by contemporary political events and that Shakespeare probably expected his original audience, at court and/or in Southwark, to see these connections.

The question which arises out of these observations is of course why Shakespeare inserted these topical allusions in his play. Was he, as Jones suggests, simply "pay[ing] a tribute to James's strenuous peace-making policy" (89) or was he trying to accomplish something else?

Balanced Treatment

To see what Shakespeare wishes to achieve by incorporating references to contemporary political events into *Cymbeline*, it is perhaps worthwhile to start by looking at how he presents these topical subjects in the play.

Milford Haven and Wales

Wales, especially the port town of Milford Haven in Wales, is allotted geographic centrality in the play. Milford is the place to which almost every one from Cymbeline's court eventually hurries. The action ends there, where every knot in the tangled plot is untied and the late Shakespearean theme of reunion, repentance and reconciliation played out. On the level of state politics, it is in Wales that Britain's victory over Rome is won, Cymbeline's magnanimous promise to resume the tribute given, and peace between the two countries declared. On a more personal level, Cymbeline is reunited in Milford with his lost heirs and reconciled with his daughter and her husband. The latter two also achieve a reconciliation between themselves. Thus in the final scene, Milford and Wales live up to Jacobean expectations of their symbolic significance, hosting revelation, reconciliation, British victory, declaration of international peace and assurance of dynastic continuation.

On the other hand, however, Milford and Wales also breed discontent and even despair. Early in the play, a complaint about the Welsh mountains is voiced by Cymbeline's two princes. To them, raised in these mountains, the place is, according to Guiderius, "[a] cell of ignorance…[a] prison for a debtor" (3.3.33, 34), and for Arviragus, a "cage" (3.3.42). Their complaint is commonplace in that it is the kind which any "poor unfledged" (3.3.27) who finds the monotony of his confined existence unbearable would voice to a parent who continually refuses him the possible excitement offered by what is beyond his daily routine. Yet such criticism is at the same time highly significant in a play written around 1610. The cave and mountains are, after all, located in Wales. Although in its details the complaint is by no means political, it nevertheless introduces into the ears of the audience a dissonant note in contrast to the triumph and glory associated with Wales and Milford.

Guiderius and Arviragus' description of the Welsh mountains—"cell", "prison" and "cage"—though intended figuratively by them, can, and maybe should, be taken literally by the audience, for, however fatherly Belarius has treated them, there is no altering the fact that the princes were abducted and are essentially hostages held in the Welsh mountains.

Moreover, growing up under Belarius' tutelage, the two boys may well have had a rather bitter resentment against the king who has wrongfully banished their "father" planted in them: "the King / Hath not deserved my service nor your loves" (4.4.24-5). Therefore Wales, birthplace of the Tudor dynasty and root of James's claim to the English throne, stands paradoxically in the dramatic plot of *Cymbeline* as the place where princes are nurtured yet at the same time held prisoner and turned against their own royal roots and identity.

The two boys' dull life in the mountains of Wales, however, pales in comparison with their sister's experience there. It is in Wales that Innogen experiences traumatizing emotional toils, falling from hope and elation to the depths of despair. Hurrying towards "this same blessèd Milford" (3.2.59) under the written instruction of Posthumus, Innogen is to discover, when she reaches Wales, that her husband has in fact intended Milford to be the place of her execution, on a charge of having "played the strumpet in my bed" (3.4.21-2). Escaping death on this occasion, she is later "poisoned" by the draught given to her by Pisanio. Waking from her drugged sleep, she finds a bloody headless corpse by her side, dressed in Posthumus' garments and sharing his physique, which convinces her that her husband has been brutally murdered. And finally, in Milford, before husband and wife can reunite, she, still in her disguise as a page to the Roman ambassador, receives a physical blow from Posthumus. Of course, it should be noted that the pain Innogen has to go through is not actually inflicted on her by anyone *from* Wales. On the contrary, the little human warmth she has had comes from Belarius and the two boys, "natives" to the place. Nevertheless, her experience *in* Wales makes this part of Britain a site of intense personal suffering for her.

Cymbeline's children's experiences in Wales introduce a rather unpleasant note to the connotations of triumph and dynastic birth which Tudor-Stuart mythology associated with the place. But more damaging still to its image is the fact that in *Cymbeline*, Milford is where the Romans land to invade Britain. Of course, letting the Romans enter Britain via Milford is an arrangement which makes sure that, as this is a play designed to end with Roman defeat, the British army can achieve this victory *in* Milford, thus allowing the port to live up to its reputation as the place of triumph and celebration in Jacobean panegyrics. The British army can also be shown to advantage, for the Roman defeat in Milford would mean that the enemy is immediately quelled, prevented from moving further inland to become a substantial threat to British independence. Nevertheless, the Romans' choice of invasion route may imply that, in the fictional world of *Cymbeline* at least, Milford is a weak spot in Britain's border defence, a threat to the country's security. The battle at Milford also puts its status as the birthplace of a dynasty under the threat of being turned into the grave of a nation's independence, especially since, before Belarius and the two princes join in the battle, the British army was actually "broken" (5.5.5). And finally, whether the Britons win or lose, the Roman invasion creates the rather awkward situation where, in a fairly ironic twist, it is Caius Lucius, the Roman emissary, rather than any Briton, who lands at Milford, in anticipation of the future Henry VII of England.

In *Cymbeline*, then, Milford and Wales play host to both human sufferings and joy, separation and reunion, death and restoration. The mountains of Wales hold princes prisoner, yet at the same time carefully nurture them. The port of Milford threatens British independence, but is also the place where Britain proves itself unconquered. It is a battlefield *and* the site where peace is declared. Cymbeline's own last words in the play sum up Milford and Wales pretty neatly. They are places where "bloody hands were washed, with such a peace" (5.6.485).

British Nationalism

Shakespeare has, in *Cymbeline*, composed one of the most exhilaratingly eulogistic speeches about Britain in the whole of his repertoire (comparable, indeed, to John of Gaunt's "This England" speech in *Richard II*) in its praise of

> The natural bravery of your isle, which stands
> As Neptune's park, ribbed and paled in
> With banks unscalable and roaring waters,
> With sands that will not bear your enemies' boats,
> But suck them up to th' topmast. (3.1.18-22)

In praising the defence offered by Britain's unique geographic position, the speech boosts British nationalism with its recollection of how Caesar was "carried [f]rom off our coast, twice beaten; and his shipping... cracked...easily 'gainst our rocks" (3.1.25-6, 28-9). However, Shakespeare undermines the effect of this speech by assigning it to the Queen, whose degenerate moral character prevents the audience from easily accepting it either as a demonstration of earnest patriotism or a manifesto of support for British nationalism on the part of the playwright.

To the virtuous Innogen, on the other hand, Shakespeare gives five lines in which she questions the protective isolation of Britain:

Hath Britain all the sun that shines? Day, night,
Are they not but in Britain? I'th' world's volume
Our Britain seems as of it, but not in't,
In a great pool a swan's nest. Prithee, think
There's livers out of Britain. (3.4.136-40)

The effect of this speech, though not marred by any question of its speaker's moral position, is undercut by the circumstances under which it is spoken. Innogen, one should remember, is not in her most sensible or stable frame of mind here. She has just learnt that her husband had ordered her killed on a false charge of adultery. Moreover, she has increased her own agony by hastily jumping to the mistaken conclusion that he wishes to clear her away for "[s]ome Jay of Italy" (3.4.48). This five-line observation on British isolation is in fact a digressive answer, in the affirmative, to Pisanio's suggestion that she should flee the country. That she should take five lines to say a "yes" is further demonstration of the intellectual and emotional turmoil she is experiencing. Considering the condition which Innogen is in when she speaks 3.4.136-40, it seems more reasonable to see the lines as expressing a desperate emotional state rather than a cool-headed political judgement. Innogen elaborates on the isolation of Britain not because she judges it a political drawback, but because she is making up her mind to leave a place where memories are painful. In other words, her expressed internationalism, though sensible by twenty-first-century standards, should perhaps not be taken too literally within the context of the play, and should not be looked on as proof of the playwright's own anti-nationalism.

Neither does the play's depiction of the battle between Britain and Rome offer much insight into Shakespeare's own position on British nationalism and pride. The British army is shown to have vanquished the Romans in Milford, but during the battle there was a moment when the majority of British soldiers were far from unconquerable or heroic. Faced with an "enemy full-hearted, / Lolling the tongue with slaught'ring" (5.5.7-8), on the British side

[t]he King himself [was]
Of his wings destitute, the army broken,
And but the backs of Britons seen, all flying. (5.5.4-6, italics mine)

The day is only saved when Belarius and the two princes join in the battle and spur the British army back into combat. It is by defeating the Romans that Britain's two lost princes have completed their passage from boyhood to manhood and regained their royal status. On the other hand, these two heirs to the British throne were nursed by a surrogate mother whose name, Euriphile, literally means "lover of Europe". The war ends with Britain distinguishing itself as a worthy rival to Rome rather than a submissive colony. But while establishing its own national identity, Britain loses its autonomy somewhat, for it chooses to resume the payment of the tribute to Rome. Again, as a result of such balanced treatment of the process and the outcome of the Romano-British war, Shakespeare, as in the case of Milford and Wales, offers no clue—or rather, too many clues—about his own personal views on the matter of British nationalism.

Cymbeline and Peace

Winning the war against the Romans puts Cymbeline in the position to magnanimously declare "[m]y peace we will begin" (5.6.459). Many scholars have suggested that, to a certain extent, Cymbeline is to be looked on as an analogue of James:

Like James, Cymbeline is peaceful, cosmopolitan and a modernizer. (Butler 51)

Imagine King James watching the play: he would have seen himself as a composite version of Cymbeline and Augustus, both a British king and a neo-Roman emperor. (Bate, "*Cymbeline*" 2243)

It seems to me likely that the character of Cymbeline—at any rate, in the final scene, with its powerful peace-tableau—has a direct reference to James I. (Jones 96)

Whether or not he had intended his title character to be understood in this light, Shakespeare may have been aware that such associations would be made and thus had possibly taken some pains to make sure that his script should not give offence. The surprisingly weak characterisation of Cymbeline, for example, makes sense when considering that the fictional king might be seen as a reference to James, since "[i]t would not do to inquire too closely into the monarch's interior life" (Bate, "*Cymbeline*" 2243). It would not do to openly question a monarch's decisions either, which is probably one reason why by the end of the play, the blame for the recent war, caused by Britain's refusal to pay tribute to Rome, has all been laid on the Queen—"We were dissuaded by our wicked queen" (5.6. 463)—who has conveniently died offstage. Jones suggests that the portrayal of the Queen as a stock evil-stepmother character is another possible attempt to distance fiction from reality, for

[i]t would have been undesirable for Cymbeline's wicked Queen to be approximated, in the minds of the audience, with James's virtuous consort, Anne of Denmark. So the Queen is made conventionally grotesque after a fairytale fashion in order to counteract the temptation to find a real-life analogue. (97)

And thus, through compromising the characterisation of Cymbeline and his Queen, Shakespeare "officiously protects" (ibid.) the fictional king from blame as well as himself from offending his real-life royal patron.

But these "protective measures" in the characterisation of Cymbeline are only half the picture. As with his presentation of Milford, Wales and British nationalism, his treatment of the king balances positive and negative connotations. Cymbeline in the final scene is "the great Western King, at the centre of things, restored to all his children and, to close all, magnanimously radiating Peace" (ibid.). But he is also the king who, by refusing to pay tribute to Rome, had broken the peace between the two countries and necessitated the war. He is the happy "mother to the birth of three" (5.6.370) by the end of the play, but it was through his own incompetence as a monarch and tyranny as a father that he had been separated from his children in the first place, having caused two to be abducted and one to run away. The two valiant heirs who have saved the day for Britain are "blood of [his] begetting" (5.6.332), but he, who has no hand in their upbringing, was himself temporarily captured by Romans in the battle.

Moreover, Shakespeare's own "protective measures" in the characterisation of Cymbeline have in fact a double-edged quality. By undercutting characterisation, the playwright keeps a discrete distance from a monarch's interior life, but at the same time makes it inevitable that his audience should speculate on this monarch's thought process and form their judgement on his kingship based on these speculations, for, without being allotted a soliloquy, Cymbeline has no opportunity to reveal his criteria in reaching his decisions. The audience might reach the conclusion, as Butler does, that

Cymbeline is peaceful, cosmopolitan and a modernizer, but his kingship is no less potent for being pacific. In his state, authority is invested in a strong and self-authorizing fatherhood. (51)

But it is equally possible that they might be sceptical, for Cymbeline's explanation that refusing to pay tribute to Rome was the Queen's idea exposes him either as an incompetent king dominated by others or, if he is using her as a scapegoat, as someone who is afraid to take responsibilities for the consequences of his own decisions. Similarly, his act of promising peace between Rome and Britain shows him both to his advantage and disadvantage. On the one hand, it shows him as a benevolent and far-seeing monarch. On the other, this peace is declared by him only after he has heard the Soothsayer's interpretation of Jupiter's tablet and understood that Britain has been promised "peace and plenty" (5.6.458), which makes it seem as if that he is merely following and announcing decisions made for him. Besides, for the most part of the final scene, Cymbeline appears to "[know] only one course of action: to threaten anyone who contradicts him" (King 149), which makes his "My peace we will begin", announced after he has recovered his family, seem more a manifestation of his good mood than of his political wisdom.

I hope that the above analyses have made it clear that in presenting Milford, Wales, British nationalism and Cymbeline's peace in the play, Shakespeare subjects these topical subjects to a kind of "balanced treatment", offering materials both complimentary and damaging to their reputation with pretty much equal emphasis.

Such ambivalence is not limited to the play's presentation of immediately contemporary concerns. It is administered to more general topics of discussion as well. Womanhood in the play, for example, is represented by both the virtuous Innogen and the evil Queen. Similarly, in its discussion of matters of loyalty, the play features Pisanio, who is both loyal and not loyal, as he proves his loyalty by not doing as he is told: "Wherein I am false I am honest; not true, to be true" (4.3.42). Belarius is another case in point: "beaten for loyalty" and thus "[e]xcited...to treason" (5.6.345, 346), he commits the crime of abducting the princes, but also does the country service by raising them up as fine warriors worthy of their royal status. The play's presentation of British and Roman qualities is equally balanced, as Britain breeds both Cloten and Cymbeline's princes, while Rome contains Giacomo alongside Caius Lucius. And finally, Jupiter, who expresses his favour in cruelty, "Whom best I love, I cross" (5.5.195), represents *Cymbeline*'s dramatisation of divine authority. In giving mortals balanced treatments, divine authority is itself in turn treated with balance, presented neither as straightforward epitome of justice nor of irresponsible caprice.

Not surprisingly, taking the cue from the abundance of topical subjects in the play, scholars have subjected *Cymbeline* to a plethora of political interpretations in an attempt to detect traces of Shakespeare's personal political sympathies. Indeed, of all the late romances, with the possible exception of *The Tempest*, *Cymbeline* seems to be the most popular for political interpretations. The conclusions these readings have reached are varied and not infrequently contradictory. Victorians saw in the play an emphasis on the qualities of womanhood and British virtues embodied in the figure of Innogen, yet contemporary critics have pointed out that the play's resolution ends with a decidedly "masculine embrace" (Mikalachki 303) as "Britain renews itself as women are disempowered or disappear" (Howard 2970). Knight suggests that *Cymbeline* presents "a national statement" (130), while David Bergeron sees the play as

> the dramatist's last *Roman* play, providing a glimpse of the Augustan era and offering a logical conclusion to the events dramatized in other Roman plays. ("Roman" 30, italics mine)

Bergeron's view is shared by Coppélia Kahn, who considers that *Cymbeline* "belongs with the Roman works" (160) and further suggests that "in this play Shakespeare pays tribute to Rome as a cultural model for Britain" (161). Jones, on the other hand, finds in the play "tribute to James's strenuous peace-making policy" (89), which apparently stands in contrast to King's conclusion that the play "allows its audiences...the opportunity to take a rather harder look at the propaganda of power" (63).

These political interpretations are all supported by substantial evidence from the play itself—Shakespeare has made sure of that by his balanced treatment. There is enough evidence to suggest that with his portrayal of Milford and Wales, the playwright is, through presenting the "darker side" of these places, introducing a dissonant note into Jacobean celebration of their symbolism, and consequently signalling his scepticism of James's views and policies in general. But it is equally possible that he is following the structural design, characteristic of the last plays, of events moving from bad to worse before turning better again. The manoeuvre thus shows Milford and Wales earning their respected status, just as characters in the plays all have to struggle to earn forgiveness, reconciliation and happiness. Similarly, with his presentation of British nationalism in the play, he seems to be either questioning Jacobean national aspirations and pointing out the paradox that the pursuit of such aspirations would "potentially [conflict] with the more pacific and internationalist determinations of Jacobean kingship" (Butler 42), or, since the play has a happy ending where British identity remains intact *and* international peace is achieved, commending a policy which strives for the realisation of both. And as for those who perceive a reference to James in Cymbeline, based on their conclusions about the latter's kingship, Shakespeare may either be praising the English king and his policies, or expressing his disapproval of them. The playwright has laid out materials for all these interpretations.

Upon first glance, *Cymbeline*'s balanced treatment of its topical subjects is not unusual in the Shakespearean canon. In providing both positive and negative materials about his subjects, the playwright participates, as he has always done, in the Elizabethan and Jacobean rhetorical tradition of arguing both sides of a question—*in utramque partem*—a habit of thinking which his education at the Stratford grammar school would have drilled into him.[4] Perhaps considerations of political discretion also contributed to Shakespeare's balanced treatment of *Cymbeline*'s topical subjects. Again, this seems to be the rule, rather than the exception, in his career. He has, after all, always been evasive where his personal opinions are concerned.

But in the case of *Cymbeline*, more than considerations of political discretion and adherence to contemporary rhetorical practice seem to be at work behind such balanced treatment, for it extends beyond the play's presentation of topical discussions and is applied to other dramatic arrangements. The play's overall plot, in terms of its choice of source material, is balanced between history and legend, the former supplying the names, background and subplot of the story and the latter the main storyline. Within that history-romance balanced plot, elements of comedy and tragedy as well as pastoral and the grotesque are allotted fairly equal proportions and given fairly equal emphasis. The lyrical sadness of the lovers' forced separation, for example, is balanced by immediate comic relief in the form of the Second Lord's mockery of Cloten and the First Lord. The grandeur of the Queen's "patriotic" speech is undercut by the laughable vulgarity of Cloten's interruptions. The beauty and tranquillity of Innogen's funeral are straightaway shattered by the horrific sight of her smearing her face with the blood from a headless corpse. And even during that poignant *and* repugnant scene where Innogen grieves over the headless body, there is an element of the comic. Her grief is "heartfelt, real, desperate and terrible—so desperate, in fact, that it may strike an audience as embarrassing and therefore funny" (King 31). The combined effect of such balanced treatment on all levels of the play ultimately manifests itself in the famous (or infamous) generic uncertainty of *Cymbeline*, as of the elements of history, romance, tragedy and comedy, none is able to override the others to become the dominant force.

Such balanced treatment, by offering the audience too many contradictory clues—and therefore effectively no clue at all—on aspects of the play, obscures the playwright's own stance on questions of the

---

[4] "Shakespeare imbibed his dialogic way of thinking unconsciously through the daily grind of exercises in the Stratford-upon-Avon classroom" (Bate, Introduction 26).

play's tone, genre or political sympathies. It thus forces the audience to form their own opinions about them.

What Shakespeare is doing to his audience here is, in a non-morally-corrupt way, a metadramatic equivalent of what Giacomo is doing to Posthumus in the deception scene (2.4): letting the listener manipulate the meaning of his words by being ambivalent himself. Of course, Giacomo is much less committed to such balanced ambivalence than Shakespeare. With material gains to consider, the Italian is not above occasionally stating his own meaning explicitly to make sure that Posthumus interprets the rest in the intended way. But it is worth noticing that in reporting his encounter with Innogen, Giacomo tells few direct lies. Apart from his account of how he gets Innogen's bracelet ("She stripped it from her arm...She gave it me" (2.4.101, 103)) and his claim that he kissed the mole under her breast, which are both barefaced lies, for most of his report Giacomo relies on the forces of rhetoric to achieve his end. Often, in fact, he speaks quite truthfully, but with an ambiguity which opens up room for alternative interpretations. In such cases he depends on the listener's, as it were, cooperation in inferring unpleasant implications from the literal meaning of his sentences. His observation that Posthumus' diamond is not hard to come by with "[y]our lady being so easy" (2.4.47), for example, is true in the sense that Innogen, in readily agreeing to safeguard his trunk in her own bedchamber, is "[m]oved without difficulty to action or belief; soon yielding, compliant; credulous" ("Easy adj., adv. and n.", Def. 12a). The slander on her character is to be completed by Posthumus, if he interprets the "easy" here with the sexual undertone of the word in "lady of easy virtue". Similarly, Giacomo's claim that

> First, her bedchamer—
> Where I confess I slept not, but profess
> Had that was well worth watching (2.4.66-8)

is also literally true, for he did indeed keep up a vigil in Innogen's bedchamber, busily noting the decorations in the room and the physical features of the sleeping princess. But the lines can also be understood to have a more sexual implication. Another such example is his swearing "By Jupiter, I had it [the bracelet] from her arm" (2.4.121), which is again true in a literal sense. He did remove the bracelet from the arm of the unsuspecting Innogen—and therefore it is safe to swear by Jupiter—but not in the way which Posthumus interprets it: that she voluntarily bequeathed it to him.

To Posthumus' credit, he has managed to resist seeing any sexual suggestiveness in Giacomo's "[y]our lady being so easy" or his claim that he did not sleep in Innogen's room. It is only after the Italian has produced the physical evidence of the bracelet that his faith in her breaks down and he begins to see more than he should from Giacomo's statements. It is significant, however, that the evidence of the bracelet is enough to shatter his trust in Innogen's chastity. Clearly this is a point with which Shakespeare wishes to illustrate how easily Posthumus' faith in his wife is overcome, for he makes him depart from his predecessors in the German tale *Frederick of Jennen* and Boccaccio's *Decameron*, both of whom succumb to the villain's deception only after the more compelling evidence of the knowledge of the wife's birthmark is presented. The playwright also, in this scene, makes it a point to contrast Posthumus' reaction with Filario's to show the rashness of the former's judgement:

POSTHUMUS O, no, no, no— 'tis true! Here, take this too.
…
FILARIO   Have patience, sir,
    And take your ring again; 'tis not yet won.
    It may be probable she lost it, or
    Who knows if one her woman, being corrupted,
    Hath stol'n it from her?
…
POSTHUMUS Hark you, he swears, by Jupiter he swears.
    'Tis true, nay, keep the ring, 'tis true. (2.4.106, 113-7, 122-3)

Posthumus' easy credulity is as much the result of his own predisposition to associate Innogen with infidelity as that of Giacomo's skilfully ambivalent language. For all his declaration of confidence in his wife's virtue in 1.4, Posthumus' language in 2.4, even before Giacomo begins to relate his experience at the British court, betrays a readiness to denounce her. It is he who, upon Giacomo's return from Britain, brings up the subject of the wager. Inquiring after the outcome of the Italian's trip, Posthumus asks in a "complacent" (Siemon 57) way: "Sparkles this stone as it was wont, or is't not / Too dull for your good wearing?" (2.4.40-1). Since the stone is given to Posthumus by Innogen, compared to her in the men's previous conversations, and offered as the wager in the bet on her chastity, it is firmly associated with her. Thus when Posthumus asks about the diamond, he is in effect asking about the outcome of the wager and thus about her chastity. This close identification between Innogen and the diamond makes Posthumus' question a curiously disturbing "either-or" choice, for whichever option Giacomo takes, Posthumus has himself provided the Italian with an opportunity to slander Innogen. If Giacomo answers that he thinks the diamond still sparkles and is not beneath his dignity to wear, it can imply that he is going to wear it—in other words, Posthumus has lost the wager and that Innogen, outwardly fair, is wanton. If, on the other hand, Posthumus is to keep the diamond, it would mean that Giacomo considers it "too dull" for his "good wearing", still implying that she is unworthy. Thus in trying to express his complacency, Posthumus betrays his subconscious insecurity. If this interpretation of this question about the diamond seems to have a somewhat "Posthumusian" quality to it in that it digs for figurative meaning in something which the speaker might mean quite literally, it is because Posthumus himself has provided the cue. A few lines earlier, in response to Giacomo's praise of Innogen's beauty, he rather vehemently states that if she is not fair and good,

> let her beauty
> Look through a casement to allure false hearts,
> And be false with them. (2.4.33-5)

Although by this he means to praise his wife's combined virtue of fairness and goodness, his way of speaking "suggests how predisposed he is to attribute whoredom to Innogen" (Butler, qtd. in NCS *Cymbeline* 135, note to l. 34).

Posthumus' easy defeat in the deception scene is a case in point of a listener's preconceived views, however unconscious, manipulating the direction of his interpretations. Innogen, to a lesser degree, is also susceptible to such injudiciousness, demonstrated by her immediately interpreting Posthumus' order for her execution as the consequence of his having fallen for some woman in Rome. The idea that Posthumus is inconstant is first suggested to her by Giacomo. Although Giacomo's blunder in suggesting that she should take her revenge by behaving wantonly herself has helped her to resist the deception in the first instance, her later remark that

> Giacomo,
> Thou didst accuse him of incontinency.
> …
> Thy favour's good enough, (3.4.45-6, 48)

shows that the Italian, though failing in persuading her to misbehave, has succeeded in planting the idea of her husband's inconstancy into her head. A mind not poisoned by the suggestion of Posthumus' falsehood would

have formed a more reasonable explanation of the situation, as Pisanio's
has:

> It cannot be
> But that my master is abused. Some villain,
> Ay, and singular in his art, hath done you both
> This cursèd injury. (3.4.118-21)

The main plot of *Cymbeline* thus rolls into action as a result of facts
being distorted through the process of interpretation. In a parallel course,
Rome and Britain's dispute over the payment of tribute has part of its root
in the two countries' disagreement on how to interpret the same historic
episode. Shakespeare juxtaposes both versions of the history of Caesar's
"conquest" (the Roman version) or "kind of conquest" (the British
version) over Britain in the same scene. With the Romans and the Britons
drawing their vastly different conclusions from the same historic event, he
illustrates once more how pre-conceived opinions dictate interpretation.

Like the Queen and Caius Lucius, who form contrasting opinions
about the same episode in history, the audience, in watching the same
performance of *Cymbeline*, might reach contesting conclusions on the
play's genre or political sympathies, as is proved by the ongoing debates
on genre and the wealth of political interpretations it has generated. And
just as Posthumus, and to some extent Innogen, falls into Giacomo's plot
by their "cooperative interpretation" of his ambivalent report,
Shakespeare's audience and readers, in reaching their conclusions, will
have fallen cooperatively into the playwright's own dramatic scheme. As
his own views on politics or genre lie shielded by the impenetrable walls
of his balanced treatment of the play's dramatic elements, any conclusion
about genre or professed political views is thus arguably a manifestation of
the spectator/listener's own pre-conceived views on the subject. As a
result, in forming an opinion—any opinion—on these subjects, members
of the audience will have contributed to the idea that in practice,
interpretation is often more a process of fitting the evidence to one's preconceived views than that of forming an opinion based on given evidence.

Ever observant of the Janus-like character of the manoeuvres of
English Renaissance rhetoric and true to his own "balancing spirit" in this
particular play, Shakespeare, while exposing the problematic process of
interpretation, is equally ready to point out the possible unreliability of
report—the other end, as it were, of communication. After all, despite
Posthumus' "cooperation" in his deception, Giacomo, who deliberately

distorts certain facts in his report about Innogen, is unquestionably the villain of the piece.

By another act of balanced treatment, Shakespeare raises the audience's awareness of the possible distortion of facts in reports: the balance between events acted out and events reported. Giacomo's intrusion into Innogen's chamber is the most obvious example. It is presented in performance in 2.2 and through report in 2.4. But since false report plays a central role in Giacomo's plot, it is inevitable that the Italian's night at the British court should be dramatised in both forms. *Cymbeline*, however, also contains a good number of episodes in which verbal report plays no apparently significant role but which are nevertheless presented both in full action and through report. Posthumus' character is both presented through what he does in the course of the play and offered to the audience in the First Gentleman and Filario's praises and the Frenchman's recollections. Guiderius and Cloten's quarrel and fight exist both in staged form and in Guiderius' account. The battle between Rome and Britain is fought on stage and immediately afterwards recounted by Posthumus. And in the epiphany scene, Jupiter's descent and ascent are both acted out in front of the audience and described by Sicilius.

Apart from these staged-and-reported episodes, the play also has several events which, though not performed on stage, are offered to the audience in multiple reported versions. The example which immediately comes to mind is of course the Queen and Caius Lucius' contesting accounts of Caesar's (kind of) conquest of Britain. But certain other less important episodes are also subjected to such multi-versioned presentation. For example, Posthumus' fight with Cloten is presented in three reported versions: Pisanio's briefing, Cloten's recollections (seconded by the First Lord), and the Second Lord's account in his asides.

While the "multi-versionedness" of these events serves a special purpose in each individual case,[5] one function they share is demonstrating how seldom facts survive intact through communication. Sometimes facts are lost when the reporter chooses not to mention them. Posthumus, for example, in recounting the battle at Milford, omits to relate his own heroic deeds in the war. Similarly, Guiderius, when he retells how Cloten insulted him, does not mention how he himself was equally insulting. At other times facts suffer from distortion which does no ill. For instance, on the Jacobean stage, Jupiter's eagle probably descended rather woodenly

---

[5] For example, Sicilius' awed description of Jupiter's epiphany and Posthumus' account of the battle probably make up for the inadequacies of seventeenth-century stage effects, while the clashes between the Second Lord and Cloten's account of the latter's fight with Posthumus offer the audience a bit of comic relief.

instead of magnificently "[s]toop[ing], as if to foot us" (5.5.210), and it is highly unlikely that it was capable of "[p]reen[ing] the immortal wing and claw[ing] his beak" (5.5.212). But Sicilius' embellished report does no harm. Not infrequently facts are contaminated because they have already been processed by the reporter's unconsciously prejudiced mind. The First Gentleman, for example, no doubt has no suspicion that Posthumus may not always be

> A sample to the youngest, to th' more mature
> A glass that feated them, and to the graver
> A child that guided dotards. (1.1.48-50)

Similarly, Cloten, being an arrogant ass, probably genuinely believes that he did wound and intimidate Posthumus when he says "[t]he villain would not stand me" (1.2.12). And finally, facts can sometimes be deliberately falsified by a reporter. When they are, such communication can do tremendous damage, as Giacomo's deception has vividly demonstrated.

These double- or multi-versioned episodes illustrating the distortion of facts in communication are to be found throughout the play, constantly reminding the audience of the possible untrustworthiness of reports. They, like the ambiguity of the play's genre and political stance, thus engage the audience in personally experiencing what the play dramatises in its main storyline: the potential perils of verbal communication.

This problematic experience of communication for the audience is consolidated by the play's liberal inclusion of apparent references to topical issues. It seems that with these topical pointers, the playwright draws the audience in, signalling to them the possible presence of discussions of contemporary politics. He further solidifies this "luring" effect by subjecting the topical subjects in *Cymbeline* to a fairly neutralised presentation, obscuring his personal views in the balanced proportions of complimentary and damaging materials, and thus forcing the audience to come to terms with the play's political stance based on their own preconceived opinions of Jacobean politics. At the same time, his consistent practice of presenting one episode in multiple versions continually alerts them to the possible distortion of facts through report and the potential dangers of interpretation. Therefore, as the audience watch the play, with its main- and sub-plots both developing as a result of problematic report and interpretation, they are made to personally experience, on a metadramatic level, the moral of the story of *Cymbeline*. The play, rather than "peculiarly" stitched together, is thus a carefully constructed entity. With his unusual employment and treatment of contemporary political topics, Shakespeare has achieved in *Cymbeline* a unity between dramatic action and metadramatic experience.

Of course, one is not saying that Shakespeare's employment of political references in *Cymbeline* is limited to using them as "baits". He might possibly have intended a political statement in the play. However, owing to his exactingly balanced treatment of these topics, without conclusive external evidence about his political sympathies—and there appears to be none, at least at the moment—it seems impossible to pin down that statement. There is, however, ample evidence to show how audiences over the ages have participated in contributing to the play's suggestion that interpretations of the same event or subject can vary significantly. While the Master of Revels in James's court (and the king himself, if he ever attended a performance) appeared to have found no political dissonance in *Cymbeline*—the play passed censorship and did not get the playwright into trouble—and Sir Henry Herbert's records show that it was "well likte" by Charles I, twentieth- and twenty-first-century scholarship tends to discover in the play a playwright "ask[i]ng fundamental questions about England's place in history, her experience with religion, and her future in the world" (King 2).

This hypothesis regarding part of Shakespeare's dramatic design in *Cymbeline* is, of course, another interpretation which may be entirely off the mark. However, one is emboldened to venture it by the playwright's own ultimate redemption of the processes of verbal communication in the last scene. Having pointed out the potential dangers of interpretation and warned the audience of the possible treachery of report, Shakespeare proceeds to undo the damage with a dramatic *tour de force* of a final scene in which restoration, reconciliation and reunion are achieved almost entirely through the agency of verbal communication. As in *Pericles*, the act of storytelling bridges the gap between the past and the present, between appearance and reality, and between what one thinks and what really is. Reports *can* reveal the truth. Giacomo, for example, eventually confesses to his deception. Similarly, interpretation *can* be correct. It is, after all, Dr. Cornelius' correct conjecture about what the Queen intends to do with the poison she orders that has made him switch the drug, thus saving Innogen. Moreover, Shakespeare also gives those who have blundered in their interpretations a second chance. Such is the case with the Roman Soothsayer, who, previously mistaking the vision of Jupiter in his dream as a sign for Roman victory, readjusts his interpretation with the help of the tablet to reveal the true meaning of the epiphany.

Cymbeline-Style

The coordination between dramatic action and metadramatic experience in *Cymbeline* is further consolidated by its linguistic style. Broadly speaking, the play is written in Shakespeare's late style established in *Pericles*. With a style which both demands audience participation in coming to terms with the language and displays a high degree of artistic control, the late verse seems to fit well with the play's dramatic scheme.

Shakespeare's late style rings as soon as the play opens:

> You do not meet a man but frowns. Our bloods
> No more obey the heavens than our courtiers
> Still seem as does the King. (1.1.1-3)

Throughout the three lines there is an incessant repetition of the "s" sound, particularly in the last line: frown*s*, blood*s*, heaven*s*, courtier*s*, *s*till *s*eem a*s* doe*s* the King. On the level of lines, except for the first sentence, the lines are enjambed, the full meaning not revealed until the last line. Both sentences are grammatically devious. The first is elliptical, omitting a relative pronoun: "You do not meet a man but [who] frowns". The second presents more of a challenge to grammatical analysis. It can be looked on either as an elliptical sentence which has removed a conjunction and a pronoun:

> Our bloods
> No more obey the heavens than our courtiers
> Still seem as [if they] do[es] the King,

or as a sentence in which the order of certain words is inverted

> Our bloods
> No more obey the heaven than our courtiers
> Still seem as [the King does].

Both explanations, however, fail to give complete grammatical satisfaction. In the first instance the sentence will be grammatically incorrect, for the "does" in 1.1.3 is inconsistent with the plural "courtiers" in 1.1.2. On the other hand, if the sentence is to be looked on as a case of inverted word order, the two halves—"Our bloods no more obey the heaven" and "than our courtiers still seem as the King does"—feel subtly uncoordinated in the negative comparative, making the listener unsure if the speaker intends by it to mean that "Our bloods do not obey the heaven any more than our courtiers still seem as the King does" or "As our bloods obey the heaven, so the courtiers still seem as the King does". It is, in short, a sentence that seems hardly able to withstand grammatical scrutiny.

Thus in the space of two sentences in three lines, many features typical of Shakespeare's late style have already emerged: incessant repetition of sound, enjambment, elliptical sentences, inverted word order and convoluted syntax. The second sentence, if interpreted as an elliptical one, also reveals Shakespeare indulging in his late impulse of being at once economical and elaborate in sentence construction, for while the ellipsis removes dispensable (to some extent) grammatical elements, the sentence complicates itself by turning a simple statement into a complex negative comparative.

The repeated "s" sound which runs throughout this passage immediately provides the background of the story, which is also the purpose of the entire speech. /S/ and /z/ are sounds at once soft and scratchy, thus introducing to the ears of the audience a sense of the hushed dissonance in Cymbeline's court. As the lines move towards 1.1.3, the "s" sound grows ever more noticeable, finally becoming audible in almost every word in the last line—in the First Folio the last word actually reads "kings" instead of "king"—the frequency of its occurrence making the scratchiness of the /s/ or /z/ overpower its softness, signalling the violence soon to break out at the British court.

Like their aural quality, the complex syntax of the three lines also helps to make the audience personally experience what their speaker is describing. The First Gentleman, to whom the lines are assigned, is basically telling the Second that in Cymbeline's court, the courtiers' faces are not faithful indicators of their own sentiments. In other words, there is something else going on beneath the surface. The way he makes the point, shrouding his simple statement with a hardly penetrable grammatical structure, conjures up the feeling that perhaps there is more behind his words, making the listener feel bewildered and uneasy, as one probably would at Cymbeline's court.

Apart from helping to illustrate its speaker's point in its immediate context, the language of *Cymbeline* also encapsulates the audience's experience of coming to terms with the action of the play. Shakespeare's linguistic style here, like his balanced treatment of generic elements and topical subjects, brings the process of interpretation to the foreground. His late impulse to both abbreviate and elaborate, in particular, poses as another act of balanced treatment which makes easy comprehension of meaning almost impossible. The impulse to be elliptical denies listeners helpful grammatical information, while the tendency to digress detains them from reaching the thesis of a sentence. The complicated, and often convoluted, sentence formation thus forces the audience to work for meaning. It is a linguistic complement to the metadramatic experience of "enforced" interpretation brought about by the playwright's neutral presentation of topical subjects as well as generic elements.

Having pushed interpretation to the foreground, the playwright's late style proceeds to consolidate, on a linguistic level, the play's argument about how interpretations of the same subject can vary from listener to listener. Although members of the audience are able to grasp the general meaning of a sentence, their understanding may be subtly different as a result of their different ways of coming to terms with the devious grammar or tortuous syntax. It is even possible that the gradual accumulation of such differences in the comprehension of single sentences will eventually contribute to the considerable differences in the understanding of the play as a whole.

1.1.1-3 once more offers a fine example of how listeners' reception of a late Shakespearean passage may vary. In this particular case, the variations in interpretation can be seen in editors' different decisions about how the two sentences should be punctuated. King remarks that "scarcely two modern editions present the text here in precisely the same way" (5). She may have exaggerated a little, for the Norton version I quoted at the beginning of the section is exactly the same as Warren's Oxford version and Butler's New Cambridge version, and only varies from Bate's Royal Shakespeare Company version in capitalising the "K" in "King". Nevertheless, it is true that editors can differ considerably in their choices of punctuation for this opening speech. The First Folio version reads:

> You do not meet a man but Frownes.
> Our bloods no more obey the Heauens
> Then our Courtiers:
> Still seeme, as do's the Kings. (qtd. in King 5)

King's own proposed version runs:

> You do not meet a man but frowns. Our bloods
> No more obey the heavens, than our courtiers'
> Still seem as does the king's. (7)

And J. M. Nosworthy's version in the second Arden series reads:

> You do not meet a man but frowns: our bloods

No more obey the heavens than our courtiers
Still seem as does the king's.

These subtle variations in punctuation, particularly in the second half of the second sentence, give subtle differences to the emphasis of the sentences, which betray the editors' subtle differences in their interpretations. The Norton (and Oxford and Cambridge) version, by its choice of "does the *King*" rather than "does the *King's*" seems to put an emphasis on Cymbeline's tyranny/authority (the courtiers obey the king in everything). The Folio, King and Nosworthy versions, however, put more immediate stress on the hypocrisy of the court (the courtiers' displayed moods imitate those of the king), of which the king's tyranny may only have been one of the causes. One is thus not surprised to see in the introduction to the New Cambridge *Cymbeline* the editor observing that "[in] his [Cymbeline's] state, authority is invested in a strong and self-authorizing fatherhood" (Butler 51), while in her analysis of 1.1.1-3 King remarking on "the protocol of the hierarchical, self-deceiving culture in which they [the courtiers] make their living" (7).

Nosworthy's substitution of the stop between the first and the second sentence with a colon, though not making much difference in a performance, brings to surface an inner logical connection between the two sentences, one which Shakespeare may not have intended to make immediately evident even in writing. Throughout *Cymbeline*, the playwright seems bent on denying his audience the visible connections between sentences or parts of a sentence. The most visible manifestation of this is his late partiality for asyndetic constructions, of which the play contains "seventy-eight instances" (McDonald, *Late* 90). *Cymbeline*'s asyndetons make the listener work to discover the logical connection between elements of speech, the same way as the dramatic coherence of the action of the play requires a degree of mental labour from the audience to uncover. Although 1.1.1-3 is not strictly speaking an asyndetic construction, it nevertheless participates in the late-style practice of weakening the logical relationships in speech. Audibly, there is no conjunction that sign-posts the connection between "You do not meet a man but frowns" and "Our bloods no more obey the heavens than our courtiers still seem as does the King", a connection which does not emerge until the words "courtiers" and "seem" (which refer semantically back to "man" and "frowns") appear.

The richness of sound, the disconnectedness of logic and the trickiness of grammar in 1.1.1-3 are to be found throughout the play. Giacomo's language contains them, as does the Queen's, Posthumus' and Innogen's. Even Cloten's occasionally display these features. It thus helps more to reinforce the immediate context of a speech and advance the dramatic purpose of the play as a whole, rather than help distinguish character from character, participating once more in Shakespeare's late practice of severing style from speaker. As we have seen in the chapter on *Pericles*, this weakening of characterisation, coupled with the complexity of the language, has the effect of making the audience aware of the artist's hand in the composition of the drama, echoing the romances' frequent reliance on divine intervention as well as revealing the playwright's artistic control.

In *Cymbeline*, this sense of artistic control is further exemplified by the way the treatment of language coordinates with the playwright's treatment of his generic elements and topical subjects in pushing interpretation to the forefront of metadramatic experience, suiting that experience to the dramatic purpose of the play. *Cymbeline*, in the end, is a dramatically coherent play composed under tight artistic control. Just as the dispersed and many threaded actions of the play are eventually superbly reassembled and straightened out in the finale, the late style and the balanced treatment in the play are masterfully coordinated to add rich layers of metadramatic experience to the process of watching (or reading) *Cymbeline*.

The play, while making full use of the late Shakespearean style, also develops certain stylistic features of its own in its effort to coordinate metadramatic experience with dramatic action and linguistic style.

Again, one can start looking for these new stylistic features in the opening lines of the play:

> You do not meet a man but frowns. Our bloods
> No more obey the heavens than our courtiers
> Still seem as does the King.

Not only does the First Gentleman's second sentence seem to resist grammatical scrutiny, it is also vulnerable to logical analysis, for it is a statement with a false premise. It so happens that our bloods do not obey the heavens—and even in the days before modern science this was known, as "it was an important tenet in astrology that the stars might incline but cannot *compel* one to any course of action" (King 7). Thus the negative comparative in the second sentence does not work, for while the courtiers' bloods do not obey the heavens, they do appear to take their cue from the moods of the king. Yet paradoxically, this complex statement with its false premise offers a further layer of suggestiveness which still reveals what may be going on at Cymbeline's court: the courtiers no more obey the king than their bloods do the heavens, but they put on an appearance of obedience.

The First Gentleman's false premise in his negative comparative reveals a linguistic feature unique to *Cymbeline*: the instability of its descriptions. That instability can be caused by false logic, as in the case of "our bloods" obeying the heavens. It can also be brought about by the speaker's implicit cancellation of a comparison. An instance of this treatment can be found in Innogen's description of the worthiness of Posthumus:

> he is
> A man worth any woman, over-buys me
> Almost the sum he pays. (1.1.146-8)

Elena Glazov-Corrigan comments on this passage that

> Imogen's portrayal of her husband treats human qualities in terms of solid objects, or monetary values, while undercutting this correspondence with an uncertain "almost". (387)

A third cause is the unstable quality or ambiguity of the referential field itself. A more well-known example of *Cymbeline*'s unstable descriptions is found in the First Gentleman's praise of Posthumus, which combines cancellation of comparison with ambiguity of referential field:

> he that hath her—
> ...
> —is a creature such
> As, to seek through the regions of the earth
> For one his like, there would be something failing
> In him that should compare.
> ...
> I do extend him, sir, within himself;
> Crush him together rather than unfold
> His measure duly. (1.1.17, 19-22, 25-7)

Having praised the qualities of Posthumus, the First Gentleman immediately cancels his praise by stating that it is insufficient. But that original praise, with its hyperbole, in fact describes nothing and tells the listener nothing, for since "he that should compare" is not offered, there is no way of knowing the exact qualities of him—Posthumus—that is compared. King writes about the First Gentleman's praise:

> The language turns itself repeatedly inside out. It moves from the world to the individual, from outside to inside, from a far extension—but one within

the confine of a single individual—to a crushing together that prevents due examination since no examination or comparison could possibly give him his due…Having struggled to work it out, we find that there is in fact nothing there. (8)

The empty praise of Posthumus' qualities has the function of encapsulating the audience's experience of coming to terms with the play itself. *Cymbeline* is a play in which appearance often fails to correspond to reality. In terms of the dramatic action of the play, the development of the plot hinges on the instability of reports, while "[t]he identity of all protagonists can only be caught in a state of transition" (Glazov-Corrigan 389). On a metadramatic level, *Cymbeline* is a play whose title character is hardly the protagonist; a play which was probably advertised to the Jacobean theatregoers as a "tragedy" but nevertheless has a happy ending; and one which, though seeming to allude to contemporary political issues, is highly ambivalent in its apparent political sympathies. Thus, like Shakespeare's employment of his more usual late stylistic features in the play, the unstable descriptions of *Cymbeline* both contribute to the enrichment of a speech's meaning in its immediate context and to the suiting of the audience's experience of play-watching to what the protagonists are going through in another form on stage.

Another stylistic feature which contributes to the dramatic-metadramatic unity of *Cymbeline* is the harshness of its language. The First Gentleman, once more, in the first scene, gives the audience a sample of what is to come

> I do *extend* him, sir, within himself;
> *Crush* him together rather than *unfold*
> His measure duly. (1.1.25-7, italics mine)

"Extend", "crush" and "unfold" illustrate a series of actions which, though meant figuratively, still provoke in the listener a sense of violence, especially considering that the object of this sentence is a "him" rather than a piece of paper or string. This sense of linguistic violence is further generated by the infamously convoluted syntax of the sentences. F. C. Tinkler has pointed out that

> [w]ith certain obvious exceptions…the verse has a hard, corrugated texture differing from that of, say *Coriolanus* or *The Winter's Tale*, in that this harshness proceeds from the persistent recreation of feeling of a particular kind of physical pain…There is an insistent feeling of brutal strain; the contours of the verse…suggest a strong compression. (6)

The language of *Cymbeline* thus recreates the physical and mental pain which its characters are going through to impose it on the audience. In a way, while the other stylistic treatments of the language force intellectual participation from the audience, this harshness of tone in the verse demands their emotional involvement. The listener is thus once more stretched between opposing forces, an effect which the balanced treatment of dramatic elements also reinforces.

Apart from its unstable descriptions and harshness of tone, *Cymbeline* also often carries Shakespeare's late style to extremes. McMullan remarks that it is "cited far more than any other play when evidence of a difficult, spiky late style is sought" (*Idea* 116). J. M. Mackail singles out the style of the play and terms it "Cymbeline [*sic.*]-style" (224), the most noticeable feature of which, according to him, is "the immense number of parentheses, and of parentheses within parentheses" (ibid.). Although the parentheses themselves are probably more the contribution of the Folio compositor than Shakespeare's own choice, they nevertheless exemplify how extremely tortuous the sentences of this play can become. Parentheses indicate digressions in speech through sudden changes of direction or inclusion of supplementary materials, which, once more, tax the listeners' comprehension, feeding them additional information while at the same time delaying their arrival at the main argument. Inevitably, digressions will stretch a simple statement into a complex and long one. And it is indeed in *Cymbeline* that long sentences, according to John Porter Houston, "increase in length over those of the immediately previous plays" (204).

"*Cymbeline*-style", then, is a style which coordinates the linguistic, dramatic and metadramatic experience of the play. In achieving this coordination, it inherits linguistically from the "*Pericles*-style" the dominant late features of ellipsis, asyndeton, repetition and complexity of syntax, which form linguistic echoes of both the play's dramatic action and the audience's metadramatic experience. It has also inherited from *Pericles* an interest in the powers of language and, in achieving the reconciliations and reunions as well as the play's dramatic coherence in its finale almost exclusively through the agency of reports, presents an acknowledgement of the good verbal communication can do.

But that acknowledgement of the positive power of language is balanced in the play by the presentation of the ill effects of false reports and prejudiced interpretations. This balanced treatment of his subject can be found throughout the play on all levels of dramatic experience: topical discussions, generic classification and linguistic style. It signals a gradual transition from the more optimistic and positive worldview of *Pericles* to the eventually more sceptical one of *The Two Noble Kinsmen*. This transition is also manifested linguistically in the frequent violence of tone in the play's verse and the instability of its descriptions.

Cymbeline also offers glimpses of things to come in Shakespeare's later plays of his last period. The structural symmetry of *The Winter's Tale*, for example, seems another form of the balanced treatment, although it is equally possible that it was really the symmetrical treatment of the past and the present in *The Winter's Tale* that preceded the balanced treatment of generic elements and topical discussions in *Cymbeline*. The often paradoxical quality of dramatised events or subjects, which results from such carefully balanced presentation, will be developed into a thematic feature in *The Tempest*. In terms of genre, *Cymbeline*'s use of Roman and ancient British history anticipates *Henry VIII*'s more decided affiliation to histories. Moreover, the play's discussion of the problematic process of the transmission of facts will be expanded into a major dramatic motif in *Henry VIII*. Finally, the pain and violence of *Cymbeline* seem to have laid the ground for the disturbing re-interpretation of *The Knight's Tale* in *The Two Noble Kinsmen*. Although one cannot say for certain that the initial inspiration for these later last plays lies in the playwright's process of creating *Cymbeline*, it seems not unreasonable to think that the legacy of the play, both in terms of its style and its dramatic arrangement, must have had been put to some use in his own later plays. After all, as has been demonstrated in the previous chapter, Shakespeare was continually reacting to his own previous work.

Cymbeline, with its "*Cymbeline*-style", both consolidates the playwright's new style and new dramatic focus ushered in by *Pericles* and develops them. It is thus an indispensable link in the ongoing process of late Shakespeare's development of his art. Incidentally, the cover art of Russ McDonald's *Shakespeare's Late Style* is a display of lines taken from the First Folio version of *Cymbeline*. Although one does not know what the artist's criteria in selecting these lines were, or whether McDonald himself was involved in the design of his book's cover, one would like to imagine that it might have been a gesture on the part of the artist or/and the author acknowledging "peculiar" *Cymbeline*'s special place in the development of Shakespeare's late style.

CHAPTER THREE

THE WINTER'S TALE

Art and Nature

Ben Jonson had no patience for Shakespeare's last romances. He calls them in the induction to his own *Bartholomew Fair* "a nest of antics...*Tales, Tempests*, and other such like drolleries" (132). He himself, Jonson declares there, will never stoop to such a degrading level, "mix[ing] his head with other men's heels", for he "is loath to make Nature afraid in his plays" (133, 131).

By accusing Shakespeare's romances of making nature afraid, Jonson is, first of all, accusing the events in the plays of being implausible and unrealistic, in other words, untrue to the laws of nature. Not only do these plays proceed through sudden movements which apparently do not operate under the logic of cause and effect, they also contain bizarre details which defy other rules of reality and nature. *Bartholomew Fair*'s induction lists a "Servant-monster" and "a nest of antics". The former probably refers to Caliban in *The Tempest*, who is more than once called a "servant-monster" in the play (3.2.3, 3.2.4, 3.2.7), while the latter may allude to the satyrs' dance in *The Winter's Tale*, since "elsewhere Jonson criticized the '*Concupiscence of Daunces, and Antickes*'" (Partridge, qtd. in Jonson 10, note to ll. 129-32). Alternatively "a nest of antics" might also be, as John Pitcher suggests, "a jibe at the scene where Jupiter hovers on his eagle over a family of ancient ghosts" (86) and therefore a passing criticism of *Cymbeline*. Possibly Jonson also had in mind the seacoast of Bohemia in *The Winter's Tale* and Prospero's magic in *The Tempest* when he refers specifically to "*Tales*" and "*Tempests*".

Shakespeare does not need Jonson to point out to him that his romances are unrealistic. In *The Winter's Tale*, he himself acknowledges the fact freely and repeatedly. Its title alone seems enough to discourage any expectation of strict realism. The piece is after all only a "tale", a fictitious piece of narrative imaginatively recounted, "[a] mere story, as opposed to a narrative of fact; a fiction, an idle tale; a falsehood" ("Tale, n.", Def. 5a). It is, moreover, not just any tale, but a "winter's tale", in other words a particularly fanciful story about sprites, goblins and supernatural phenomena told to while away long winter evenings. And as the play is not just *a* winter's tale but *the* winter's tale, it announces itself to be the ultimate fanciful and artificial story whose own mode is the excuse for its unaccountably jealous husband, turns of events which depend on chance, and statue that comes to life.

In some ways *The Winter's Tale*, or at least the first three acts of it, can be looked on as the fanciful "sad tale", deemed "best for winter" (2.1.27), which Mamillius is just starting to tell when he is interrupted at the beginning of Act 2. The young prince has just begun narrating his tale of sprites and goblins with "[t]here was a man...[d]welt by a churchyard" (2.1.31-2) when a man, his father, bursts in on the scene. Leontes, eventually losing his family and spending sixteen years of his life in daily mourning and penitence upon Hermione's grave, can easily be that man who dwells by the churchyard in Mamillius' sad tale for winter. And although no goblins or sprites turn up in the course of *The Winter's Tale*, the first three acts do contain the account of a spirit, the onstage appearance of a bear, and the mention of "fairy's gold" (3.3.112). Considered thus, it is almost as if Mamillius has a status as a sort of chorus figure, verbally preparing the audience for what they are about to witness as the plot unfolds. I hasten to add that with this I am not suggesting that somehow the real playwright-figure or the agent of control in the piece is Mamillius rather than Paulina, Time, Nature or the god Apollo. What I do want to suggest is that by having Leontes rushing in just as Mamillius is starting to tell his tale, Shakespeare creates a situation in which subsequent events are heralded by an act of storytelling—storytelling, moreover, by a little child who, in relating his tale (were he given the chance) would very probably be incoherent at times and overly imaginative throughout, which reiterates the message already imparted by the title of the play: that *The Winter's Tale* can be anything but a realistic piece of art aimed at faithfully reproducing nature.

While one must do a bit of "over-imagining" oneself to see Mamillius as the Chorus which ushers in the dramatisation of the winter's tale in the first half of the play, no such exercise is required for one to perceive the figure of Time as the Chorus who introduces the audience to the tales in the second half. Time's appearance on stage is designed for more than the purpose of announcing that sixteen years have passed, for if the playwright merely wishes to inform the audience that a considerable temporal gap stands between the end of Act 3 and the start of Act 4, Camillo's remark that "[i]t is sixteen years since I saw my country" (4.2.3) at the opening of the second half would be sufficient. Shakespeare, however, makes a point of introducing Time to the audience. Time is directed onto the stage first of all as a visual intrusion into the action of the play. The sight of an abstract concept personified on stage dispels any false impression or expectation of realism that members of the audience may have formed in spite of the Oracle, the tempest and the bear.[1] Moreover, in having Time come up as a director-figure who arranges plot manoeuvres, Shakespeare foregrounds the idea of authorial manipulation. Time's "fast forwarding" of the story reminds the audience that the play's dramatic arrangements are determined by a playwright according to his own design rather than that of nature, who, like Time, "o'erthrow[s] law, and in one self-born hour / ...plant[s] and o'erwhelm[s] custom" (4.1.8-9).

Not only does Shakespeare acknowledge his play's unrealism by its title, tableaux of storytelling, and the personified Time, he also has the characters call the audience's attention to the incredibility of the events they are witnessing. During her trial, Hermione declares plainly that she cannot comprehend Leontes' sudden jealousy: "My life stands in the level of your dreams" (3.2.79). And Leontes, in answering bitterly that "[y]our actions are my 'dreams'" (3.2.80), reveals to some extent the illusory nature of his "reality". Antigonus, although deciding that he would be "squared" (3.3.40) by the vision of Hermione, acknowledges that "[d]reams are toys" (3.3.38). "Toy" here is usually interpreted as "trifle", perhaps more in the sense that it is

> [a] false or idle tale, told (a) to deceive, cheat, or befool, (b) to divert or amuse; a lying story, a fable, a fiction; a jest or joke; a foolish, trivial, or nonsensical saying ("Trifle, n.", Def.1)

---

[1] Of course, the bear itself may have been realistic, in the sense that a real bear may have been employed in the original production. To this day it remains a debatable issue whether the King's Men used a bear or merely presented the audience with an actor in a bear costume. But whether real or fake, the bear makes a startling intrusion upon the scene. If any member of the audience has been inclined to take the play as a non-fanciful tragedy as a result of the seriousness and pathos of events presented so far, the bear will have probably jolted him or her out of that inclination, as it is inevitable that its appearance will induce an emotional response very different in kind from that to the trial scene or the news of Mamillius and Hermione's deaths. Thus in effect, the bear, whether represented by a live beast, an actor or some form of artificial contrivance, joins the Oracle, the tempest and the figure of Time in signaling the play's participation in the romance tradition and thus its inherent unrealism.

than that it is small and unimportant. Antigonus resolves to follow the orders of this trifle "superstitiously" (3.3.39). In other words, he is going to believe in it, but also knows that his belief is invested in an illusion.

These reminders of incredibility and incredulity become all the more prominent towards the end of the play, in the reports and discussions about Perdita's return. Prior to Florizel and Perdita's arrival at the Sicilian court, Paulina declares that the prospect of finding Perdita again is

> as monstrous to our human reason
> As my Antigonus to break his grave
> And come again to me. (5.1.41-3)

And when the lost princess is indeed restored to her father, the gentlemen at court discussing the reunion voice their incredulity by comparing the event to an old tale: "This news which is called true is so like an old tale that the verity of it is in strong suspicion" (5.2.25-6). Indeed, its incredibility even exceeds that of an old tale, for "[s]uch a deal of wonder is broken within this hour, that ballad-makers cannot be able to express it" (5.2.21-2). The circumstances surrounding Antigonus' death also come to light during the reunion, upon which the Third Gentleman's comment is that it is "[l]ike an old tale still, which will have matter to rehearse though credit be asleep and not an ear open" (5.2.55-6). It is a comment which works both within the context of the play and metadramatically. Within the plot, it is the onstage audience's response to Antigonus' bizarre death as a real event which took place sixteen years before. Outside the story, it is Shakespeare's self-observation on the bear sequence as well as perhaps his articulation of the offstage audience's possible reaction to the episode.

The gentlemen also mention that the royal party is going to see a statue of Hermione in Paulina's keeping. The statue sequence is the final scene in *The Winter's Tale*. It is also Shakespeare's final reiteration of his play's distance from realism. Some still debate whether Hermione literally dies and is resurrected in this scene, or whether she has been alive all along. I myself think that Hermione's "thou shalt hear that I…have preserved myself to see the issue" (5.3.126, 128-9) is pretty clear in implying that she does not die in 3.2. But either way, the statue scene has little to do with artistic realism. If Hermione, as some believe, is restored from death to life here, then Shakespeare is presenting his audience with a miracle which is clearly no true reflection of the order of nature. If, on the other hand, she has been alive these sixteen years, then the audience is not in fact watching a piece of art coming to life. There is no statue, and therefore the kind of mimetic realism in art represented by the mastery of Giulio Romano described by the gentlemen and exulted by the spectators at the beginning of 5.3 in fact has no bearing on the dénouement. Northrop Frye remarks that "whatever Romano's merits, neither he nor the kind of realism he represents seems to be very central to the play itself" ("Recognition" 241).

Frye goes on to say that "the literary equivalent of realism is plausibility...There is little plausibility in *The Winter's Tale*" (ibid.). Indeed, what Shakespeare is doing in this play is building his story upon implausibility and then continually directing the audience's attention to it. He either does it overtly, through the play's title and stage devices such as the figure of Time, or subtly, through allusions to old tales in in-text comments about dramatic events. The result is a play which clearly displays a self-consciousness about its implausibility and artificial nature.

While most members of Shakespeare's original audience would have been alerted to the unrealistic nature of the play by the frequent mention of "tales" and what Frye calls "ridiculous and outmoded devices" ("Recognition" 242), the "intelligentsia" among them who knew their Aristotle or Sidney—Ben Jonson, for instance—would have discovered more transgressions of the rules of nature. When Jonson in *Bartholomew Fair* accuses Shakespeare's last plays of making nature afraid, he not only means that they contain presentations of improbable details and implausible sequence of events, but also that they ignore and upset artistic rules of drama which aim at keeping products of art within nature's laws. This is particularly true of *The Winter's Tale*. The verb "discover" in the first sentence of this paragraph is perhaps not the best word to describe the experience of the Jonsons in the audience, for it implies effort or unexpectedness, while in fact the play's construction is so flagrantly "false" that it fairly accosts them at every turn with its negligence of proper, neo-Aristotelian rules of dramatic composition.

Jonson has not time nor space to go into details about Shakespeare's transgression of these rules in the induction of *Bartholomew Fair*, but his predecessor in the neo-classical school, Sir Philip Sidney, has devoted a few passages his *Defence of Poesy* on the subject of "silly" drama. The points he raises there might serve as an index. Although this criticism had been written some twenty years before Shakespeare started drafting his last plays and was in fact directed at popular English drama of the 1570s, it feels as if it could have been written *after* Sidney had attended one of the performances of *The Winter's Tale*.

For the neo-classical scholars, a good piece of drama must above all observe rules of the unity of time and of space. Sidney writes that these are

> the two necessary companions of all corporal actions. ...[T]he stage should always represent but one place; and the uttermost time presupposed in it,

should be, both by Aristotle's precept, and common reason, but one day. (73)

But sadly, the ignorant playwrights of his time conceived of such fantastical plots that shattered the unity of space, where

> you shall have Asia of the one side, and Afric of the other, and so many other under kingdoms, that the player, when he comes in, must ever begin with telling where he is, or else the tale will not be conceived. Now shall you have three ladies walk to gather flowers, and then we must believe the stage to be a garden. By and by, we hear news of shipwreck in the same place, then we are to blame if we accept it not for a rock. Upon the back of that comes out a hideous monster with fire and smoke, and then the miserable beholders are bound to take it for a cave: while, in the mean time, two armies fly in, represented with four swords and bucklers, and then, what hard heart will not receive it for a pitched field? (ibid.)

They also overturned the unity of time by dramatising stories in which

> two young princes fall in love; after many traverses she is got with child; delivered of a fair boy; he is lost, groweth a man, falleth in love, and is ready to get another child; and all this in two hours' pace. (73-4)

And apart from their indifference to the unities, contemporary plays on the London public stage pained Sidney with their abuse of genre. These were

> neither right tragedies nor right comedies, mingling kings and clowns, not because the matter so carrieth it, but thrust in the clown by head and shoulders to play a part in majestical matters, with neither decency nor discretion; so as neither the admiration and commiseration, nor the right sportfulness, is by their mongrel tragi-comedy obtained. (75-6)

It is not hard to see how Jonson's neo-classical artistic sensibilities were outraged or to imagine how Sidney's would have been by *The Winter's Tale*. It is in this particular piece that almost every one of these indiscretions of dramatic construction seems to have made an appearance. The setting of the story, though not exactly expanding the continents of Asia and Africa, is in two kingdoms hundreds of miles apart. The switch of the story's location from Sicilia to Bohemia is indeed announced by a player as he comes in, expressed in the form of an inquiry if the "ship hath touched upon / The deserts of Bohemia" (3.3.1-2). The figure of Time in the next scene performs a similar function in informing the audience that the action of the next part will take place "in fair Bohemia" (4.1.21). A hideous monster does come out from backstage, rapidly succeeded by the account of a shipwreck. In terms of temporal movement, the plot spans no less than sixteen years, during which time a queen is indeed got with and delivers a fair child, who is lost and, by the time it is returned to its parents, in love and upon the threshold of marriage, presumably ready to get another child—and all these in two hours' pace. And finally, in terms of genre, *The Winter's Tale* is neither a comedy nor a tragedy. It is dominantly tragic in the first three acts, largely comic in the fourth, and ends with a happy reunion tinged with pathos in the fifth. Kings are mixed with clowns. And in that the presence and doings of the clown-figure Autolycus do not really precipitate the plot in anyway (he is in fact completely removed from the Lambs' prose version in *Tales from Shakespeare*, with no ill effect on plot coherence), it might be said that at least one "non-majestical" character in the play is there because he is "thrust in by head and shoulders" for the purpose of making mirth rather than because "the matter so carrieth it".

Years after Shakespeare had died, Jonson, in a conversation with the Scottish poet William Drummond, famously remarked that the playwright "wanted art". *The Winter's Tale*, in terms of its mixture of tragedy and comedy and its serious negligence of classical regularity, certainly seems to be an example which justifies Jonson's comment. But while it does seem to present a playwright wanting art, it also bespeaks one wanting it by choice rather than by ignorance, for to have been able to write a play in "the wrong way" with such thoroughness and, as it were, precision, suggests a man familiar with the neo-classical theory—especially the version voiced by Sidney—on dramatic composition, not one who is altogether ignorant of these rules. [2] Indeed, one can almost picture Shakespeare having a copy of *The Defence of Poesy* by his side as he worked on *The Winter's Tale*, double-checking now and again to make sure that every undesirable feature observed by Sidney was written into his new play. Of course, whether or not he was continually referring to Sidney's work as he wrote his own one cannot know, but it does seem that in *The Winter's Tale* he is ignoring rules of "proper" dramatic construction by design. These ostentatiously rule-upsetting artistic arrangements fairly flaunt the play's disinclination to be true to nature in the face of the literati, just as repeated references to old tales and the use of out-dated stage devices carry the same message across to the general audience.

---

[2] *The Comedy of Errors* and *The Tempest*, one of Shakespeare's earliest works and one of the last, show that the playwright was knowledgeable about and able to conform to the classical unities at both ends of his career.

Shakespeare, then, is both aware of, and apparently wants his audience to be equally alert to, how much *The Winter's Tale* has deviated from the order of nature in its dramatic details, in the story's want of plausibility, and in the play's deliberate disregard for neo-classical rules of dramatic construction.

Jonson's choice of phrasing in describing the unrealistic and unruly nature of Shakespeare's last plays, "to make Nature afraid", is more than a comment on how the playwright's art fails to be true to nature. In alluding to nature's frightened reaction to these plays, he is also expressing the concern that these fantastical stories, by disobeying nature's rules and creating an alternative reality, would in turn have a negative effect on nature and reality.

Jonson in fact has an ally in the play itself who would second his opinion. Perdita is quite in earnest in her worries about art's negative effect on nature. Were she among the audience watching this or any other late Shakespearean romance, she would probably be even more critical than Jonson was, for these plays, in pushing the plot forward through "contrived turns of fate, accidents and pretended magic" (Pitcher 61), appear to compete with nature in creating an impossible alternative reality which overturns natural orders. Perdita does not believe in art tampering with nature in any way. Because she has

> heard it said
> There is an art which in their piedness shares
> With great creating nature, (4.4.86-8)

she bans streaked gillyflowers from her garden. She is equally dismissive of art's ability to arouse admiration and passion where they should not. In answer to Polixenes' request that she make her garden "rich in gillyvors" (4.4.98), Perdita stoutly refuses by saying that

> I'll not put
> The dibble in earth to set one slip of them,
> No more than, were I painted, I would wish
> This youth should say 'twere well, and only therefore
> Desire to breed by me. (4.4.99-103)

For her, it is unacceptable that gillyflowers, which ought to be single-coloured by nature, should gain streaks through horticultural art, or that love should be inspired by the art of makeup.

Of course, streaked gillyflowers in themselves are quite harmless, as indeed is rouge or lipstick. What can make nature afraid, however, is the cumulative effect of art's attempt to modify it according to men's will. Therefore, in rejecting streaked gillyflowers and expressing unease about the delusional powers of makeup, Perdita is displaying a concern for "the damage art may do to Nature when it forces it to become what the mind desires" (Pitcher 56). One has to say that in this respect she is quite forward-looking, as the twenty-first century, with its worries about health risks caused by genetically-modified food, countless cases of hazardous cosmetic surgery, and other human-inflicted damage on nature, fully justifies, hundreds of years later, her wise fastidiousness in insisting on the artlessness of her garden.

In harbouring an aversion to art's audacity to compete with nature in creating an alternative reality, Perdita, besides showing foresight, also unconsciously (and perhaps instinctively) relates back to her own origin, for she is herself, though of course she does not realise it at the time, a victim of art's negative effect on nature. She was separated at birth from her parents and deprived of her royal status because of her father's sudden unjustifiable conviction that her mother had committed adultery. In the loose sense that art is the product of the mind—art is imagination expressed, while imagination is the product of the mind—Leontes' sudden jealousy and its disastrous consequences can be looked on as *The Winter's Tale*'s more detailed presentation of Perdita's side of the argument in the art-nature debate: that art can have severely negative effects on nature.

In coming to terms with the tragic first half of the play, much research effort has been (and still is) put into investigating causes of Leontes' apparently inexplicable outburst of jealousy. Theories about patriarchal fears, social space, and sexual provocations abound. However, whether the Sicilian king's violent suspicion should be interpreted as an expression of "Oedipal anxieties and repressed homoerotic desires" (Snyder and Curren-Aquino 24), or as "a type of spatiotemporal derangement of the ethos of gift, hospitality, and expenditure" (Bristol 154), or as an understandable reaction to the provocative implications of the sight of Polixenes elaborately highlighting, while standing beside a visibly pregnant Hermione, the fact that his stay has lasted nine months (Coghill 31-3, my summary), the nature of Leontes' eventual conviction of Hermione's guilt remains the same: a construction out of his imagination. By skipping over the dramatisation of a cause for his suspicion—which, were it included, would have taken up much plot space and stage time, as the other two famous jealousy plots in the canon have proven—Shakespeare directs, as it were, the limelight on the stage-by-stage unfolding of the king's process of constructing Hermione's guilt, a process which Frye terms "a parody of a creation out of nothing" ("Recognition" 243).

The play's presentation of Leontes' rapid descent into jealousy and, to all intents and purposes, madness officially starts with his

> Too hot, too hot:
> To mingle friendship farre is mingling bloods.
> I have *tremor cordis* on me. (1.2.110-2)

Of course, during a performance, depending on the director or/and the actor's interpretation, Leontes might show signs of discomfort or anxiety well before this speech. But in print, this is the first clear indication that he suspects foul play between his wife and his friend. Up to this point he has been either cordial, or, when Hermione, at his own request, is trying to persuade Polixenes to stay, silent in the background, but now he unleashes his suspicion, in language already fairly vehement, in this aside to the audience.

As is the case with Posthumus in *Cymbeline*, once the suspicion of a wife's infidelity rears its head, it is little time before it turns into fierce conviction. Leontes rapidly moves on to the next stage in his construction of Hermione's guilt. After the initial "budding" of his jealousy, he proceeds to weigh the "evidences". But since his assessment mainly involves interpreting gestures exchanged between Polixenes and Hermione on the premise that the two *are* having an affair, not much weighing is really involved. In his eyes, they are

> paddling palms and pinching fingers,
> …and making practised smiles
> As in a looking-glass; and then … sigh[ing], as 'twere
> The mort o'th'deer, (1.2.117-20)

while in reality Polixenes is probably simply lending an arm or hand to Hermione in a gentlemanly spirit. Hermione would then of course acknowledge her gratitude, with a smile and perhaps a few words. Again, as etiquette dictates, Polixenes would probably smile back in response. It is, potentially, all perfectly innocent and above board. But to Leontes, who already has an opinion and is suiting the evidence to his interpretation, such gestural exchange is quite enough to incriminate. What he is starting to do as he speaks these lines is, in a way, to bend nature to his will, forcing it to become what he thinks it is.

Leontes' act of reconstructing nature involves not only warping what he sees into the shape of what he believes it to be, but also forcing *himself* to become what he thinks he is. As Wilson Knight puts it, Leontes is "a man tense, nerving himself to believe, to endure—more, to *be*—the hideous, horned, thing" (82). This process of moulding himself into the Leontes of his imagination is displayed in his soliloquy-like conversation with Mamillius:

> Can thy dam—may't be?—
> Affection, thy intention stabs the centre.
> Thou dost make possible things not so held,
> Communicat'st with dreams—how can this be?—
> With what's unreal thou coactive art,
> And fellow'st nothing. Then 'tis very credent
> Thou mayst co-join with something, and thou dost—
> And that beyond commission; and I find it—
> And that to the infection of my brains
> And hard'ning of my brows. (1.2.139-48)

This passage has been called, and in my opinion not at all unjustly, "the obscurest passage in Shakespeare" (Van Doran, qtd. in Pafford, "Appendix I" 165) and the "passage which no one has been able to read" (Stewart, qtd. in ibid. 166). Interpretations of it are many and varied, depending on how an editor or reader understands the keyword "affection". It is very likely, however, that during a performance, spectators, particularly if they are hearing the lines for the first time, would have no time nor spared attention to make much sense of these lines at all. Polixenes' immediate question, "What means Sicilia?" (1.2.148), though not exactly directed at Leontes' private musings, nevertheless probably voices the audience's incomprehension. But even if the exact meaning of the passage is lost on them, the knotted language and the choice of words ("possible", "dreams", "unreal", "nothing", "credent" and "something") would convey to the listeners a sense of how Leontes is struggling between the possible and the impossible, the real and the unreal, and nothing and something. It is also clear from the last few lines that the result of this struggle is that he becomes convinced by the unreal, accepts the impossible, and believes that there is something. He has in fact, through this mess of a reasoning process, himself planted the horn upon his brows.

Closer examination of the speech enables a clearer insight into Leontes' process of hardening his brows. Different interpretations of the word "affection", as I have mentioned, will result in fairly divergent ways of understanding the speech's meaning. One thing that remains unchanged, however, is the fact that Leontes, by the end of his meditations, has completely submitted his reality to the rule of his imagination.

Most editors take "affection" to mean "passions", though no unanimous conclusion has been reached on what and whose passions he is brooding on. One possible interpretation is that by "affection" he is alluding to Hermione's "lustful passions". In this case, roughly translated, his argument probably runs thus: "since lust can cause people in the throes of such passions to engage themselves in imaginary relationships with an entirely non-existent person, it is conceivable that it will lead them to transfer that pretended relationship onto a real-life one". One must confess that this in itself sounds quite logical as a statement. However, despite the appearance of logical reasoning, the passage in fact shows that Leontes is rapidly losing his faculty of reason, for, notwithstanding his pose of logical meditation, he is arbitrarily confirming his suspicion of Hermione's faithlessness upon "evidences" gathered from a piece of general observation which is by no means the indisputable truth. That in his argument, he immediately jumps from acknowledgement of the possibility of a scenario—"'tis very credent / Thou *mayst* co-join with something" to establishing his case, the non-sequitur "and thou *dost*", once again demonstrates that he is not suiting his judgement to reality, but bending reality to his judgement. Moreover, in believing that an imaginary physical relationship induced by strong passion can attach itself to real-life objects and manifest itself in the external world, he displays a firm conviction of imagination's rule over nature, which prepares for his eventual arrival at the belief that his imagination is the only truthful reflection of nature, a state of mind which becomes evident during his conversations with Camillo and, later, Paulina and Antigonus. In short, reading this passage in the light of "affection" meaning Hermione's lustful passions reveals a man bent on constructing his wife as an adulteress and himself a cuckold. For him, what imagination deems possible is as good as a confirmation of reality.

Another possible explanation of the "affection" here is that Leontes is alluding to his own jealousy. If so, then whatever else he may be thinking of, he is also at the same time making an effort to come to terms with his own bitter suspicion. He reasons that since strong jealousy, partaking dream's power ("communicate" here meaning "to have a common part or share" ("Communicate, v.", Def. II 6b)), can make possible things normally held impossible, in other words give existence to that which has no existence ("nothing"), it is then, to him, very plausible that that which has no physical existence may join onto that which exists in reality ("something") and effectively become reality itself. In short, it is entirely creditable that his groundless jealousy should have a ground. This is horrible logic, of course, and founded upon a serious confusion of imagination and reality. Leontes' association of "affection" with "dreams" puts the premise of his argument strictly within the realm of imagination, for although the impossible can indeed be made possible by dreams, it only remains so as long as one is dreaming. Once one wakes up, reality steps in and undoes imagination's work. Similarly, jealousy may propel someone to conceive the inconceivable, but, unless there is solid evidence of betrayal, the idea remains just a thought in this person's mind instead of a solid fact in the external world. Leontes, however, heedless of the boundary between the imagined and the real, forces his "dream logic" upon reality in the second part of his argument and concludes that imagination can be unconditionally applied to objects of physical reality. So in the end, what he has accomplished through his "reasoning" is the same as what he has done in interpreting Hermione and Polixenes' "paddling fingers and pinching palms": he is suiting nature to his imagination. According to his reasoning, the idea of an adulterous Hermione should fit the real Hermione, just as the idea of a cuckolded Leontes can be applied to the real Leontes. He has thus reasoned himself into a horned man.

That his fantasy should so fit the present state of affairs, Leontes confesses, infects his brain. H. C. Goddard remarks that in declaring so he has "hopelessly confuse[d] cause and effect", for "the truth of course is the other way around: it is the infection of the brain that has fitted the fantasy to the present instance" (qtd. in Pafford, "Appendix I" 166). Another reading of the passage, however, suggests that Leontes is initially aware that he may have a delusional brain, but rather than wisely refraining from making any judgement as a result of this awareness, he grows to believe that this "affection" has in fact given him unique insight into truth which no one else in the Sicilian court has. This reading is proposed by Pitcher, who suggests that "affection" here, rather than referring to someone's passion or jealousy, in fact has a more technical meaning of brain fever and delusion. This psycho-medical meaning of the word, according to him,

> derived from the Latin *affectio*…It was a kind of severe mental sickness, a seizure with recognizable physical symptoms: agitation followed by palpitations, feverish sleeplessness and exhaustion, all of which Leontes experiences (e.g. 1.2. 110-11; 2.3.1-2, 8-9, 30-8). (41)

In this reading, in 1.2.139-48, Leontes starts out clearly aware that a diseased brain may produce hallucinations, but switches halfway from a comparatively sensible diagnosis of his own mental condition to a sudden acceptance of the hallucinations produced by his mind. The sudden switch is probably the result, Pitcher suggests, of his uttering the sexually-charged words "nothing" and "something" so that "saying these words, with their powerful sexual meanings, makes Leontes think of adulterers having sex" (ibid.), which makes him lose his reason altogether. From this point onwards, he is firmly in the grips of his own imagination, believing that "his mental breakdown leads him to divine the truth of things, because his unsettled mind is a stronger source of truth than anything outside him" (42).

Whether or not Leontes starts out thinking his brain is infected is still debatable, as is whether his mental balance is finally tipped over by the sexual implications of "nothing" and "something". However, Pitcher's observation that Leontes has in the end come to view his mind as *the* source of truth is shrewd. 1.2.139-48 marks his completion of his construction of an alternative reality in which he is cuckolded. The rest of the first three acts, before the news of the loss of his son and wife shocks him back to his senses, sees him moving into that imaginary reality and categorically denying as well as destroying the real world around him.

Leontes' procedures in annihilating reality include, first of all, pronouncing anyone who does not see what he thinks he sees a traitor, a liar and/or a fool. Among his victims are Camillo, Antigonus and Paulina. Camillo, by remarking that Polixenes has changed his mind about going for the honourable reason of wishing to "satisfy your highness, and the entreaties / Of our most gracious mistress" (1.2.234-5), draws upon himself the verdict that he is either "not honest", "a coward" or "a fool" (1.2.244, 245, 249). And when he refuses to acknowledge that Leontes' accusation is just, the king calls him a liar and heaps insults and accusations on him:

> You lie, you lie.
> I say thou liest, Camillo, and I hate thee,
> Pronounce thee a gross lout, a mindless slave,
> Or else a hovering temporizer, that
> Canst with thine eyes at once see good and evil,
> Inclining to them both. (1.2.301-6)

Leontes continues this almost childish way of rejecting a second opinion after Camillo flees the Sicilian court with Polixenes, which to him is concrete proof of Hermione's transgression. He responds to Antigonus' entreaties that he should see reason by cutting him short with

> Cease, no more!
> You smell this business with a sense as cold
> As is a dead man's nose (2.1.152-4)

as well as commenting that "[e]ither thou art most ignorant by age / Or thou wert born a fool" (2.1.175-6). He calls the lords collectively "[a] nest of traitors" and "liars all" (2.3.82, 146), while his names for Paulina are "[a] mankind witch", "[a] most intelligencing bawd" and "[a] callat / Of boundless tongue" (2.3.68, 69, 91-2). This is by no means an exhaustive list of his insults, but I think it is sufficient to show how the man is doggedly determined to make his imagination his reality. Lack of constructive argument or solid evidence presents no obstacle to him. He simply denounces reality as a traitor and a fool.

Paulina succinctly and accurately diagnoses Leontes' condition:

> I'll not call you tyrant;
> But this most cruel usage of your queen—
> Not able to produce more accusation
> Than your own weak-hinged fancy—something savours
> Of tyranny. (2.3.116-20)

Something else which savours of tyranny is Leontes' stout refusal to take counsel of any sort. Apart from denying anyone who attempts to reason with him the possession of adequate intelligence or integrity, he states out loud that he does not need a second opinion. He makes it very clear to the lords that he calls on them not because he requires advice or that proper government requires him to convene a council, but because he is gracious enough to enlighten them:

> Why, what need we
> Commune with you of this, but rather follow
> Our forceful instigation? Our prerogative
> Calls not your counsels, but our natural goodness
> Imparts this; which, if you—or stupefied
> Or seeming so in skill—cannot or will not
> Relish a truth like us, inform yourselves
> We need no more of your advice. (2.1.163-70)

Similarly, he sends for the Oracle of Apollo not in order to seek guidance for himself, but so that he can

Give rest to th'minds of other such as he,
Whose ignorant credulity will not
Come up to th'truth. (2.1.193-5)

When it turns out to contradict his false accusations, Leontes simply adds
the Oracle to his list of liars and traitors: "There is no truth at all i'th'
oracle…This is mere falsehood" (3.2.138-9).

The sight of Leontes asserting his royal "rights" reminds the audience
that he, besides being a delusional individual, is at the same time a king
with prerogatives, and as such has the power not only to deny reality, but
drastically to modify it to the point of destruction. And destroy it he does.
Ever since he has convinced himself of Hermione's infidelity in the
"Affection" speech, besides verbally abusing his courtiers, Leontes has
been acting upon his conviction. He orders Polixenes to be poisoned,
removes Mamillius from the care of Hermione, throws his wife in prison
despite her heavy pregnancy, instructs Antigonus to exile the queen's new-
born child, and subjects Hermione to a public trial. The results of these
actions are catastrophic. Apart from the poisoning scheme, which is
thwarted by Camillo's refusal to collaborate, all the other measures reap
death, loss and despair. Antigonus is devoured by a bear in Bohemia.
Perdita is lost. Mamillius dies fearing for his mother. Hermione apparently
dies. The kingdom now faces an heirless future which may entail chaos,
war and yet more deaths. Leontes' construction of an alternate reality is
finally complete.

Leontes' case, in certain ways, greatly resembles the process of artistic
creation. It starts out as an idea, a fancy, a sort of highly subjective
interpretation of certain aspects of nature. It is then given a shape by the
artist—usually as a painting, a statue, a poem, a piece of music, or a
drama—though in Leontes' case his fancy is manifested in acts of
imprisonment, exile and trial. The finished artistic product usually has
some degree of impact on nature, bringing aesthetic pleasure or shock to
the ear and/or eye, or perhaps giving its audience a new, though not
necessarily better, perspective on nature. Leontes' "artistic production"
certainly has an impact. It almost completely destroys the real world at the
Sicilian court. In presenting the case of Leontes' self-inflicted tragedy,
which not only tortures the "artist" but also the innocent others around
him, *The Winter's Tale* offers an elaborate support for Perdita's
scepticism, expressed through her rejection of the cultivated streaks on
gillyflowers, of art's effect on nature when human beings seek to bend the
latter to their will.

During the debate in Act 4, Perdita's doubts about art's interference with nature meet with Polixenes' counter-arguments, which appear to be equally reasonable and valid. Polixenes attempts to persuade her to raise gillyflowers by maintaining that art is in fact nature, for

> nature is made better by no mean
> But nature makes that mean. So over that art
> Which you say adds to nature is an art
> That nature makes. (4.4.89-92)

Thus a gardener might undertake to change gillyflowers' natural colour-schemes, but ultimately the streaks on the flowers can only be formed through the power of nature itself.

Polixenes' is a "sound humanist view" (Frye, "Recognition" 241). It is also in a way infallible, for human beings are, after all, nature's creation themselves, and the materials they are working with fundamentally elements of nature, so that in a sense all art and artificial products are ultimately products of nature, or nature's way of making a difference to nature. Thus Aristotle argues that what one means by art perfecting nature is really that nature perfects itself: "a doctor doctoring himself: nature is like that" (qtd. in Pitcher 54).

Of course, conventionally a distinction is still made between human creation—art—and nature's own. Nevertheless, in the age-old debate about the relationship between art and nature, a good number of thinkers have concluded that the two are not separate. Plato writes in his *Laws* that a good legislator "ought to support the law and also art, and acknowledge that both alike exist by nature, and no less than nature" (qtd. in ibid.). Similarly, Sidney states in *The Defence of Poesy* that

> [t]here is no art delivered unto mankind, that hath not the works of nature for his principal object, without which they could not consist, and on which they so depend, as they become actors and players, as it were, of what nature will have set forth. (12)

Art, in short, is dependent on nature and, as such, can be considered ultimately a part of nature.

Polixenes' argument that "art is nature", like Perdita's doubts about art's negative effect on nature, is elaborately enacted in *The Winter's Tale*, in this case by the statue episode. As has been discussed earlier, Paulina's presentation of Hermione in the last act involves no real statue. Thus, rather than a scene showing art becoming nature, it is one which depicts nature improving nature in the guise of art. Leontes' eventual redemption from his sin comes not in the shape of stone miraculously coming to life, but in that of the living Hermione posing as a statue which responds to his repentance by "hang[ing] about his neck" (5.3.113). In a very literal way, where the "statue" of Hermione is concerned, the art *is* simply just nature.

During the debate in 4.4, Polixenes elaborates upon what he means by "art is nature" by a horticultural example. He explains to the shepherdess that art, rather than harming nature, is nature's way of improving on itself:

> You see, sweet maid, we marry
> A gentler scion to the wildest stock,
> And make conceive a bark of baser kind
> By bud of nobler race. This is an art
> Which does mend nature—change it rather; but
> The art itself is nature. (4.4.92-7)

To this Perdita responds by admitting "[s]o it is" (4.4.97), though still stoutly refusing to allow "nature's bastards" to have a place in her garden. It has been observed that it is hardly surprising that Polixenes fails to persuade Perdita, as he hardly seems to have convinced himself with the example of grafting, judging from his furious refusal to marry his son Florizel, "a gentle scion", to what he perceives as a lowly shepherdess, "the wildest stock". Most consider that this ironic twist rather undermines the forcefulness of his defence of art. Technically, however, Polixenes' opposition to the union of Florizel and Perdita only proves that all do not practice what they preach. The validity or lack of validity of his two arguments—that art is nature, and that art can have mending effect on nature—remains intact.

Although Polixenes' argument is not backed by his own actions, the idea that art improves on nature is supported in the play by a scenario in, again, the final scene. Apart from Hermione's "statue", which is simply nature disguised as art, 5.3 incorporates other forms of more straightforwardly "man-made" art, namely drama and music. Rather than simply informing the party that Hermione has been alive all along, Paulina stages the reunion as a theatrical spectacle, complete with the drawing of curtains, plot suspense and background music, with herself as narrator, guiding the spectators through to the climatic moment of revelation. Paulina's stated reason for this manoeuvre is that

> That she is living,
> Were it but told you, should be hooted at
> Like an old tale. (5.3.116-8)

The artistic frame in which nature is put, then, is considered to be able to add credit to nature's own incredible truth and thus help it to communicate.

But Paulina's drama serves an even more important purpose than just assisting nature to tell its tale. Her theatrical imitation of a miracle puts across to the spectators the message that "[i]t is required / You do awake your faith" (5.3.94-5)—faith, not simply in the impossible (which Leontes already amply had sixteen years before), but more importantly in a person other than oneself (for example, trusting that Paulina can indeed ask the stone to come to life), in wonder and thus in divine justice. These "three faiths" are reminders to audiences both on and off the stage, but to Leontes in particular, that lack of faith in one's God and fellow men may have devastating consequences. Leontes' case has made this abundantly clear, for it is his serious distrust of his wife and friend, of his counsellors and of Apollo's Oracle that has victimised his son, daughter, queen, courtiers, kingdom and, of course, himself. Such reminders serve to warn him against relapsing into tyrannical self-assurance now that he has had his family (what is left of it) back and has secured the kingdom's future. The lesson is driven home through the dramatic spectacle's step-by-step arousal of expectation, astonishment, remorse, wilder expectations, and finally wonder and joy. Such effects probably would not have been achieved were Hermione's preservation only reported as a matter of fact. Therefore art, in helping nature to communicate its wonders, also improves nature, in this particular case curing Leontes of his lack of faith in anything other than his own mind.

Apart from reminding both the on- and off-stage spectators of the importance of faith in divine justice, miracles and their fellow men, when the playwright has Paulina require the king's party to awaken their faith, he himself is also making an appeal for another kind of faith to his own audience: an appeal for faith in art. If the first three acts' presentation of Leontes' imaginative construction is a portrayal of "artistic creativity" going wrong, the statue scene balances that negative representation with a positive one which shows art doing good. In *The Winter's Tale*, the late romances' signature ending of reunion, restoration, reconciliation and revelation is achieved directly through Paulina's theatrical efforts, a combination of representational and performative arts. This scene, where art is given centre stage, lifts the mood of the play not only from the tragedy of the first three acts, but also from the "earthiness" of the merry sheep-shearing festival onto a level that is heartwarming, solemn and sublime.

Thus, Perdita and Polixenes' debate on art and nature extends beyond the thirty or so lines of exchange initiated by Perdita's rejection of cultured flowers. A debate about the relationship between art and nature in fact runs throughout the play. Both Perdita and Polixenes' positions receive a correspondent elaboration in the events of the plot. Perdita's suspicion about art seems to have been justified by Leontes' destructive imaginative construction of his wife's infidelity, while Polixenes' point about art's beneficial effects finds its support in the statue scene.

It therefore would seem that, similar to his presentation of topical discussions in *Cymbeline*, here Shakespeare is also endeavouring to give the art-nature debate balanced treatment. Dramatic arrangements in the debate scene in 4.4 in particular and other parts of the play in general certainly contribute to the appearance of ambivalent presentation. [3]

---

[3] The balanced treatments of the debate include, first of all, undermining each party's argument by each's own action. Without this twist, hypothetically speaking, to the audience, at the time of 4.4, Perdita's argument should carry much more weight than her opponent's. For one thing, the play's elaborate support for her argument—in the form of Leontes' fateful "artistic construction"—has already been presented, while Polixenes' still awaits elaboration. For another, the girl, with her youth, beauty, modesty and innocence, would be much easier for the audience to sympathise with than Polixenes, who is potentially a threat to the happiness of the younger generation. Therefore, should a debate between the two be presented without some twist of circumstances, it is likely that the audience would conclude that the playwright's own view on art and nature sides with Perdita's. To prevent this, Shakespeare takes care to add in dramatic details which reduce the forcefulness of each's argument. Polixenes, as we have seen, jeopardises his own persuasiveness by refusing to marry his son, a prince, to Perdita the shepherdess. Similarly, Perdita, knowing Forizel to be of noble birth and believing herself to be a commoner, in accepting his proposal of marriage is really putting into practice the horticultural art of grafting which she has hitherto kept assiduously out of her own garden.

Another aspect of the debate scene which balances the forcefulness of the arguments against and for art's effect on nature is the fact that both Perdita and Polixenes are "in disguise", in other words made up by art. Perdita is decked out in splendour for the festival like a goddess or queen. Polixenes is dressed in lowly garments as a commoner. To the audience, who are in the know, Perdita's festival costume in fact reveals her true identity as royalty, while Polixenes' hides his as the king and Florizel's father. Thus in another ironic twist, Perdita, who does not think much of makeup and art, is really enacting Polixenes' argument that art is nature. On the other hand, Polixenes, who believes that art and nature are one, in seeking to cover nature with art, is in a way emphatically differentiating between the two.

However, in *The Winter's Tale*, the respective forcefulness of the presentations of art negative and positive is in the end not neatly balanced, but in fact tipped over in art's favour. The statue scene, one should remember, is strategically placed at the very end of the play. Thus the sense of joyous solemnity achieved through art is what would presumably remain the freshest in a spectator's mind as the play closes. It is also probably the view of art which the playwright wanted his audience to take home with them.

At work in tipping over the balance are not only the statue scene's resemblance to a divine miracle and its strategic position at the closing of the play, but also the scene's invocation of classical tales about the power of art. In having Hermione restored to her husband in the guise of a statue coming to life, Shakespeare reanimates the Ovidian tale of Pygmalion, whose own statue, this time a genuine piece of artistic creation out of ivory, also comes to life. Pygmalion's story is first of all an illustration of "one of Ovid's favourite ideas, the power of art to equal or indeed outdo nature" (Kenney 434), as Pygmalion

> With marvelous triumphant artistry
> …gave [his ivory] perfect shape, more beautiful
> Than ever woman born. (Ovid, Book X 299-301)

This statue is able to inspire him, who is

> Horrified
> At all the countless vices nature gives
> To womankind (294-6)

with love—a case of the power of artistic creation scoring over that of nature. The Pygmalion story also shares with the last scene of *The Winter's Tale* a stress on the importance of faith. Pygmalion's "faith in Venus" (Crider 153) is instrumental in bringing his artwork to life. Had he not gone before the altar to pray to the goddess for a bride who would be the living image of his statue, however superior his craftsmanship, the

---

The play's more elaborate presentations of the relationship between art and nature also seem to be constructed with balance in mind. The much-commented-on diptych structure of the play not only marks a somewhat even split between winter and summer, past and present, the older generation and the younger, and tragedy and comedy, but also art's destructive power and its regenerative effect. After all, the whole story of *The Winter's Tale*, in a sense, is triggered by a destructive act of artistic construction, and eventually resolved by one that mends.

ivory statue would remain ivory. In other words, "Pygmalion's art is necessary for Galatea's metamorphosis, but it is insufficient. Prayer is required" (ibid.). Thus, with its invocation of the story of Pygmalion, the statue scene in *The Winter's Tale* makes its message about the positive power of art and the importance of faith doubly forceful.

Triply, as a matter of fact, for the statue scene not only has the story of Pygmalion at its back, but that of Orpheus as well. One should not overlook the fact that in *Metamorphoses*, the story of Pygmalion is told by Orpheus, the bard of Rhodope. Like that of Pygmalion in his tale, Orpheus' own experience first of all demonstrates the power of artistic excellence. His songs are not only able to make others forget their own sufferings—

> So to the music of his strings he sang,
> And all the bloodless spirits wept to hear;
> And Tantalus forgot the fleeing water,
> Ixion's wheel was tranced; and Danaids
> Laid down their urns; the vultures left their feast,
> And Sisyphus sat rapt upon his stone— (Ovid, Book X 48-53)

but also move the gods of the Underworld to such an extent that they give him back his Eurydice, as

> The Furies' cheeks, it is said, were wet with tears;
> And Hades' queen and he whose scepter rules
> The Underworld could not deny the prayer. (55-7)

As in the Pygmalion tale, the art of the poet triumphs over nature, giving life back to the lifeless.

But the Orpheus-Eurydice story, unlike that of Pygamlion, is ultimately tragic. Ignoring the terms of Eurydice's release (that he should not look back until they are out of the Underworld), Orpheus turns back his eyes and Eurydice is immediately lost to him once more, this time forever. What makes the fate of Orpheus a contrast to that of Pygmalion is that, while the latter has demonstrated a faith in Venus, the former does not entirely trust Hades and his queen. "Orpheus' faith is not as strong as Pygmalion's" (Crider 157). The story of Orpheus' own experience in the Underworld, therefore, while exulting art's power to move even nature, at the same time puts its emphasis, through Orpheus' personal tragedy, on the importance of faith. Art can imitate and move nature; but for it to become nature, faith is needed.

The Pygmalion-Galatea story is told by Orpheus after the "double death" of his Eurydice. In granting Pygmalion his bride, Orpheus is in a way envisioning an alternative ending to his own tragic experience. But more importantly, by telling the tale of a fellow artist who shares his own great craftsmanship but not his distrust in the gods, he is reflecting upon his own experience and summarising his lesson. In short, he is educating himself through art, in this case in the form of narrative poetry. Thus, in Ovid's *Metamorphoses*, while the presentation of Orpheus' experience in the Underworld tells of art's power to win over nature and how that power only lasts while faith is upheld, scenes of his tale-telling after retreating with a broken heart to Rhodope demonstrate art's ability to make sense of and perhaps improve on nature.

By installing at the end of his play a scene which reanimates the Pygmalion and Orpheus stories, Shakespeare is effectively portraying three examples which support Polixenes' argument that art is and can mend nature: Orpheus' story of Pygmalion, Ovid's story of Orpheus, and Shakespeare's own of Hermione and Leontes. Similarly, when Paulina requests her audience that they should awaken their faith, she is not only putting her own message across, but also passing forward appeals for faith in love and art from Pygmalion, Orpheus, Ovid and Shakespeare. The rich literary associations of the statue scene therefore add weight to the forcefulness of its defence of art, enabling it not only to balance but moreover to override the negative presentation of art's damage to nature in the case of Leontes' maddened fancy—which after all occupies three acts in a five-act play—thus overcoming the audience's instinctive allegiance to the aversion of art expressed by Perdita, with whom their sympathy might instinctively lie.

The final scene's association with the poetry of Orpheus, the resurrection of Hermione in the form of a play-within-the-play, and the fact that Shakespeare himself was a playwright make one suspect that the statue scene's appeal for faith in art, while applicable to all branches of artistic creation, may have been specifically made on behalf of narrative art, particularly drama, which is a blend of poetry, old tales, physical action and music. A survey of the dramatic arrangements of the play seems to lend support to this speculation. Shakespeare, apart from installing a dénouement which brings a solution to the plot in the form of an awe-inspiring theatrical event, appears to have made the act of tale-telling and/or poetry-making a source of solace in times of distress (particularly to the audience) throughout the course of the play.

The first instance of this comes at the beginning of Act 2 in the form of Mamillius telling a winter's tale to the womenfolk. Before this happy domestic scene, the audience have been confronted by the obsessive suspicion of Leontes and his vicious plan of having Polixenes poisoned. Fleetingly short though it is, the sight of Mamillius in the act of entertaining the ladies with his fantastical tale nevertheless temporarily relaxes the mood of the play from the brooding tension of the first act. It is also the last snatch of light-heartedness the audience is allowed before the end of Act 3.

Mamillius' tale, as we have seen, is cut short by Leontes' entrance. For the next two acts the audience and the Sicilian court are put through a whirlwind of distressing events culminating in the deaths of the young prince, the queen and Antigonus. Release from the winter of Sicilia eventually comes in the shape of Autolycus singing his merry ballads. After the grotesque scene with the storm and the bear, and after Time has waved sixteen years away, he enters singing about daffodils and springtime and proceeds to tell tall tales about himself to the Clown. Later he also makes an appearance at the Old Shepherd's place, this time selling his ballads, which share with Mamillius' winter's tale (and Shakespeare's own) the quality of being incredible:

> Here's one to a very doleful tune, how a usurer's wife was brought to bed of twenty money-bags at a burden, and how she longed to eat adder's heads and toads carbonadoed. (4.4.253-5)

Although Autolycus as a character has little bearing on the progress of the play—as has been mentioned, the plot operates smoothly without him—he and his farfetched tales framed in poetry do play an important role in shifting the play from its tragic half into the predominantly comic mode in which it will remain.

The jarring note in the otherwise merry Act 4 is struck by Polixenes as he reveals his identity and opposes the union of Florizel and Perdita, promising punishment which rivals in violence and cruelty those issued by Leontes sixteen years ago. This crisis, of course, is finally averted when it is revealed the shepherdess is really Sicilia's lost princess. Shakespeare, instead of directly dramatising this reunion, has it brought to the audience in narrative form. They are presented with the spectacle of Gentlemen of the Court relating to each other the miraculous event which has taken place. In other words, to the audience, the solution to Act 4's crisis comes once more in the form of storytelling.

The climax of, and resolution to, the whole play, as has been discussed at length, comes in the form of a carefully planned play-within-the-play.

Much has already been said in earlier paragraphs about the final scene's association with drama and poetry, so I shall not go into it again here. But I would like to point out that *The Winter's Tale*, like its predecessor *Pericles*, ultimately ends with the prospect of more rounds of storytelling, as Leontes closes the play with

> Good Paulina,
> Lead us from hence, where we may leisurely
> Each one demand and answer to his part
> Performed in this wide gap of time since first
> We were dissevered. Hastily lead away. (5.3.152-6)

Tales and poetry, then, retain their positive power not only throughout the action, but also beyond the two hours' traffic of the play.

The Winter's Tale's pattern of averting a disaster (or a potential one) by a sort of "story session" brings to mind the dénouements of Shakespeare's other two romances, *Pericles* and *Cymbeline*, where the act of storytelling (or verbal exchange of information) takes centre stage and functions more or less as a solution to the accumulated complexities of the plot. However, the format here in *The Winter's Tale* is vitally different from that of the other two plays in one respect, which is that storytelling, or any other form of manipulation of verbal communication, does not really initiate the tragedy in the plot here. Unlike Pericles, whose misfortune is set off by Antiochus' daughter's riddle and furthered by Dionyza's lie about Marina, and unlike Innogen and Posthumus, who both fall prey to Giacomo's perfidious reports, Leontes' doubts about his wife are not put into his head by false information supplied by a third party. They are entirely self-inflicted. Moreover, Shakespeare has arranged it so that, in print at least, it is not clear what has given rise to his jealousy. It might well be some words, but it might also be a look, a gesture, or nothing at all. The point is that in the tragedy of *The Winter's Tale*, there is no interested beguiler sabotaging by telling deliberately false stories. The only character in the entire play remotely resembling a Giacomo or Dionyza is Autolycus, whose tales of misfortune (plus his acting skills) trick the Clown into pitying him. But while his act of storytelling is immoral, it is not portrayed as evil. For all his roguery, Autolycus is paradoxically quite a likeable character. And his ballads, as we have seen, do much to alleviate the suffocating tension of the first three acts. Thus in this play, unlike in *Pericles* and *Cymbeline* where words and tales are presented as both decidedly damaging and ultimately restorative, the destructive potential of stories is never fully unleashed. Tales in *The Winter's Tale* are associated with the ludicrous and the miraculous, but not with the evil. Shakespeare's attitude towards storytelling as a human activity therefore seems to be much more firmly positive in this piece.

Metadramatically, *The Winter's Tale* itself is, of course, an elaborate narrative told by its dramatist and a company of actors. Shakespeare makes sure that his audience is fully and constantly aware of the fact by drawing attention to the artificiality of the dramatic arrangements. Out-moded devices like the bear and Time and consistent references to the incredibility of old tales impress upon them that they are watching the telling of a story, and moreover a story fictive rather than realistic. Thus while the mode of the play, dramatised romance, asks for the audience's "willing suspension of disbelief" (Bullough 155) in taking in the plot, the play's dramatic details, by continually reminding them of the fictional nature of the narrative—in effect highlighting the boundary between the real and the imaginary—at the same time checks the complete liberation of their imagination. In other words, the playwright presents to the audience an alternative universe (and possibly a better one, with its assurance of divine justice, triumph of true love and reward for sincere penitence), but prevents them from becoming fully immersed in it, so that they do not repeat Leontes' mistake of living in an imaginative construction.

Shakespeare's way of making art ostentatiously artful in *The Winter's Tale* is, in a way, also a resolution to Perdita's—and Jonson's—fear of art making nature afraid. Perdita's worry is that art, in daring to presume to share great nature's creating power, may in the end mistake its subordinate status and bend nature at will, thus ultimately bringing destruction upon nature. But a piece of art like Shakespeare's play, in being both self-consciously and almost flauntingly artful, clearly distinguishes between the artificial and the natural, and thus successfully prevents both its creator and its public from committing the folly of confusing imagination with reality. In fact, in watching *The Winter's Tale*, the audience is subjected to an experience not unlike Orpheus' as he, living in the misery of having lost Eurydice due to his own lack of faith, sings to himself the happy tale of Pygmalion gaining his Galatea. Orpheus is soberly aware of reality and at the same time drawing solace from, as well as being chastened by, glimpses of a more idealistic but clearly imaginatively constructed alternative. In parallel, the audience are continually made conscious of the improbability of *The Winter's Tale*'s plot details, but at the same time can enjoy themselves and, hopefully, learn, amongst other things, to awaken their faith from watching the play. An unrealistic tale, in the end, helps those living in the real world make better sense of it. In other words, nature is not made afraid by this tale about the edifying effect of tales, but rather made more comprehensible.

While Orpheus consoles and teaches through his narrative poems, Shakespeare does so through the medium of drama. In making dramatic storytelling the major medium for revealing and penetrating reality in *The Winter's Tale*, the playwright is both following and developing Sidney's argument about the supremacy of poetry in *The Defence of Poesy*. For Sidney, poets stand apart from the other artists in that they are not tied down by nature but in fact "grow, in effect, into another nature: in making things either better than nature bringeth forth, or quite anew" (13). This second nature created by poets, according to him, is in fact even better than the original, for while "her [nature's] world is brazen, the poets only deliver a golden" (ibid.). The merit of this poetic golden world lies mainly in its ability to teach through delighting. Shakespeare, with the in-text example of Paulina's theatrical triumph and the metadramatic one of his dramatisation itself, is claiming the same status and power of artistic supremacy for the dramatists. They are also somehow free of the subjugation of nature—they are free to add a seacoast to Bohemia, conceal the not-easily-concealed survival of a "dead" queen, or make an heirless king live sixteen years without a consort—and can create a "golden world" better than brazen reality, as in the latter divine justice seems not assured, love does not always triumph, and repentance does not guarantee restoration and reconciliation. In delighting his audience with the story of *The Winter's Tale*, the dramatist also makes them see reality more clearly and thus in effect "teaches" them a new way of considering, and experiencing, the real.

Similarly, with the composition of *The Winter's Tale* in particular and the last plays in general, the playwright is also suggesting that what poets can put into poetry, dramatists can animate to great effect on stage, frequent geographical changes and great temporal gaps included. After all, Aristotelian classicists' objections to the disregard of the unities arise mainly out of the concern that leaps of time or switches of setting may interfere with an audience's comprehension of the plot. With clear (and often subtle) announcements of transitions, however, comprehension is not a problem for the audience, as Forman's accounts prove.[4] Thus, as long as careful treatment is applied, the points of faulty construction which Sidney finds in his contemporary theatre in fact become opportunities for Shakespeare. They, because of the broadness of time, space and action implied, help to extend the plot from the imitation of "one action", as

---

[4] Forman's account of *The Winter's Tale* can be found in Chambers, E. K. *William Shakespeare: A Study of Facts and Problems*. Vol. 2. 1930. Reprint. Oxford: Clarendon Press, 1951. 340-1. 2 vols. Print. Although he left out a few details, Forman's summary of the basic plot is sound.

defined by Aristotle, to an imitation of life, which is itself, in a manner of speaking, one continuous action spanning space and time. Moreover, it is Aristotle himself who writes that

> the limit as fixed by the nature of the drama itself is this: the greater the length, the more beautiful will the piece be by reason of its size, provided that the whole be perspicuous. (*Poetics*)

Shakespeare's deft stagecraft assures perspicuity and enables him to enact what Sidney deems acceptable in his own *Arcadia*—high-born princes dancing with lowly shepherds and mythical fawns, beasts jumping out without warning from nowhere, and love stories spanning more than one generation—successfully on stage, releasing the audience's imagination but at the same time preventing it from wandering unchecked, thus avoiding what Aristotle and Sidney fear—incomprehension—as well as what Perdita and Jonson dislike—imagination taking over. The result is one play whose disregard for the classical unities brings it richness and magnitude, which in turn give it beauty.

As has been mentioned near the beginning of this chapter, Shakespeare's thorough application of what Sidney deems as ignorant and unacceptable dramatic arrangements in his play appears to be a deliberate gesture. It is a gesture which serves the purpose of his play, for by keeping his narrative unrealistic, he is able to impress upon his audience that they are, like their onstage counterparts, attending a series of "storytelling sessions" which are entertaining as well as edifying. It also expresses the play's ultimate conclusion about the relationship between art and nature, which is that the former, as long as it remains self-conscious about its deviation from the latter, rather than harming nature, in fact helps people understand it better.

The Winter's Tale's engagement in the art-nature debate is in keeping with Shakespeare's general concern about art, particularly dramatic art, displayed in the last plays.[5] Both *Pericles* and *Cymbeline*, as demonstrated in earlier chapters, in a way develop around the destructive and restorative powers of language and theatre. *The Tempest*, as we shall see in the next chapter, appears to have taken its cue from *The Winter's Tale*'s last scene and focuses its action around the "theatrical arrangements" of Prospero, who is a sort of combination of storyteller, magician and dramatist. *Henry*

---

[5] It is also possible that the extensive presentation of the art-nature debate in *The Winter's Tale* is Shakespeare's contribution to a topical discussion, as "just around the date of *The Winter's Tale*, the art and Nature debate had come alive again" (Pitcher 55), stimulated perhaps by the development of experimental science.

VIII employs dramatic spectacles extensively. And *The Two Noble Kinsmen* is, again, the retelling of an old tale.

Moreover, Shakespeare was probably using *The Winter's Tale* as a response to Jonson's criticism of his recent work, though not specifically to the "making nature afraid" comment, as that only came after the production of *The Tempest*. Jonson had started accusing Shakespeare of "pander[ing] to and ruin[ing] popular taste" (Pitcher 60) by his inattention to artistic rules around 1600. It is generally believed that *The Tempest*, with its strict conformation to the unities of time and space, was Shakespeare's retort to Jonson's criticism of his ignorance of the classical rules. It seems that *The Winter's Tale* may have been another such response. Through the play's extensive references to the works of Sidney, Jonson's forerunner, the playwright demonstrated that his "lack of art" was by choice and with purpose rather than by ignorance. More importantly, he made a case for ostentatiously unrealistic art, showing that it could be equally efficacious in communicating the truths of nature. Considering the continuing popularity of Shakespeare's wildly "flawed" romances today and the relative indifference shown to Jonson's own rule-conforming comedies, it seems that Shakespeare's neo-classicist colleague was either very wrong in his verdict about nature's reaction to his rival dramatist's art, or very right about how he had utterly "ruined" popular taste.

Linguistic Realism?

While few dispute that in terms of plot manoeuvres *The Winter's Tale* is not what one would call realistic, opinions concerning its characterisation, specifically the relationship between speech and characterisation, are divided. One school of thought argues that, unlike his treatment of the plot, Shakespeare's characters are imbued with realism, with each individual's speech tailored to suit and reflect his or her character. A. D. Nuttall, for example, is of the opinion that the dialogue in *The Winter's Tale* is "acutely naturalistic" and "without parallel in the Romances" (*Winter's* 16). J. H. P. Pafford writes that "all characters…use language which gives a strong illusion of reality" and that "[t]he language characterizes both speaker and scene...throughout the play" (lxxxvi). Similarly, A. F. Bellette remarks that in this play—indeed in all the last plays—"[e]ach person speaks in a way which is most directly expressive of his or her nature" (65).

On the other hand, in direct contrast to these views are those of scholars such as S. L. Bethell, Anne Barton and Russ McDonald, who believe that, in keeping with Shakespeare's late habit of separating character and speech, *The Winter's Tale*'s dramatis personae collectively speak in a late-Shakespearean style, rather than respectively in a Leontes-, Paulina- or Florizel-style. Bethell comments that "there is little attempt to indicate character by giving a particular type of verse permanently to a particular stage personage" (23). Barton, using Leontes' "I have drunk, and seen the spider" speech (2.1.38-55) as a starting point, proceeds to suggest that Shakespeare's concern in the last plays is to "express situation before character" ("Leontes" 138) and that he

> in his Last Plays, destroyed that close relationship between language and dramatic character which had seemed the permanent achievement of his maturity. (136)

McDonald agrees with Barton in her estimate of the playwright's late style, and points out that stylistic features which one tends to associate with the speeches of one particular character in one particular frame of mind are in fact to be found in abundance in the language of other characters harbouring other kinds of emotion.

On the whole I am more inclined to agree with the latter school of thought. Style and speaker in *The Winter's Tale* are mostly separated, as they are in *Pericles* and *Cymbeline*. While it is true that one is unlikely to confuse the speeches of, say, Paulina with those of Leontes, I believe that such distinction is more the result of differences in matter rather than manner. A comparison between some examples will, I hope, illustrate the point.

I suspect that the impression that characterisation is reflected in linguistic distinctions in the play is mainly caused by the compatibility of Shakespeare's late style with the mental state of Leontes in his jealousy. The late stylistic feature of repetition, both of sounds and words, for example, seems a perfect illustration of a darkly obsessed mind capable of only one line of thought:

> Come, captain,
> We must be neat—not neat, but cleanly, captain.
> And yet the steer, the heifer, and the calf
> Are all called neat. —Still virginalling
> Upon his palm? —How now, you wonton calf—
> Art thou my calf? (1.2.124-9)

> Go play, boy, play. Thy mother plays, and I
> Play too; but so disgraced a part, whose issue
> Will hiss me to my grave. Contempt and clamour
> Will be my knell. Go play, boy, play. (1.2.188-91)

Apart from the obvious lexical repetitions of "captain", "neat", "calf", "play" and "will", in these two extracts there are also subtler reiterations of sounds: the liquid /l/ in "cleanly", "calf", "all", "called", "still", "virginalling", "palm", "play", "will" and "knell", the combination sound of /ɔ:l/ in line 1.2.127 "all called…virginalling", the hissing /s/ in 1.2.189-90's "disgraced", "issue" and "hiss", and finally, the harsh constant /k/ that runs through the two speeches which are in fact quite some sixty lines apart in the play, "come", "captain", "cleanly", "calf", "contempt", and "clamour".

Incessant repetitions in speech, however, though possibly a hallmark of the language of the crazed Leontes, are not confined to the speeches of the Sicilian king in his unreasonable jealousy. They, and especially the subtle reiteration of sound, are also an important feature in the speeches of other characters whose personalities are perceptibly different from his, and who are speaking under fairly dissimilar circumstances, as for example, in Hermione's dignified defence during her trial:

> Sir, spare your threats.
> The bug which you would fright me with, I seek.
> To me can life be no commodity.
> The crown and comfort of my life, your favour,
> I do give lost, for I do feel it gone
> But know not how it went. My second joy,
> And first fruits of my body, from his presence
> I am barred, like one infectious. My third comfort,
> Starred most unluckily, is from my breast,
> The INNOCENT milk in its most INNOCENT mouth,
> Haled out to murder, (3.2.89-99)

or when Florizel speaks to Perdita at the beginning of the sheep-shearing festival:

> Thou dearest Perdita,
> With these forced thoughts I prithee darken not
> The mirth o'th'feast. Or I'll be thine, my fair,
> Or not my father's. For I cannot be
> Mine own, nor anything to any, if
> I be not thine.[6] (4.4.40-5)

It may be observed that not only the "technique" of syllabic repetition is adopted by both Hermione and Florizel on very different occasions, some

---

[6] I have marked the "th"s pronounced /ð/ in bold and /θ/ in italics.

of the elements of repetition are shared as well. Hermione's speech in court, for example, shares with Leontes' two speeches the incessant reiteration of the /s/ and /k/ sound, while Florizel repeats his /f/'s and /m/'s, as Hermione does. One can go on listing such instances of syllabic or semantic repetitions in *The Winter's Tale*, but I think the two examples, Hermione on trial and Florizel in love, are adequate to show that such repetitions are not the exclusive properties of the language of the crazed Leontes.

On a syntactic level, the elliptical, digressive and often ambiguous quality of Leontes' speeches in the first half of the play is often believed to be specially tailored to demonstrate his disordered mental state, as in the following example:

> Ha' not you seen, Camillo—
> But that's past doubt; you have, or your eye-glass
> Is thicker than a cuckold's horn—or heard—
> For, to a vision so apparent, rumour
> Cannot be mute—or thought—for cogitation
> Resides not in that man that does not think—
> My wife is slippery? (1.2.269-75)

Seen in print, the first thing a reader would notice is the repeated appearance of dashes: three pairs in seven lines. In other editions they may have been replaced with round brackets, though it is possible that neither was Shakespeare's original choice. However, despite the uncertainty of these punctuation marks' authenticity, they are not out of place here, as pairs of dashes and brackets are visual markers of divagations in thought and speech—and Leontes' is one very digressive speech. His point, when one strips away the added-in contents between the dashes, is to ask if Camillo has any suspicion that Hermione is false, as grammatically this whole seven-line speech is but one not overly complex question: "Have not you seen or heard or thought, Camillo, that my wife is slippery?". But instead of asking it straight out, the king leaves his listeners suspended in the air, expanding the simple question to its present size by a series of parenthetic phrases in which he insists why Camillo must have seen, heard and thought that Hermione is unfaithful. The resulting speech, in postponing the audience from getting to the point in the final line, reflects a Leontes whose mind is not working as clearly and as straightforwardly as a reasonable man's should. At the same time, it also shows him, despite this feverish and chaotic mind, doggedly set on establishing the guilt of Hermione, for with the help of these fairly abusive parenthetic phrases he is not so much asking for an opinion as forcing out a concurrence from

Camillo. It is an impression of the mental condition of the present Leontes consistent with that given by previous speeches like the obscure "Affection" soliloquy.

However, as is in the case of repetitions, characters other than the jealous Leontes also frequently digress, interpolate themselves, and (consciously or unconsciously) keep their listeners in suspense when they speak. For instance, the sober Leontes in the second half of the play also occasionally inserts parenthetic phrases or sentences that slightly change the direction of what he is saying, albeit in a much less ostentatious manner:

> Most dearly welcome,
> And your fair princess—goddess! O, alas,
> I lost a couple that 'twixt heaven and earth
> Might thus have stood, begetting wonder, as
> You, gracious couple, do; and then I lost—
> All mine own folly—the society,
> Amity too, of your brave father. (5.1.129-35)

However, where in the former case the interpolated phrases serve to reveal the obstinate unreasonableness of a jealous tyrant, the change of direction in the speech here has the opposite effect of showing a Leontes, struck by the youth and beauty of Perdita, wisely and sincerely regretting and repenting his own folly.

An example which can equal Leontes' earlier speeches in the extremity of interpolation and suspension comes from Paulina's torrent of admonitions to the king in the third act:

> PAULINA   Woe the while!
>   O cut the lace, lest my heart, cracking it,
>   Break too.
> A LORD   What fit is this, good lady?
> PAULINA [to LEONTES] What studied torments, tyrant, has for me?
>   What wheels, racks, fires? What flaying, boiling,
>   In leads or oils? What old or newer torture
>   Must I receive, whose every word deserves
>   To taste of thy most worst? Thy tyranny,
>   Together working with thy jealousies—
>   Fancies too weak for boys, too green and idle
>   For girls of nine—O think what they have done,
>   And then run mad indeed, stark mad, for all
>   Thy bygone fooleries were but spices of it.
>   That thou betrayed'st Polixenes, 'twas nothing.
>   That did but show thee, of a fool, inconstant,

> And damnable ingrateful. Nor was't much
> Thou wouldst have poisoned good Camillo's honour
> To have him kill a king—poor trespasses,
> More monstrous standing by, whereof I reckon
> The casting forth to crows thy baby daughter
> To be or none or little, though a devil
> Would have shed water out of fire ere done't.
> Nor is't directly laid to thee the death
> Of the young prince, whose honourable thoughts—
> Thoughts high for one so tender—cleft the heart
> That could conceive a gross and foolish sire
> Blemished his gracious dam. This is not, no,
> Laid to thy answer. But the last—O lords,
> When I have said, cry woe! The Queen, the Queen,
> The sweet'st, dear'st creature's dead, and vengeance for't
> Not dropped down yet. (3.2.170-200)

Like Leontes' question to Camillo in 1.2, it is immediately noticeable that Paulina's tirade here also contains a fair number of dashes which signal interpolations. But more strikingly, almost the whole of the speech (ll.173-98) is in fact technically a digression, for upon being asked by the lord "What fit is this?", Paulina's immediate answer should be that the queen is dead, the announcement of which is also her ultimate object in coming into the room. But instead of getting straight to the point, she expands her announcement by asking what tortures Leontes has in store for her since he has shown quite a talent for cruelty in his treatment of Polixenes, Camillo, baby Perdita, Mamillius and the queen. She lists the violence the king has done to these people and interpolates the course of this accusation to qualify points, for example what Leontes' jealousy really was, or how truly honourable, considering his age, Mamillius' thoughts were. It is not until the very last sentence in this 31-line torrent of a speech that she delivers the news of the "death" of Hermione. And even then she delays the actual announcement, calling the name of the queen twice and dwelling on her qualities: "The Queen, the Queen, / The sweet'st, dear'st creature", before finally revealing the news. Therefore, stylistically speaking, both Paulina's speech here and Leontes' question to Camillo quoted earlier share, amongst other things, the striking quality of heavy interpolation and suspension.

But, where Leontes' interpolations and grammatical suspensions appear to reflect a mind slipping out of control, here in Paulina's speech the same features can be looked on as having the contrasting effect of revealing cool calculation. The speaker is in perfect control of her logic and rhetoric. For one thing, although the beginning of the speech—

questions about the king's plans to torture her—appears to be a great deviation from the purpose either of answering the lord's "what fit is this" or of announcing the queen's "death", it nevertheless ties in logically with the rest of the speech, for Paulina's purpose of introducing the "torture motif" is to remind Leontes one by one of the acts of violence he has committed against all those who love and serve him, culminating in the greatest crime of all, the murder, in effect, of the queen. For another, all the delays in listing Leontes' previous crimes add weight and impact to the final revelation and throw all the speech's force into the "fact" of death. McDonald writes about this speech that

> [a]s the tirade unfolds, we perceive that Paulina's joint purposes are intertwined: she will simultaneously condemn Leontes and reveal his most appalling crime. The first objective waits upon the second...Every line looks forward explicitly or implicitly to the climax. ("Poetry" 322)

Moreover, this structure which delays the announcement of "death" also suggests that Paulina has envisioned and weighed the situation before opening her mouth. She is sure that the king, anxious to know how the queen does, will hang upon her every word until he gets the information he wants. Thus if she reserves the news of the "death" of the queen until the very end, her admonitions will be listened to. On the other hand, if she immediately tells of her "death", Leontes would probably be too stunned to take notice of anything else. Besides, all these other crimes would seem to pale in magnitude and significance in comparison with this last one that it might seem rather futile to list them *after* the revelation of Hermione's "death". Her deviations and interpolations, then, are techniques calculated to achieve maximum rhetorical effect.

However, this analysis of the effect of her employment of deviations and suspensions is rather based on the presumption that Paulina, contrary to Leontes, is in possession of her senses and probably knows by now that Hermione is not in fact dead. But if one is to suspend for a moment the impression, created by what Paulina has done so far (standing by the queen, endeavouring to persuade the king to see reason, and scolding him when he obdurately pronounces the new-born babe a bastard), that she is sane, resourceful and a good rhetorician, it would be equally possible to see this speech as the reflection of a mind possessed by grief and indignation, so that its speaker is no longer conscious of the conventions of conversation, indulges herself in speaking out loud what she thinks, and does not get to her point, which sounds not unlike what Leontes is doing in 1.2. Similarly, if one forgets for a moment that Leontes' jealousy is unfounded and his suspicion erroneous, it is not impossible to conclude that his speeches in the first act, rather than revealing a muddled and obsessed brain, in fact present a king whose faculties of reasoning remain more or less intact and who is coolly estimating the situation, as indeed some scholars believe him to be: "Leontes' words are not the ravings of insanity but a careful meditation on the relation of experience to certitude" (Knapp 270). Therefore, in the case of characterisation and language in *The Winter's Tale*, it is our pre-formed opinion of the character—formed mainly through observing their actions and the content, instead of the manner, of their speech—that leads us to perceive the effect of their language. It is not their linguistic style that offers us insight into their character but vice versa.

Other features of Shakespeare's late style are, like repetition and divagation, to be found throughout the play, in the language of most characters instead of restricted to the speeches of one in particular. Thus, as in the cases of *Pericles* and *Cymbeline*, verse style does more to distinguish the play from Shakespeare's earlier comedies and tragedies than to differentiate character from character within the same play.

Although the language in *The Winter's Tale* is largely non-speaker specific, there is one exceptional example which appears to support the claim for consistency between language and speaker. This is found, not between the differences in speech between one character and another, but rather between that of one particular character in the two different halves of the play. This one particular character is, of course, Leontes.[7] And there

---

[7] The Old Shepherd's language is also occasionally used as an example of character-specific style in *The Winter's Tale*. Although his verses still display many of the traits of the late Shakespearean verse (most noticeably metrical irregularity, elisions and ellipsis, and enjambments), syntactically they tend to have a simpler, more straightforward quality rarely found in the language of royalties. Bethell, though of the opinion that verse style and characterisation are generally separate in the play, remarks on the exception of the case of the Shepherd, "whose rural common sense and simple piety are at times thrown into relief by a type of verse relatively nearer to ordinary speech" (23).

But the example of the Old Shepherd's *verse* rather seems to work both ways. It is true that syntactically, its simplicity seems to reflect its speaker's rustic background. Yet on the other hand, the fact that for a considerable part of the fourth act he is speaking in verse might also be looked on as further proof that Shakespeare at this stage in his career was indeed not particularly concerned with the consistency of linguistic style with the character of its speakers, for, had he wished to mark out the difference of the Shepherd from the court people, the most obvious and efficient way would be to stick to convention and have him speak prose throughout.

is indeed a noticeable change in his way of speaking as he moves from the first three acts to the miraculous last act, or, as Bethell puts it, "[t]here is less difference in the quality of the verse between Leontes and Perdita than between Leontes jealous and Leontes penitent" (23). This change in language, however, is not brought about by dramatic adaptation of syntactical or "acoustic" style. Shakespeare still has Leontes elide, omit his relative pronouns and conjunctions, alliterate, interpolate, and employ enjambments in the last act, though admittedly less ostentatiously so than in Acts 1 to 3. Instead, Leontes' change of style is mainly achieved through his changed diction. As Jonathan Smith points out, the Sicilian king in the first half of the play, in selecting his words, is wont to go to extremes, either speaking mainly in Anglo-Saxon monosyllables—as McDonald puts it, "the language of blood" ("Poetry" 318)—or Latinate polysyllables. Two thirds of the latter appear in *The English dictionary, or the new interpreter of* hard *English words* (emphasis mine) compiled by Shakespeare's contemporary Henry Cockeram. Moreover, a great number of these are placed in this dictionary under the section where Cockeram

> insert[s] (as occasion served) even the mock-words which are ridiculously used in our language, that those who desire a generality of knowledge, may not be ignorant of the sense even of fustian-terms, used by too many who study rather to be heard speake, than to understand themselves. (Cockeram, qtd. in Smith 319)

Putting it another way, these are words that are pompous and supercilious to the point of unintelligibility. In contrast, the Leontes in the last act "has found the true language of a king...unequivocal, purged now of the pseudo-rational phraseology and the portentous" (Smith 326). What Latinate words he uses fall within the range of common usage and are not to be found in the dictionary of hard English words. As a result, the sense of emptiness of meaning, of speaking with manner but without matter is removed from the speeches of Leontes in the second half of the play. This change in diction marks Leontes' transformation from a pompous, self-absorbed and not infrequently gibbering tyrant to a humble and penitent ruler.

This difference in treatment of Leontes' language in the two halves of the play seems to support both the suggestion that Shakespeare here is suiting language to characterisation, and the theory, expounded in the chapters on *Pericles* and *Cymbeline*, that the playwright in the last plays is in the habit of using language to characterise the structure of the play, as this change in style also reflects the plot's move from the oppressive wintry first half to the light-hearted glorious second. This, I suggest, is because in *The Winter's Tale*, much of the plot in fact develops around the mental health (or lack of it) of one character, Leontes. This is especially evident in the first three acts, where his unreasonableness is the dominating force which propels the story forward. Similarly, the miraculous dénouement would not work, and probably would not even take place, had Leontes' mental state remained the same. Therefore, because in the case of the Sicilian king, characterisation and plot development are intertwined, Shakespeare's late style, with the added effect brought about by differences in diction, is able to illustrate both character development and plot structure. In other words, in *The Winter's Tale*, due to the fact that the development of the character of Leontes and that of plot has a kind of cause-and-effect relationship, in addition to its parallels with the structure of the plot and actions of the play, linguistic style also has the additional function of enhancing characterisation.

The *Winter's Tale* is thus distinguished from *Pericles* and *Cymbeline* in having a relatively focused plot which evolves around the development of one single character, who also strings together the main- and sub-plots of the story. That last clause sounds rather like a redundant qualifier, except that it is indeed necessary, for in *Pericles* and *Cymbeline*, despite their episodic structure, in their respective plots there is nevertheless one character whose involvement in all the episodes enables some semblance of unity to the story but whose mentality experiences either very little or absolutely no development during the course of the play. Pericles, because he technically commits no sin in the whole of *Pericles* (despite my previous discussion of the possibility of considering him succumbing to the sin of despair), need not and does not develop his character; while Cymbeline, although his personality can do with a good deal of improvement, remains exactly the same as he was before his experience of the Romano-British war and the temporary loss of his daughter. Indeed, almost no major character in *Pericles* experiences any great personal spiritual development. In *Cymbeline*, Posthumus, like Leontes, does transform from a jealous husband to a penitent one, but he is not "central" to the whole plot in the way that Leontes is to *The Winter's Tale*. The present play's intertwining of the transformation of Leontes and development of the plot thus appears to mark Shakespeare's development in dramatising the genre of romance, shifting gradually from conformity to the episodic structure of prose romance to a more focused way of narrating these stories which span time and space. This technique he would explore further in *The Tempest,* in which the events taking place on different parts of the island are directly in the control of the omniscient Prospero, whose development from a man wholly confident in his art-derived power to one who is disillusioned about art's capacity to bring about change determines the movements of both the main- and sub-plots.

It is also this focused quality of the narrative that helps to create the impression of "naturalness" or "realism" in the language in *The Winter's Tale*. Because Leontes' feverish mental state is at the centre of two thirds of the play, and because Shakespeare's tortuous, elliptical, incantatory and often obscure linguistic style is well-suited to the portrayal of the tormented mind, the play avoids giving the impression, as *Cymbeline* unfortunately does to some, that "the tone is frantic for little evident reason" (Kermode, *Language* 265). Instead, it is not surprising that an audience would form a general impression of realism of linguistic presentation in the tragic half of the play, since the plot is essentially built upon and propelled forward by Leontes' brooding madness. Moreover, a slight moderation on the part of the playwright in the succeeding comic half—introducing Autolycus' ballads and the Clown's prose, as well as changing Leontes' diction—easily throws into relief the quality of simplicity of the pastoral scenes and the wonder of the reunion episodes, again creating the impression of realistic character- or mood-specific speech, even though syntactically speaking much of the verse in the second half displays ample features of the late style found in abundance in the tragic first half.

"Naturalness" and "realism" of speech not only refer to the way in which language reflects occasion and, in the case of Leontes, characterisation, but also to the closeness of dramatic language to "natural" conversation. Certain linguistic features typical of Shakespeare's late verses do in fact contribute to creating an impression of the latter. Metrical irregularities, feminine endings and enjambments seem to be the most obvious examples, for, after all, no one in real life really speaks in perfect iambic pentameter—or in verse at all, for that matter. Similarly, interpolations which break up the progress of a sentence or passage help evoke a sense of spontaneous, rather than studied or recited, speech. In a way, they are also "realistic", for few in reality when speaking impromptu for more than three or four minutes are able to manoeuvre from one point to another without occasionally wandering off the subject.

However, in speeches which contain elements for naturalistic effects mentioned above, artistic control is nevertheless evident. Metrical irregularities, feminine endings and enjambments, however natural-sounding, are in the end variations to the rhythmic-scheme of the iambic pentameter and are thus to be found in verses, which only the characters created by a playwright would be using as the default form for communication. Moreover, the "naturalness" created by these late-style features is balanced, if not frequently overshadowed, by the excessive artificiality of another set of late-verse features: heavy alliterations, internal rhymes and semantic repetitions. Similarly, most of the speeches with frequent interpolations "spoken" by characters in the play inevitably leave the audience with the impression that they are evidently recitations of pieces of writing penned by someone who has thought them through, for in spontaneous communications in real life, no one who interpolates him- or herself as frequently and elaborately as Leontes and Paulina do is likely to successfully and seamlessly return to his or her main clause.

This "double-quality" of naturalness/realism and artificiality in the verses of *The Winter's Tale* is a linguistic reiteration of the play's treatment of the subject of art and nature. As the play's dramatic arrangements flaunt the tale's unrealistic nature, this language calls attention to its own artificiality, thus helping the playwright to further impress upon the audience that they are in the theatre watching and listening to fictional characters. Its efforts at imitating natural speech, on the other hand, remind the audience of the relationship between art and nature, as the presentation of characters speaking with an intensified rhetorical control and musicality not often found, but often desired, in reality once more demonstrates, through this artistically-produced "natural" language, that good art is the golden version of brazen nature.

To sum up: on the whole, the linguistic style of *The Winter's Tale* is similar to that of *Pericles* and *Cymbeline*, with frequent elisions, alliterations, internal rhymes, semantic repetitions, ellipsis, divagations, suspensions and other features characteristic of Shakespeare's late style. These features are to be found throughout the play in the language of different characters speaking under different circumstances, so it is possible to conclude that, for the most part, linguistic style is not directly linked to characterisation here, and is, in Hallet Smith's words, used not so much as to "characterize the speaker as dramatize the occasion" (qtd. in Barton, "Leontes" 136). However, the case of the languages of Leontes jealous and Leontes penitent proves an outstanding exception to the rule, where a marked change can be perceived in the speeches of the king in his two phases, an effect achieved largely through differences in diction. This, I suggest, is closely related to Shakespeare's development of the way of dramatising romance, switching tentatively from a mostly episodic narrative to one which evolves around the spiritual development of a central character. Since "occasion" and "character" in the case of Leontes are intertwined, language which dramatises the occasion takes on the additional function of characterising the speaker. It is an experience that we will encounter again in *The Tempest*.

The verses in *The Winter's Tale* also re-enact on a syntactic and semantic level one of the main themes of the story: the relationship between art and nature. Their often almost flaunting display of artistic control echoes the play's frequent allusion to its own unrealistic nature, while at the same time the sense of naturalness achieved through such control reinforces the play's conclusion on the subject of art and nature, which is that self-conscious art produced with good intention does no harm to, but can improve on, reality. Moreover, by evoking almost contradictory responses to their quality and effect, the verse of late Shakespeare, in its services rendered to the making of *The Winter's Tale*, proves once more the enduring topicality of the investigation into the relationship between art and nature.

CHAPTER FOUR

THE TEMPEST

Ineffective Art

The date of *The Tempest* is relatively uncontroversial. At present, it is more or less established as written in 1611, situated chronologically in the Shakespearean canon after *Cymbeline* and *The Winter's Tale*.

Because one does not know for certain whether *Cymbeline* or *The Winter's Tale* is the earlier of the two, it is equally difficult to ascertain whose immediate successor *The Tempest* really is. But, whether closer to *Cymbeline* or *The Winter's Tale* in date, *The Tempest* certainly *feels* closer to *The Winter's Tale*, with their shared romance elements of seas, tempests, exotic settings and *fin amour*, than to the more generically ambiguous *Cymbeline*. And in one aspect at least *The Tempest* has definitely inherited more from *The Winter's Tale*: its extended discussion of the subject of art. This is not to say that *Cymbeline* does not concern itself with art. As Chapter 2 has demonstrated, the matter of language and interpretation—marks of civilised human activity, and therefore wider *ars humanitas*—is a central theme and concern of the play. But, while *Cymbeline* explores this subject with subtlety, *The Tempest* follows *The Winter's Tale* in almost flaunting its concern with art and its power.

The Tempest intensifies the discussion. It greatly increases the frequency with which its audience's attention is drawn explicitly to art. The earlier play's signalled engagement in the discussion consists of a formal debate in Act 4 and the presentation of the absolute climax of its dénouement in the form of a play-within-the-play. *The Tempest*, not to be outdone, also presents a formal and philosophical reflection on art in the fourth act (Prospero's "Our revels are now ended" speech) and a theatrical gesture in the dénouement (the "discovering"—in the sense of withdrawing a cover or, in this instance, throwing open a curtain—of the spectacle of Ferdinand and Miranda playing at chess). Moreover, rather than confining such evident concern with art to one or two episodes, this play spreads it liberally across the acts by installing a protagonist, Prospero, who more or less embodies art (I shall qualify this statement later) and an "episodic" plot which is essentially a series of dramatic productions, placed one after another, planned and directed by him.

As Anne Barton puts it, "[a]lmost all the action of *The Tempest* is the contrivance of Prospero" (Introduction 11-2), in this respect the present play might be looked on as a greatly extended version of the last scene of *The Winter's Tale*, where narratives and theatrical spectacles take centre stage. After all, the whole of *The Tempest* is, in a way of speaking, the dénouement of a "regular" romance like *The Winter's Tale*. Prospero's theatrical productions are, like Paulina's presentation of the drama of Hermione's resurrection, the coda to a story which began more than a decade before. Shakespeare, then, has taken Paulina's short play-within-the-play and extended it into a series of narratives and dramas which take up a whole play instead of a couple of scenes. Thus, while in the earlier play, the discussion of art is made obvious only half-way through and then put aside before it is once more brought under the limelight in the final scene, in *The Tempest* the audience is confronted with and made aware of it from start (or, to be more accurate, from the second scene) to finish.

The present play also expands the scope of the "art" under discussion. "Art" in both *The Winter's Tale* and *The Tempest* can be summarised as referring to products of the human imagination or human intervention in the course of nature. But, although Perdita and Polixenes' debate touches on horticulture, and Leontes' mental construction of Hermione's guilt demands that the audience consider art in a broader sense than the fine arts, the main and obvious manifestations of art in *The Winter's Tale* essentially take the form of narratives and theatricals. In *The Tempest*, however, "art" not only refers to fine arts such as Prospero's theatrical and narrative efforts and Ariel's music, but also to language and discourse, magic powers, and the liberal arts (or knowledge and virtue gained through the study of books). These branches of art are important plot devices which form part of the premise of the story (Prospero's devotion to the study of the humanities and his mastery over magic) as well as serve as the means (magic, narratives and dramatic productions) by which he completes his project. They are also recurrent topics (the acquisition of language and the nature of theatrical art, for example) in characters' conversations and reflections. Thus, while the overarching plot is a theatrical production under the directorship of Prospero, made up of various episodes where theatricals and narratives are put to specific use by the magician, the gaps between the actions and major episodes are also filled with reminders of, references to and reflections on the nature and the power of art.

Much of the Art[1] in *The Tempest* can be directly related to Prospero. Indeed, it is with reference to him that the subject is first brought up in the play, as Miranda opens 1.2 with "If by your *art*, my dearest father" (1.2.1, italics mine). Art is the source of Prospero's power, for his control over the island and its inhabitants is established through and enforced by the use of magic, which in turn he has gained from his devoted study of his books, volumes containing the wisdom of the liberal and arcane arts. Art is, in the sense that it is the epitome of civilised human activity and represents an attempt to give form or bring order to wild nature, also the ultimate goal of his project, for his object is not only to reclaim his usurped dukedom and secure dynastic union between Milan and Naples, but also, to quote Robert Egan, "to purge the evil from the inhabitants of his world and restore them to good" (175) and thus establish an ideal moral order. To achieve this goal, Prospero makes full use of Art, exercising his magic in producing forms of Art, mostly narratives, music and theatrical performances which incorporate both visual spectacles and aural effects, to complete his project. Art, in short, is the source, means and object of his authority. And thus it seems not overly exaggerating to say that the play's protagonist more or less exists on and through Art.

The bulk of the action presents the audience with the mage's procedures in pushing through his project, in other words, his use of Art. From the first scene to the last, many of the important and most memorable episodes are essentially Director Prospero's "shows". The tempest in the first scene is a highly realistic theatrical production conjured up by Ariel under the magician's instructions (Art as a means of transporting a person or persons to a designated spot). A good part of the next scene is a "storytelling session" dominated by Prospero, where he relates to Miranda his life before their exile, reminds Ariel of his experience in the hands of Sycorax the witch, and enumerates Caliban's past and present sins (Art as a demonstration of authority and medium of didacticism). Later in the same scene he has Ariel lure Ferdinand with music to the spot where the latter and Miranda will be struck by the sight of each other and, as he hopes, fall in love (Art as a means of transporting a person or persons to a designated spot). In the third act the "three men of sin", Alonso, Antonio and Sebastian, are made to watch a horrific show where an enticing banquet suddenly vanishes in thunder and lightning, replaced by a harpy calling itself and its fellows "ministers of fate" (3.3.61) (Art as a medium of didacticism). In the scene which immediately follows,

---

[1] From now on I shall refer to "Art" in *The Tempest* with a capital "A", in order to do justice to its multi-layered significance and its omnipresence in the action and conversations of the play.

Prospero puts on for the benefit of the young couple a masque celebrating their betrothal, "a most majestic vision" (4.1.118) (Art as a medium of didacticism). The masque is broken off midway as he remembers and leaves to attend to Caliban, Trinculo and Stefano's revolt, which he first delays by distracting their attention with the spectacle of glittering garments hung in the woods, and later thwarts by setting spirits, transformed into dogs, on them—one might say, not without a little malignant humour, that the three are presented with a "hunting scene" (Art as a display of authority and power). In the final act, Prospero's theatricals are less elaborate, consisting mainly of revelations: dramatically revealing himself as the Duke of Milan to the spell-bound Neapolitans and revealing to Alonso the sight of Ferdinand and Miranda engaged in a game of chess (Art as a medium of didacticism).

   The Tempest has a happy ending complete with the essential elements of a Shakespearean romance. The sinners repent and ask for forgiveness. The sinned-against forgive. The older generation achieves a reconciliation long overdue. The younger finds love and looks forward to the blessings of married life. The dynastic future of kingdoms is secured through a dynastic union. What is lost is restored and reclaimed. As such happy resolutions are ostensibly brought about by Prospero's Art, it would seem that *The Tempest*, having followed *The Winter's Tale* in conspicuously incorporating discussions of Art into the dramatic action, has also inherited its ultimate optimism for Art's power. A more careful inspection, however, will reveal that the case is not so straightforward. Art in *The Tempest* is not as powerful or as effective as it appears on the surface.

   Although it seems that it is through Art that Prospero derives his authority and control over the island, Art's power is not the effective force in the implementation of his plans. The success of his project of reclaiming Milan lies not in Art's power to influence or to instruct, but in his unhesitating use of violence for coercion. Peeling away the "Artistic wrappings" of the magician's narratives and theatrical spectacles, it is not difficult to see that the real force of control comes from violence, mostly in the form of verbal threats, sometimes in physical torture, and occasionally as frightening sights which torment the mind rather than the body.

   The first of these, the lightest form of violence, Prospero reserves for his nearest and dearest. Even Miranda receives a "Silence! One word more / Shall make me chide thee, if not hate thee" (1.2.479-80) from her father for trying to plead for Ferdinand. Ariel is threatened with being "peg[ged] in [an oak's] knotty entrails till / Thou hast howled away twelve winters"

(1.2.297-8) into ceasing to complain about not being given his promised liberty. Similarly, Ferdinand, as the future son-in-law, is warned against pre-marital sex with:

> No sweet aspersion shall the heavens let fall
> To make this contract grow; but barren hate,
> Sour-eyed disdain, and discord, shall bestrew
> The union of your bed with weeds so loathly
> That you shall hate it both. (4.1.18-22)

Although the same lesson of continence and chaste love is later expressed through the more aesthetically pleasing and elaborate form of the masque, Prospero clearly considers it essential that the performance be prefaced with this crude warning.

Only on Caliban and later his conspirators does Prospero directly bestow physical punishment. In 1.2 Prospero tells Caliban that he would

> rack thee with old cramps,
> Fill all thy bones with aches, make thee roar,
> That beasts shall tremble at thy din (1.2.372-4)

should he not do as he is told. This threat, unlike the ones thrown at Ariel, Ferdinand and Miranda, is apparently no empty one, for in the opening of 2.2 Caliban complains bitterly about the ill treatments he has received. As at this point he is talking to himself and not trying to impress the cruelty of the magician upon anyone within the play itself (the audience off the stage is another matter), his words should probably be accepted as more accurate than exaggerated. His plea, when he mistakes Trinculo for one of Prospero's spirit minions, that he not torment him is urgent and impassioned, once more attesting to the severity of the mage's physical punishments. Later, when his attempt on Prospero's life fails, it is ordered that goblins should

> grind their joints
> With dry convulsions, shorten up their sinews
> With agèd cramps, and more pinch-spotted make them
> Than pard or cat o'mountain. (4.1.254-7)

Judging from Ariel's "Hark, they roar!" (4.1.257), this instruction is duly carried out.

Towards the castaways, who are Prospero's main targets in his afternoon's project, the magus's violence is generally of a more

psychological kind. He prefers, in their case, to commit violence upon
their spirits. That Alonso's party should end up on the island in the first
place is the result of the magician's theatrical violence: they are swept into
his power by a tempest conjured up by Ariel under his instructions.
Although the storm itself is physically harmless and "[n]ot a hair perished"
(1.2.218) in it, the terror, despair and subsequent sorrow of those caught
up in it are as real as that of the victims of any real catastrophe. Later, on
the island, the weary and hungry party is greeted by a banquet which
vanishes in thunder and lightning as they approach. But, even worse than
the experience of Tantalus, they are confronted by a harpy which accuses
them of crimes against the former Duke of Milan. Their terror is further
amplified by the eerie spectacle of strange shapes, which materialise to
"*dance with mocks and mows*", accompanied by probably equally creepy
"*soft music*" (Stage Direction 3.3). This experience leaves the three
"distracted" and the rest of the party "mourning over them, / Brimful of
sorrow and dismay" (5.1.12, 13-4).

   Most of Prospero's violence-backed Art (or Art-wrapped violence)
reaps satisfactory immediate results. Ariel begs pardon and promises
dutiful service:

> Pardon, master.
> I will be correspondent to command,
> And do my spriting gently. (1.2.298-300)

Ferdinand obediently undertakes his task of log-bearing and readily vows
that nothing shall

>   melt
> Mine honour into lust to take away
> The edge of that day's celebration. (4.1.27-9)

Caliban, for all his complaints and curses, goes about the island collecting
firewood as he is ordered. And of the three men of sin, at least one, Alonso,
registers the harpy's warnings:

>   It did bass my trespass.
> Therefor my son i'th' ooze is bedded, and
> I'll seek him deeper than e'er plummet sounded,
> And with him there lie mudded. (3.3.99-102)

   In contrast to the success of these violence-backed Artistic productions,
those of Prospero's Artistic gestures which involve no direct force or

coercion are considerably less effective. They evoke no great change in their audience, either in terms of their courses of action or in their views. Prospero's three narratives in 1.2 are in this sense utter failures. The first of these relates to Miranda his deposition and exile by the treachery of a brother. But it is questionable how much of it is really registered by the listener. Although Miranda seems to have followed the narrative quite closely during the "session", as is reflected by the proper responses she makes,[2] her subsequent actions suggest that much of Prospero's story is finally lost on her. Falling in love at first sight with Ferdinand and being almost immediately afterwards made aware, by his self-introduction, of his identity as the son of the King of Naples, she suffers none of the qualms, which Juliet does in a similar situation, about falling in love with an enemy of the family. Indeed, not only does she "[show] no sign of connecting him with the story she has just heard, she seems genuinely perplexed by Prospero's unfriendliness" (Barton, Introduction 11). In the final scene, when she sees Alonso's court party, Miranda exclaims with delight:

> O wonder!
> How many goodly creatures are there here!
> How beauteous mankind is! O brave new world
> That has such people in't! (5.1.184-7)

Apparently, Prospero's tale about the treacheries and evils in the world at large has not made much impression on her either. Of course, her untroubled love for Ferdinand and admiration for the "brave new world" are a reflection of her innocence and inherent goodness. However, they are at the same time a testament to the failure of Prospero's narrative to conform his daughter's response to history to his own.

Prospero's narrative to Ariel in the same scene is equally ineffective in achieving its desired goal of inducing him to willing service. Ariel only responds to the account with "yes" or "no" or, when a non-monosyllabic reply is explicitly demanded of him, a curt answer mostly in incomplete sentences and never exceeding four words. It is not until Prospero resorts to verbal threat of imprisonment that the spirit promises to be obedient and not grunt about freedom.

The use of narrative to establish control over Caliban is even more futile. Prospero's (and Miranda's) account of Caliban's attempted assault

---

[2] Prospero's constant demand for attention is perhaps more a manifestation of his "bossiness" than her inattention.

on the girl's honour and accusation of ungratefulness evoke no sense of guilt or resolution to repent on the part of the listener, only the regret that

> O ho, O ho! Would't had been done!
> Thou didst prevent me; I had peopled else
> This isle with Calibans. (1.2.352-4)

Indeed, in this episode Prospero is rather beaten on his own turf, or at least greatly challenged, for it is Caliban who initiates the use of narrative for the justification of authority. He contests Prospero's rule over himself and the rest of the island by claiming the place to be his inheritance from his mother Sycorax, stating that it is Prospero the new-comer, rather than himself the host, that has responded ungratefully to kindness and hospitality. Moreover, Caliban directs his attack straight at the ultimate medium of narrative art, language, and dismisses it as useless and worthless, his only "profit on't / Is I know how to curse" (1.2.366-7). In the end, as is with Ariel, Prospero has to resort to threat of physical torment to regain control over him. Once more, pure Art has failed to achieve its desired effect, rescued only by the force of violence.

Even verbal violence, however, does not always produce the expected results. Ariel and Caliban can be subdued by verbal threats of violence because they have experiences of such violence and know that Prospero is capable of realising such threats. To someone who does not know about the magician's powers, however, verbal threats are, in a way of speaking, merely theatrical gestures which make imaginative use of language. Such must have been Ferdinand's immediate impression, during his initial encounter with Prospero, of the old man's threat about ill treatment. Verbal threat in this case, rather than intimidating the listener into immediate submission, makes him put up a fight: "I will resist such entertainment till / Mine enemy has more power" (1.2.469-70). And so it is with more solid power—a charm that freezes the prince's motions— rather than that of language, that Prospero finally manages to bring Ferdinand to submission.

While the above examples reveal that in this play, Art is in fact more or less helpless unless backed by more substantial forces like violence or magic spells, there are things which even such violence-supported Art cannot accomplish. Prospero's ultimate goal, that of establishing moral order, fails, as the afternoon's series of drunken riots and attempted revolts, fratricide and regicide show, and as Antonio and Sebastian's indifference to forgiveness and aloofness from reconciliation in the last act also confirm. Despite the mage's Artistic efforts, the drunkards remain intoxicated and the degenerate amoral.

Unlike in *The Winter's Tale*, where art is ultimately shown to have a positive influence on nature, in the present instance, Art, even when it is strengthened by unhesitant use of violence or potent magic, is presented as essentially powerless against the dictate of nature. The two or three hours of the play witness Prospero's gradual realisation that his Artistic attempts are futile. The realisation first begins to dawn on him when the remembrance of Caliban's revolt makes him break up the betrothal masque. As the spirits and the pageant vanish into thin air, Prospero remarks on the illusory and transitory nature of performative art and, indeed, reality itself:

> Our revels now are ended. These our actors,
> As I foretold you, were all spirits, and
> Are melted into air, into thin air;
> And like the baseless fabric of this vision,
> The cloud-capped towers, the gorgeous palaces,
> The solemn temples, the great globe itself,
> Yea, all which it inherit, shall dissolve;
> And like this insubstantial pageant faded,
> Leave not a rack behind. We are such stuff
> As dreams are made on, and our little life
> Is rounded with a sleep. (4.1.148-58)

This is his first step towards disillusionment in Art's power, the realisation that Art, and indeed human life itself, are but "such stuff as dreams are made on".

The second step is his acknowledgement that Art can do little in the case of Caliban:

> A devil, a born devil, on whose nature
> Nurture can never stick; on whom my pains,
> Humanely taken, all, all lost, quite lost. (4.1.188-90)

Admitting defeat, the magician locates the root of his failure in Caliban's incorrigible nature as the product of the union between a witch and a devil. Ways of "nurture" both humane and violent have been used in the effort to force some morals into him, but all in vain up to this point. Caliban still retains his essential beastliness. He made an attempt to violate Miranda's virginity, curses in his newly acquired tongue, easily switches allegiance, and has no scruples about plotting murder. Prospero thus comes to the conclusion that because Caliban is the outcome of a union so alien to humanity that it is futile to expect that Art of any form, liberal or violent, can change him for the better. Jan Kott calls this realisation "the climax of Prospero's tragedy" (*Contemporary* 334). While I believe that the real climax of the magus's tragedy comes later, Kott is certainly right in pointing out the bitterness and poignancy of the moment, particularly of the lines "my pains, / Humanely taken, all, all lost, quite lost". It is probably this great sense of defeat and recognition of the essential powerlessness of his source of power in the upbringing of Caliban that accounts for Prospero's sudden burst of "passion / That works him strongly" (4.1.143-4) in the middle of the masque, one which bewilders Miranda and Ferdinand and has puzzled many a Shakespearean scholar, who cannot comprehend why the magician should be thus disturbed by a "revolt" which he can quell with a flick of his wand. The revolt itself is no threat to Prospero, but doubts that his source of power might not in fact be as omnipotent as he believes are.

Kott takes Prospero's frustrated exclamation at 4.1.188-90 to be the climax of his tragedy because "[o]nly after this scene will he break and reject his magic wand" (*Contemporary* 334). The reason why I disagree with him is that at this point the mage has not yet witnessed the full extent of his project's failure, nor is he completely disillusioned with the power of Art. Furthermore, he has yet to properly comprehend the cause of his failure. With 4.1.188-90, Prospero only admits failure in the specific case of Caliban and concludes that nurture has no effect on the likes of him because, not being fully human, he is beyond the reach of human Art. The magician, however, seems still to have retained enough faith in Art's power of influence over his fellow human beings to resort later to "some heavenly music" (5.1.52) and the dramatic revelation of Ferdinand and Miranda. Indeed, his magnificent declaration of the decision to abandon magic sounds "more like a great assertion of power than a withdrawal from efficacy" (Bloom, *Invention* 683) and more like a reaffirmation of the power of Art than a statement of disillusion. Moreover, even as he prepares to abjure magic, he makes use of it, for the court party is still held in his power under his spells and will be put into the magic circle which he has drawn and awakened by the heavenly music which he has summoned. And he still has Ariel, who is as good as a magic staff, indeed, who *is* his "magic staff". Thus despite his declaration that he shall

> break my staff,
> Bury it certain fathoms in the earth,
> And deeper than did ever plummet sound
> I'll drown my book, (5.1.54-7)

Prospero has not yet renounced Art altogether. And note that he is only going to drown his book, not his book*s*. It is possible to interpret the choice of the singular as implying that he is merely going to abandon one volume—the one containing the magic spells perhaps?—but not his library, not the whole range of liberal arts. Besides, his observation to Ferdinand about performative art being a fading illusion, profound though it is, might only be an expression of a passing frustration brought on by the thought of Caliban's revolt. No sooner has he finished remarking that life is "rounded with a sleep" than he adds

> Sir, I am vexed.
> Bear with my weakness. My old brain is troubled.
> Be not disturbed by my infirmity.
> …A turn or two I'll walk
> To still my beating mind, (4.1.158-60, 162-3)

as if to persuade Ferdinand, as well as himself, not to take what he has said to heart and that his faith in Art *can* be restored after "a turn or two".

Not wholly giving up on Art also means that at this point in the play, Prospero has yet to learn that Art, the source of his power, is also the source of his failure. His pursuit of Art, when he was still Duke of Milan, was the cause of his neglect of temporal duties and thus an indirect stimulus for Antonio's ambition for power as well as provider of opportunity for usurpation. More importantly, his better familiarity with books than with his fellow men means that Prospero's moral vision, which he seeks to implement on the island through the force of Art, is founded rigidly on an ideal, with little consideration for practicality. Egan observes that "[h]is years of seclusion in his library have instilled in him a moral perspective rooted not in the real world but in the ideals of his art" (176). Prospero's moral world is one in which evil does not exist, where brothers do not abuse their trust and turn against their kin, lovers abide by the rules of chaste love and continence, reason governs all, and Art is the highest form of power. In short, his moral vision is as unrealistic and impractical as Gonzalo's Golden World. But whereas the latter contents himself with merely talking about his Arcadia, Prospero has spent not only the three hours on the afternoon of the tempest but in fact his twelve years on the island trying to establish his moral utopia. Even his final acknowledgement of forgiveness to Antonio still bespeaks this sense of rigid moral idealism, for unlike Innogen or Hermione's forgiveness, Prospero's is not one of compassion or goodwill, but a choice dictated by rational thinking, formed on the intellectual understanding that "[t]he rarer action is / In virtue than in vengeance" (5.1.27-8). This is why his forgiveness to Antonio sounds forced. Indeed, it sounds like anything but forgiveness. And he still hates the thought of acknowledging Antonio as a brother: "you, most wicked sir, whom to call brother / Would even infect my mouth" (5.1.132-3), for in his moral absolutism if

> his brother act[s] contrary to the ideal of a brother, then his brother [is] not a brother but some alien, inhuman being of evil, to be dealt with as an enemy. (Egan 176)

But all this Prospero has yet to realise. For now, rather than accepting reality, he still denies it, though not by ignoring it or treating it as something entirely mouldable by his Art. Instead, when reality intrudes upon him during his pageant and upsets his mood, he temporarily descends, in the "Our revels now are ended" speech, to nihilism, declaring that reality is, like a performance, but a fading illusion. A turn or two, however, will still his beating mind and more or less restore his faith in Art, which he will proceed to use to quell Caliban's revolt before abjuring the magical part of it, probably preparatory to his return to the non-magical society of Milan. The rest of the elements of his Art, plus some lingering magic, he will continue to work on the Neapolitan party, in the hope that although he has failed with the devil-born Caliban, he might yet succeed with his fellow human beings.

Prospero, however, is wrong in his restored confidence, as he is wrong about the nature of Caliban. By the end of the last act, which is also the last step in his project, those who have shown themselves to have benefited from the afternoon's experience are Ferdinand, Alonso and Caliban. Ferdinand, who is naturally noble and good, promises to respect Miranda's virginity and is enthusiastic about the moral vision demonstrated in the masque. Alonso, who is not evil or base in the way that Antonio and Sebastian are, repents and asks for forgiveness. Caliban, who is in fact "the lowest and the highest human, the rebel and the man with music in his soul" and who furthermore has "the capacity to sympathize with other beings which humanism took to be one of the highest capacities of man" (Bate, *Soul* 138), vows to be wise and seek for grace.

On the other hand, the truly degenerate among the party, Antonio and Sebastian, and their buffoonish counterparts Stefano and Trinculo, show no sign of remorse or repentance. Trinculo and Stefano are unashamedly drunk and only complain about the bodily pains they are suffering, not once showing the faintest realisation that this pain and their heinous plan are connected. Antonio has remained emphatically unresponsive to his brother's reprimand and forgiveness. It is difficult to imagine his silence as resulting from shame rather than indifference or even contempt, for later when he does speak, he, together with Sebastian, still smirks and jests at others' expense, an indicator, no doubt, of the two men's incorrigibility, for it has been observed that "Shakespeare never puts habitual scorn into the mouths of other than bad men" (Coleridge, qtd. in Bate, *Romantics* 533). It is clear these two have not been purged of their sin.

It would seem that the verdict is in: Art is powerless against the dictates of nature, any sort of nature, human or bestial. Those who have a natural tendency towards goodness, however well-buried, might be responsive to Art's influence. The degenerate shall remain degenerate. Similarly, as the nature of the world's inhabitants remains essentially unchangeable by Art, so the workings of the world stay uninfluenced by Artistic efforts. The mechanism of history remains far from Prospero's idealistic moral vision and still develops around the theme of struggle for power, often entailing murder, revolt and violence. In fact, during the three hours on the island, the mage has seen his own history repeated twice, the first in the form of Sebastian's attempt, under the inducement of Antonio, at fratricide and regicide, and the second in Caliban, Trinculo and Stefano's clumsy plan of *coup d'état*. Prospero's Art is able to prevent death in both cases, but not the attempts at murder for the sake of power themselves. In a way of speaking, his intervention in the two coups, especially the one hatched by Antonio and Sebastian, might be looked on as a gestural attempt at rewriting, now that he is Artistically potent, his own humiliating history. But his super-human intervention is itself a proof that history cannot be changed by human efforts. As Kott observes:

> Prospero's staff makes the history of the world repeat itself on a desert island. Actors can play that history in four hours. But Prospero's staff cannot change history. When the morality play is over, Prospero's magic power must also end. Only bitter wisdom remains, (*Contemporary* 325)

the bitter wisdom that the homeward journey will end in the old Milan and Naples, where violent struggle for power is a law of the world and cannot be so easily averted now that he has broken his staff and released Ariel.

Therefore, although Prospero has successfully regained his dukedom and secured his daughter's marriage, his three-hour (or twelve-year) Art project can at best be called half a success. Its ultimate goal of implementing his moral vision and establishing a truly "brave new world" is not and cannot be reached. So it is that when Miranda wonders with delight at the sight of the court party, Prospero has only four bitter words in reply: "'Tis new to thee" (5.1.187). The world is new only to Miranda, who has never properly known it. It remains the same old evil world to

Prospero, not only in the sense that the wicked in it are incorrigible, but also that the mechanism of history remains unchanged by his Artistic efforts. "'Tis new to thee"—Prospero has finally admitted defeat, accepted reality, and lost his faith in Art.

"'Tis new to thee." This, for me, is the climax of Prospero's tragedy. This quiet line contains his full realisation and admission that his whole afternoon's—whole life's, in fact—pursuit has been futile, his disillusionment in the power of Art, his frustration that the world he had wished to make anew remains stubbornly as it ever was, his regret that he cannot offer his daughter a "brave new world", and his uneasiness about the prospect of his innocent child trying to survive in such a treacherous world. In the end, Art's greatest effect in *The Tempest* is to reduce a fervent believer of its power to disillusionment.

After this remark, Prospero will have no more theatrical gestures. The little magic he employs is no longer his liberal-arts-derived magic, but Ariel's purely "natural"—in the sense that it is not gained from library studies—supernatural power. And even that magic only seeks to offer "calm seas" and "auspicious gales" for the return journey. No more Art as a display for authority or medium for didacticism is involved.

In fact, after "'Tis new to thee", Prospero remains relatively silent in the rest of the last scene. He does speak and not too infrequently. But he is no longer the dominator of conversations and narratives that he used to be, a sign that he has relinquished his Artistic control over perspectives. He actually advises that the past should not be dwelt on, a complete reversal of his former take on history. And when Gonzalo interprets the afternoon's event in his own way and suggests its morals be "set…down / With gold on lasting pillars" (5.1.210-1), Prospero makes no response, not attempting to contradict Gonzalo's interpretation, nor showing enthusiasm for the proposed use of Artistic didacticism.

When Prospero does offer to tell his story, he no longer seems to be employing it as an agent of moral reform. At first, he says his object is to

> resolve you,
> Which to you shall seem probable, of every
> These happened accidents. (5.1.251-3)

However, he cannot "deliver all" (5.1.317) as promised, for he can hardly reveal his secret studies, lest it be known that he was responsible for the Neapolitans' afternoon's misery, nor dwell too much on the cause of such sufferings. Therefore one can foresee no great moral lesson in this upcoming narrative, for it is in the parts which he cannot relate that the moral lies. Prospero himself probably realises that he cannot explain much as well, for when near the end of the play he once more promises to tell his tale, he further humbles its object to "mak[ing] it [the last night on the island] / Go quickly away" (5.1.307-8), or, in other words, to serve as pleasant pastime. And still later, in the epilogue, Prospero—for the actor is still in character here—once more mentioning his project, finally reduces its goal to "to please" (Epilogue 13).

But it is likely that Prospero's upcoming narrative cannot achieve even that comparatively unambitious goal. While *Shakespeare's* presentation to the audience of Prospero's project, whose immediate attraction lies in the exciting episodes which *Prospero* would have to conceal from *his* Neapolitan audience, can please, it is extremely doubtful whether the duke's upcoming bland abridged version can really help pass the time pleasantly away. Thus, unlike in *Pericles* and *The Winter's Tale*, where the prospect of an after-show "story session" among the characters promises further restorative effect, in *The Tempest* it is merely a form of entertainment with no such guaranteed efficacy. For all we know, Alonso and his party might be reduced to sleepiness by Prospero's narrative, as Miranda has been in 1.2.

In a manner of speaking, Prospero's Artistic efforts in *The Tempest* are not unlike Leontes' process of confirming Hermione's guilt in *The Winter's Tale*. Both attempt to construct reality according to their "artistic" vision, artistic in the sense that it is a product of the human imagination. But while Leontes' artistic construction is destructive, and thus at least has an effect, Prospero's is merely ineffective. *The Winter's Tale*'s discussion of art centres on whether it has a negative or positive influence over nature, taking it for granted that either way it will have an impact. *The Tempest*, however, questions that premise and shows Art to be in fact ineffective, powerless against reality and nature.

And so by the end of *The Tempest*, Art, once believed by Prospero to be the ultimate pursuit in life, the controller of natural elements and the moulder of reality, is finally reduced to a form of entertainment, of whose ability to please its producer cannot be certain. Prospero asks to be released from it, or else his "ending is despair" (Epilogue 15). The audience obligingly claps. The show is over.

It is worth noting that the play's duration is roughly the same as Prospero's three-hour dramatic project. Moreover, in Shakespeare's day, it probably also started at about two or three in the afternoon and ended at six. When the playwright, who usually plays freely with time, suddenly keeps his dramatic clock exactly the same as that in reality, the consciousness of the design cannot be missed. It draws the audience's attention to the close parallel between the play world and the real. After three hours' futile Artistic endeavour at establishing a better world, Prospero will return to one which remains the same, just as after three hours in the theatre, the audience would return to life as it was before *The Tempest* began. "Life begins again, in the same way as before the tempest, before the performance, for characters and audience alike" (Kott, *Contemporary* 296). Art has not accomplished much in either world. *The Winter's Tale*'s appeal for faith in art is already in the past. And the past is not to be dwelt on, according to Prospero in the last act. Thus, after three romances which seek to establish art—particularly performative art—as a positive force in influencing the affairs of man (of course, all the time keeping a cool head about its potential problems and limitations), Shakespeare's treatment of the medium of his livelihood seems to be shifting back towards the other side of the balance.

Treacherous Language

Consistent with Shakespeare's practice in the last plays, the matter of language, or verbal communication, is a major dramatic concern in *The Tempest*. Like its treatment of the broader subject of art, the play visibly signals its preoccupation with the more specific matter of language. In the three preceding plays, Shakespeare's engagement in the discussion is rather subtly indicated, usually by the important position which rhetorical manipulation of words (in the form of riddles, letters, songs and ballads, and narratives) holds at key moments of the plot. *The Tempest*, while inheriting such a practice, develops it by explicitly drawing the audience's attention to the subject through direct comments on language and communication in the characters' conversations.

During the first two acts, the playwright more than once specifically alludes to the matter of language by having a character or characters pass a comment on or strike up a discussion about it. In the first act, for example, Caliban bluntly contests the view that he should be grateful for his acquisition of language, famously remarking that

> You taught me language, and my profit on't
> Is I know how to curse. The red plague rid you
> For learning me your language! (1.2.366-8)

Apart from this, twice, on separate occasions, a character is shown to register surprise at the discovery that a "native" of the island actually speaks his tongue. Ferdinand, upon hearing Miranda speak, exclaims: "My language! Heavens!" (1.2.432). Similarly, in the next act, Stefano wonders at Caliban's linguistic competence: "Where the devil should he learn our language?" (2.2.63-4). It has been pointed out that despite the appearance of Welsh in *Henry IV* and French in *Henry V*, this is in fact "new", for "never before in Shakespeare's plays have characters called such attention to the fact that they might *not* speak the same language" (Garner 177). But perhaps the most elaborate direct emphasis on the verbal medium comes at the beginning of Antonio's attempted political seduction of Sebastian, where the two demonstrate a self-conscious awareness of the act of speaking itself:

> SEBASTIAN   What, art thou waking?
> ANTONIO Do you not hear me *speak*?
> SEBASTIAN   I do, and surely
> It is a sleepy *language*, and thou *speak'st*
> Out of thy sleep. What is it thou didst *say*?
> This is strange repose, to be asleep
> With eyes wide open; standing, *speaking*, moving,
> And yet so fast asleep.
>   …Thou dost snore distinctly.
> There is *meaning* in thy snores.
>   …Prithee, *say* on.
> The setting of thine eyes and cheek *proclaim*
> A *matter* from thee. (2.1.205-11, 213-4, 224-6, italics mine)

Such high-frequency references to language, together with more substantial elaboration on the subject throughout the play (Prospero's long narrative in 1.2, or Antonio and Sebastian's wordplay, for example), push to the forefront the play's thematic attention to the problems of language and communication.

Language and verbal communication are presented in *The Tempest* in rather an unfavourable light. A quick survey of the plot reveals that of all the major dramatis personae, the four whose use of language can be said to constitute a dramatic motif all employ it in such a way as to leave an unpleasant impression on the audience regarding the act of speaking: Prospero threatens, Caliban curses, Sebastian jeers, and Antonio seduces. Moreover, significantly, communication remains imperfect even in the final dénouement. This is noticeably contrary to the pattern in the previous last plays where harmonised verbal communication reflects the achievement, or the prospect, of understanding among characters, an essential part of the final restoration and reconciliation. In *The Tempest*, however, we see what Barton describes as a "compartmentalized" ending, in which

[d]istinct groups of characters meet at last, but they do not really communicate with one another, and the magician who has ordered these revelations and discoveries is still essentially alone. (Introduction 40)

Such arrangements appear to imply a sceptical, or at least disappointed, attitude towards verbal communication and language, which is consistent with the play's reserved view on the power of art in general.

In 2.2, after his initial surprise at a native's ability to speak his language, Stefano offers Caliban liquor and tells him that "[h]ere is that which will give language to you" (2.2.78-9). A moment later, handing the bottle to Trinculo, he asks the latter to "[k]iss the book" (2.2.121). The direct association of language with alcohol not only echoes Caliban's expressed contempt for the acquisition of speech, but also ridicules Prospero and Miranda's efforts spent on training him to speak, since liquor gives language as effectively as, if not more so than, methodical education. The equation of "the bottle" and "the book" takes the comparison a step further. No longer is language merely the result of intoxication, but is in fact the demon drink itself, for if the bottle is the book, then by implication liquor language. This is not a nonsensical comparison that merely ridicules language, but in fact points to a likeness that truly exists between it and alcohol, which Antonio and Sebastian's use of language in the previous scene (more about this episode later) has already fully demonstrated. Alcohol has the potential to intoxicate and muddle the brain, while language possesses the ability to confuse communication and to arrest the thinking process. Moreover, this equating of the book with the bottle might be looked on as suggesting that the world is not to be made comprehensible or organised by the efforts of language. Wine bottles contain substance which may upset order. Thus by implication, books, the bottle's equivalent, assemblages of language, must fail in their intended mission of giving a recognisable shape to events.

Stefano's metaphor in fact succinctly summarises the play's presentation of language. In *The Tempest*, language is either ineffective, or effective in a treacherous and potentially destructive way. Unlike in the earlier last plays, where verbal communication, despite its faults and dangers, is finally a restorative force, most of the major episodes in this drama explore and demonstrate the negative side of language, whose image remains unredeemed even in the final act.

The play in fact opens with a portrayal of language's powerlessness to effect change. Much has been said about how the Boatswain's words introduce the theme of authority, to the effect that it almost crowds out from critical attention the fact that the scene also vividly presents a failure of verbal communication. Stripped of the thunder and the storm, 1.1 is essentially a conversation between two parties, neither of which is able to induce the other to take in its side of the argument. The Boatswain's language, impressively subversive as it is, fails to keep the courtiers, Gonzalo in particular, below decks. At the same time, the lords, be their language gentle and mild—"Good, yet remember whom thou hast aboard" (1.1.17)—or blustering and insulting—"A pox o'your throat, you bawling, blasphemous, incharitable dog!" (1.1.36-7)—equally fail to elicit from the Boatswain the marks of respect which they believe their social superiority demands.

For most of the scene, Gonzalo, ever optimistic, derives comfort from the thought that the Boatswain "hath no drowning mark upon him; his complexion is perfect gallows" (1.1.25-6), an idea which he clings to, repeating it four times in the short 1.1 and once more in 5.1 when the mariners are rejoined with the rest of the party. Although it does turn out that the Neapolitans, including the Boatswain, are not destined to drown this time, Gonzalo's almost obsessive repetition of the idea nevertheless invites ridicule, as does his blind optimism founded upon a proverb—words—which is hardly the infallible truth and cannot dictate the course of nature.

As language fails to change the attitude or actions of one's fellow men, it is hardly surprising that it should be powerless against the forces of nature. The Master's instructions and the mariners' prayers cannot prevent the ship from sinking, nor can the assertions of a king's authorities, for, after all, "[w]hat cares these roarers for the name of king?" (1.1.15-6). The powerlessness of language upon the occasion is summarised in the mariners' "All lost! To prayers, to prayers! All lost!" (1.1.46). Even as the power of language is called on for rescue, in the same breath its inadequacy is proclaimed—"all is lost". Coherent language is finally drowned in the babble of indistinct voices and the howl of the tempest as the ship goes down. Verbal challenge to authority, verbal assertion of authority, proverbs and prayers, all fail to rescue the crew from the terror of 1.1.

After the first scene's introduction to the idea of language's powerlessness, either against the will of one's fellow men or the force of natural elements, subsequent episodes pick up on the idea and develop it at length. One major demonstration of the ineffectiveness of language, Prospero's narratives in 1.2, has already been analysed earlier. Indeed, his language throughout the play, despite its speaker's being presented as a figure of control, when unsupported by supernatural power, is mostly ineffective. It fails to change the nature or perspectives of its listener; fails to civilise Caliban; fails to reform Antonio or Sebastian; and will fail to "deliver all" when the party retires to his den to hear his accounts of the afternoon.

A similar portrayal of verbal language's inadequacy to effect a change in the listener's attitude is found in Gonzalo's futile attempts, in 2.1, at comforting the grief-stricken Alonso. Gonzalo first points out that their misfortune, though great, is not uncommon and that their survival in fact calls for joy. Finding Alonso unmoved, he further develops the "causes for joy" theme and draws attention to the miracle of life. Alonso still inconsolable, Gonzalo changes tactics, trying to distract the king from broodings on the loss of his son by talking of his plans if he were to develop the island. However, though spoken with the best intentions, his verbal sketch of the Virgilian Golden World cannot lift the listener from his grief. Indeed, they make no sense at all to Alonso, who, amidst repeated but futile demands for silence—"Prithee, peace" (2.1.9); "I prithee, spare" (2.1.25); "Prithee, peace" (2.1.127); and "Prithee, no more" (2.1.170)—reproachfully protests that "You cram these words into mine ears against / The stomach of my sense" (2.1.105-6) and later flatly states that "[t]hou dost talk nothing to me" (2.1.170).

The entire episode is a case in point of how verbal communication fails to achieve its object. On the one hand, Gonzalo's persuasion cannot lighten the heart of one who refuses to be consoled. On the other, the king's verbal orders cannot silence one who is determined to talk. What finally ends this frustrating communication is the onset of drowsiness brought about by Ariel's supernatural power. Silent slumber immediately accomplishes what words have failed all along to effect. Gonzalo falls asleep and thus finally grants Alonso his peace. And Alonso in his drowsiness seems to have felt the first surge of joy since the tempest. "Wondrous heavy" (2.1.194) are his words before he drifts into sleep, the adjective "wondrous" perhaps marking as much a sense of surprise at the sudden onset of drowsiness as a pleasant sense of relief or hope at the possibility that "mine eyes / Would, with themselves, shut up my thoughts" (2.1.187-8).

Gonzalo's process of comforting Alonso in 2.1 is incessantly and mercilessly interrupted by Antonio and Sebastian, who let no opportunity to ridicule slip through their fingers. That Gonzalo's well-intended words of comfort should draw from the two not sympathy or help but scorn and laughter is another demonstration of the failure of speech to achieve its expected perlocutionary effect. Similarly, that about a hundred lines after Gonzalo's description of his world where "[t]reason, felony, / Sword, pike, knife, gun, or need of any engine" (2.1.160-1) are not to enter, Antonio and Sebastian are standing over him with a sword ready to strike points not only to the impossibility of his utopian vision, but also the futility of his narrative.

In terms of their inability to make Alonso less miserable, it can be said that Gonzalo's words are merely ineffective. But Alonso's response, "You cram these words into mine ears against / The stomach of my sense", points to the possibility that they do in fact have an impact, as they succeed in achieving the exact opposite of their original intension and make the listener more wretched. Gonzalo's talk of survival and the future probably makes the already grief-stricken king more acutely aware of the loss of his son and a stable future, thus driving him further into himself and his misery. Stanton Garner writes that Alonso's protest here reflects how "[t]he medium intrudes with an almost physical bluntness" (179) upon his grief, its effect not unlike rubbing a wound with salt.

Gonzalo's unintentionally injurious language thus demonstrates that *The Tempest* offers not only examples of ineffective language, but also of language which has the capacity to do ill. To this category Caliban's use of language clearly belongs. Despite his expressed contempt for it and dismissal of the benefits of its acquisition as merely allowing him to curse, language has been for Caliban a useful instrument of expression and a source of power. After all, without it, he probably could not have given Prospero and Miranda as much of a headache as he does now. His ability to express his curses in a recognisable verbal medium makes sure that his resentment and malice are unequivocally passed on to and registered by them, something which mere howls or growls would not have accomplished so effectively. Nor would mere wordless noise, however much hatred was boiling beneath it, have been able to disturb or hurt its listener so forcibly as worded curses can. His language provokes gentle Miranda into her most ungentle speech (1.2.354-65, "Abhorrèd slave…") in the play, apparently so out of character that some editions have consequently attributed—wrongly, in my opinion—the lines to Prospero. Miranda's uncharacteristically violent speech and Prospero's vehement threats in response to Caliban reflect how fully his verbal curse has been registered and how greatly it has disturbed. It is as Derek Traversi observes, language in *The Tempest* can be "the cause of a dangerous extension of the capacity for ill" (232).

Language's extension to the capacity for ill is more fully and explicitly demonstrated by Caliban's conspiracy with Stefano and Trinculo. Again, as much as Caliban detests language, it is his ability to speak it that allows him to make an attempt to actually carry out the vicious plan he harbours.

Without the medium of language, he would not have been able to talk to the other two in the first place, let alone direct them on how they should proceed.

Although Caliban is no master manipulator of language, he instinctively knows what to say. His version of the island's history, his detailed verbal sketch of the desirability of it and Miranda, and his thorough description of how they can get rid of Prospero combine to reconcile Stefano and Trinculo to the revolt he proposes. Caliban starts by reintroducing his version of history: "As I told thee before, I am subject to a tyrant, a sorcerer, that by his cunning hath cheated me of the island" (3.2.40-1). Language here, as Prospero's narrative does in 1.2, manipulates perspective. In presenting the island as rightfully his, Caliban gives justification to the coup which he is about to suggest, perhaps also counting on the story as a boost for the other two's morale, as "justice" is after all on their side.

But the most effectively persuasive aspect of Caliban's use of language is his ability to describe, in an intensely visual manner, visions which are not immediately present. His linguistic competence in this respect has in fact already been demonstrated earlier by his vivid curses:

> As wicked dew as e'er my mother brushed
> With raven's feather from unwholesome fen
> Drop on you both! A southwest blow on ye,
> And blister you all o'er! (1.2.324-7)

This is savage, certainly, but also in its way quite "poetical" and certainly expressive. This expressiveness he now employs to describe the island's riches,

> I prithee, let me bring thee where crabs grow,
> And I with my long nails will dig thee pig-nuts,
> Show thee a jay's nest, and instruct thee how
> To snare the nimble marmoset. I'll bring thee
> To clust'ring filberts, and sometimes I'll get thee
> Young seamews from the rock; (2.2.159-64)

what happens when Stefano takes possession of Miranda,

> She will become thy bed, I warrant,
> And bring thee forth brave brood; (3.2.99-100)

as well as how Stefano should proceed to kill Prospero,

> 'tis a custom with him
> I'th'afternoon to sleep. There thou mayst brain him,
> Having first seized his books; or with a log
> Batter his skull, or paunch him with a stake,
> Or cut his weasand with thy knife. Remember
> First to possess his books. (3.2.82-7)

Caliban's intensely concrete verbal images make what is absent almost immediately present, creating for its intended listeners an impression that "[t]o obtain Miranda and total rule, all Stephano must do…is to assent to the verbal image" (Garner 182). The bewitching quality of his language successfully elicits from Stefano his hearty agreement to the coup: "Monster, I will kill this man" (3.2.101). And, were their rival not a magician with almost omnipotent power, even if they failed to actually take over the island, they might have caused significant damage. Language is indeed a dangerous instrument which extends the capacity for ill, in this case almost allowing abstract ill will to manifest itself and have an impact.

But Caliban is after all only an average user of language. The power of his speech derives from its "sincerity", for this language is the honest expression of what its speaker has actually seen (the beauty of Miranda, the resources of the island), truly believed (that Prospero is a usurper), honestly felt (his hatred for Prospero), and probably repeatedly rehearsed in his head (the procedures of killing Prospero). It is thus a transparent language where the ultimate motive behind the utterances is easily discernible. It is also a language of the emotions, which is probably why it is Caliban, of all people, who speaks one of the most lyrical passages in the whole of *The Tempest* (3.2.130-8 "The isle is full of noises…"). This language, intended to communicate its speaker's true feelings and desires, although performed to ill purpose in the case of Caliban, does not threaten, on the whole, the reliability of verbal communication itself.

It remains for a seasoned manipulator of language like Antonio or Sebastian to demonstrate the ultimate harm it can do: to render communication itself unstable and/or unreliable. Antonio and Sebastian's language, unlike Caliban's, is one of the intellect. It is elaborate and full of wit, but it reveals little, apart from confirming for the audience its speaker's truly degenerate nature, which, on the other hand, seems not to have been registered by its onstage listeners. One never finds out for sure, for instance, from Antonio's words, the true motive behind his efforts to persuade Sebastian to get rid of Alonso. It is in fact Sebastian who supplies a motive for regicide:

One stroke
Shall free thee from the tribute which thou payest,
And I the King shall love thee, (2.1.288-90)

which, even for him, seems rather an afterthought that justifies the murder
than what motivates it. And to this Antonio himself makes no response.
His language reveals little but achieves much. Under his employment,
words become a truly powerful instrument for evil.

In 2.1, language's capacity to bar communication is first demonstrated
by Antonio and Sebastian's frequent interruptions to Gonzalo's efforts of
comforting Alonso. While Gonzalo's verbal comforts may have hurt its
listener unintentionally, manipulated by these two, language becomes a
vehicle which serves their calculated purpose of injury and ridicule. They
seize on language's ambiguity and richness and turn them into derisive
jokes which humiliate:

ALONSO   Prithee, peace.
SEBASTIAN [*to* ANTONIO] He receives comfort like cold porridge.
    (2.1.9-10)

GONZALO When every grief is entertained that's offered,
  Comes to th'entertainer—
SEBASTIAN A dollar. (2.1.16-8)

ADRIAN It must needs be of subtle, tender, and delicate temperance.
ANTONIO [*to* SEBASTIAN] Temperance was a delicate wench.
SEBASTIAN [*to* ANTONIO] Ay, and a subtle, as he most learnedly
    delivered. (2.1.42-5)

The connection between a word, its pronunciation, its meaning and the
context of its utterance is severed. Alonso's anguished plea for "peace" is
ridiculously and arbitrarily linked to "pease-porridge". Gonzalo's
"entertainer of grief" is interpreted literally as a paid performer. And
Adrian's remark about the good climate of the island, "delicate
temperance", is twisted into a reference to a voluptuous wench. In
severing word, pronunciation, meaning and context, and in violating
conversational rules with continual interruptions, Antonio and Sebastian's
almost nonsensical badinage disrupts the normal processes of conversation,
obtruding twisted interpretations upon an utterance, and thus obscuring
communication. They use their skill with words to impress upon a
miserable audience their superior wit and, in circumventing meaning,
destroy a proper verbal intercourse.

Such wordplay has the power to collapse communication, for they disclose nothing, and, furthermore, in heavily fragmenting others' verbal intercourse, turn these efforts into nothing as well. Antonio and Sebastian say much but communicate little, for their language is "non-referential...sever[ed]...from a concern for truth" (Garner 179). In addition to obscuring their own communication, the two's interruptions also upset Gonzalo's plan of comforting Alonso, cutting his argument into incoherent pieces and further complicating those pieces with puns. Thus Alonso's "Thou dost talk nothing to me" probably is as much evidence of the ineffectiveness of Gonzalo's persuasion as of the effective destructiveness of Antonio and Sebastian's interruptions.

And Antonio is about to further demonstrate how much words can actually accomplish. With the sheer power of verbal persuasion, in about a hundred lines, he successfully plants the idea of usurpation into Sebastian's mind, convinces him of the perfect plausibility of the plan, and prompts him into immediate action.

Antonio starts by introducing an illusion: "My strong imagination sees a crown / Dropping upon thy head" (2.1.204-5). He also insists that he is merely voicing a thought which Sebastian secretly entertains, despite the fact that never once before did the latter display an inclination for usurpation and that he seems genuinely surprised, if not horrified, at Antonio's suggestion. Antonio talks of Sebastian's "secret desire" as a matter of fact and not as his, Antonio's, conjecture:

> If you but knew how you the purpose cherish
> Whiles thus you mock it; how in stripping it
> You more invest it! (2.1.220-2)

The statement is uttered with such confident assuredness that Sebastian ceases to protest that his "hereditary sloth" (2.1.219) prevents him from entertaining any ambition for power. Of course, it is equally possible that Sebastian does indeed, perhaps unconsciously, have his eyes on the throne. But whether guilty or not guilty of this desire for power, it is finally Antonio's words that lodge the idea of usurpation firmly in his head. If Sebastian unconsciously wishes to usurp, Antonio's language, in helping to give shape to this thought, awakens that desire which is so dormant that its own entertainer has not been aware of it. If, on the other hand, usurpation has never entered Sebastian's head, Antonio's way of talking about something not in being as if it is succeeds in transforming "nothing" into being, convincing his listener that usurpation is indeed what he desires.

This way of talking of an illusion as if it is a reality is one of Antonio's specialities. Not only is he able to talk Sebastian's desire for usurpation into being, in a similar fashion he turns the imaginary act of usurpation itself into a sort of reality. His description of usurpation is founded on the verbal presentation of Alonso's death and its consequences, which he elaborates and imparts to Sebastian in well-rounded details:

> Say this were death
> That now hath seized them; why, they were no worse
> Than now they are. There be that can rule Naples
> As well as he that sleeps, lords that can prate
> As amply and unnecessarily
> As this Gonzalo. (2.1.256-61)

> Here lies your brother,
> No better than the earth he lies upon
> If he were that which now he's like—that's dead. (2.1.276-8)

With Antonio's vivid verbal sketch, sleep is metamorphosed into death, "like" becomes "is", and illusion is set down for the listener as an almost already realised act. Language thus blurs or confuses the boundary between imagination and reality.

It is worth noting that in persuading Sebastian to usurp, the tenor of Antonio's arguments concentrates not on illustrating in minute detail the beneficial consequence of usurpation,[3] nor does he really adopt the strategy of spurring his listener into action, like Lady Macbeth before him, by harping on the subject of manly courage. His trump card is to mould reality according to his will through language. By presenting the sleeping Alonso as already dead and thus the prospective process of usurpation an already smoothly accomplished event, his words charm Sebastian into taking the uncertain future for the definite present and the probably impossible for the absolutely possible, triumphantly turning him from "standing water" (2.1.217) to flowing water—and fairly rapid flowing water at that.

Another manifestation of Antonio's verbal dexterity is that he is capable of giving his language a poetic quality which not only has an almost lyrical aural effect, but, more importantly, gives tangibility to abstractions. This linguistic treatment is most clearly evident in his

---

[3] Antonio merely mentions, in a fairly general sort of way, that "out of that 'no hope' / What great hope have you!" (2.1.235-6) and, with just a little more detail,

> And look how well my garments sit upon me,
> Much feater than before. My brother's servants
> Were then my fellows; now they are my men. (2.1.268-70)

description of the distance between Claribel's Tunis and their island or Naples:

> She that is Queen of Tunis; she that dwells
> Ten leagues beyond man's life; she that from Naples
> Can have no note—unless the sun were post—
> The man i'th'moon's too slow—till new-born chins
> Be rough and razorable; she that from whom
> We all were sea-swallowed, though some cast again— (2.1.242-7)

> A space whose every cubit
> Seems to cry out "How shall that Claribel
> Measure us back to Naples? Keep in Tunis,
> And let Sebastian wake." (2.1.253-6)

Rather than blandly stating that "Claribel is so far away that she cannot know nor intervene", Antonio vividly illustrates this distance. According to him, to reach Claribel, it would take the time for a new-born babe to grow a beard. It is a distance that literally begs Sebastian to supplant Alonso. Similarly, in talking about his own benefits from the deposition of Prospero, Antonio, instead of presenting the enjoyment of power as an abstract concept, gives it a very solid and visual shape: the better-fitting clothes he is now wearing. And when answering Sebastian's doubts about conscience, he dismisses it, again with an image, as less of a threat than a sore on one's heel. In short, his language solidifies abstract concepts. By providing enough solid details to turn abstract concepts into concrete images, this rhetorical sleight of hand helps him convincingly blend illusion and reality.

Another of Antonio's rhetorical strategies consists in seizing upon a metaphor or concept offered by his listener and elaborating upon it. As in

> SEBASTIAN   Well, I am standing water.
> ANTONIO I'll teach you to flow.
> SEBASTIAN   Do so. To ebb
>   Hereditary sloth instructs me. (2.1.217-9)

By recycling metaphors which the other has already employed, the speaker makes it easier for his verbal consolidation of abstract concepts to get across, for it means that he need not introduce new images which might take time for the listener to digest, but instead can use language which is, as it were, immediately on the same wavelength of the intended audience's thought process. Such method thus creates a sense of genuine communication and solidarity, of shared understanding and motive, reflected in the employment of the same metaphor. This is a familiar Shakespearean method for expressing likemindedness or demonstrating mutual understanding, used before, for example, during the first meeting of Romeo and Juliet, or when Hermia and Lysander take turns to elaborate on the rough course of true love.

Here in *The Tempest*, however, that sense of mutual understanding often is but an illusion, for in elaborating upon expressions initiated by Sebastian, Antonio usually shifts, or altogether transforms their meaning to suit his own purpose. One telling example involves the word "sleep". It is first brought up by Sebastian when he comments upon the strange sleepiness which has possessed the rest of the court party. It appears with considerable frequency in Sebastian's own speeches, but always referring to slumber, drowsiness or the effects of such drowsiness:

> I find
> Not myself disposed to sleep. (2.1.197-8)

> It is a sleepy language, and thou speak'st
> Out of thy sleep. What is it thou didst say?
> This is a strange repose, to be asleep
> With eyes wide open; standing, speaking, moving,
> And yet so fast asleep. (2.1.207-11)

Antonio, rather than protesting that he is wide awake and perfectly sober, pounces on the keyword "sleep" and makes full use of it. For the rest of the scene "sleep" becomes a recurrent motif in his language, no longer implying the natural condition of temporary repose, but taking on instead the meaning of "remaining stagnant" and, almost in the same breath, shifting to indicate "death":

> Thou letst thy fortune sleep, die rather. (2.1.212)

> Say this were death
> That now hath seized them; why, they were no worse
> Than now they are. (2.1.256-8)

> what a sleep were this
> For your advancement! (2.1.263-4)

> Here lies your brother,
> No better than the earth he lies upon
> If he were that which now he's like—that's dead. (2.1.276-8)

A similar example is found in his manipulation of the implications of the word "hope", skilfully turning its usage from reference to "hope for the survival of Ferdinand" to "hope for Sebastian's great advancement and its limitless benefits". Again, it is Sebastian who first brings up the word:

> SEBASTIAN   I have no hope
> That he's undrowned.
> ANTONIO   Out of that "no hope"
> What great hope have you! No hope that way is
> Another way so high a hope that even
> Ambition cannot pierce a wink beyond,
> But doubt discovery there. (2.1.234-9)

In some ways, Antonio's verbal strategy here is essentially the same as that employed when he and Sebastian interrupt Gonzalo, which is pouncing on a word and arbitrarily changing its meaning from what the original speaker intended. Of course, here it is done with greater subtlety and finesse, and for a more serious purpose. In interrupting Gonzalo, the purpose of such wordplay is to ridicule, and its effect a disruption of regular communication. Here the object is to seduce and its effect the creation of a semblance of genuine communication. But either way, both Gonzalo before and Sebastian now are victims of such verbal treatment, their own meaning and its effect manipulated by another. The process of communication they are involved in is in fact one-sided.

Antonio contains all these rhetorical strategies within an almost classic structure of syllogistic argumentation. Proposition: I see you sitting on the throne of Naples. Support: a) Ferdinand is dead, Claribel faraway, and Alonso as good as dead; b) the rest of the party will "take suggestion as a cat laps milk" (2.1.284). Conclusion: You are as good as the King of Naples. From this structure, conventionally employed in rational reasoning, Antonio's persuasion derives a considerable but false sense of logical argumentation, enough to cover up the flaws in the argument from listeners like Sebastian who only hear the arguments once instead of having, as readers do, the privilege of scrutinising them in print. For one thing, Alonso is merely asleep, not dead. For another, Antonio only suggests dispatching Gonzalo and Alonso, but there is no guarantee that the lords Adrian and Francisco will meekly "take suggestion as a cat laps milk". Indeed, it would be hard for them not to suspect foul play when they see the sword wounds on Alonso and Gonzalo. But most importantly, the logical structure of the argument obscures the (almost) pointlessness of the proposed enterprise. After all, what is the point of killing Alonso to inherit the crown when it is fairly unlikely that they should ever return to

Naples? In this respect their plan of usurpation is in fact more ridiculous than that of Caliban, Stefano and Trinculo, even though the trio's planned coup is often seen as a grotesque parody of Antonio and Sebastian's plot. In wishing to assassinate Prospero, Stefano and Trinculo at least have the relatively "practical" objective of becoming ruler of the *island*. But Antonio is explicit in proposing that Sebastian become king of distant Naples. However, the syllogistic structure of his persuasion projects so strong an impression of logical and careful consideration that Sebastian, who has the sense to pause and consider the problem of conscience, never once questions the practicality of the proposition. And so it is that the cleverly manipulated form of speech is able to communicate as much as, if not more than, the actual content of the speech itself. In other words, Antonio's successful seduction of Sebastian reflects that often the way in which something is said has much more force than the "something" itself.

The episode where Antonio verbally seduces Sebastian into contemplating the double sin of regicide and fratricide takes *The Tempest*'s discussion of the matter of language onto a more disturbing level. No longer is language merely an honest expression of feeling and thought or an ineffective tool unable to change much, but in fact a potentially dangerous force capable of manipulating communication, severing meaning and words, confusing reality and illusion, planting desires, and prompting actions according to its speaker's design. In this respect Antonio's language is a much more domineering power than even Prospero's theatrical productions. It in fact vies in effectiveness with the sorcerer's violence-based magic. Prospero's magic, however, will have been abandoned by the end of the play, whereas Antonio's verbal dexterity, in spite of his relative silence in the last scene, shall in all probability be retained and brought back to Milan. It is a disquieting prospect.

Equally disquieting is the conversation between Ferdinand and Miranda near the end of the play:

> MIRANDA Sweet lord, you play me false.
> FERDINAND No, my dearest love,
>   I would not for the world.
> MIRANDA Yes, for a score of kingdoms you should wrangle,
>   And I would call it fair play. (5.1.174-8)

It is disquieting not only because of the troubling connotations of the phrase "play me false", but more importantly, Miranda's use of language seems to demonstrate that she has already begun to undergo the inevitable loss of innocence which her life in the Neapolitan court shall result in. The short conversation shows a Miranda, who once tended to speak directly and in simple language—"I would not wish / Any companion in the world but you" (3.1.54-5); "Do you love me?" (3.1.67); "My husband then?" (3.1.88)—now beginning, not unlike Antonio and Sebastian, to take notice of the gap between speaking and meaning and to play with words: "Sweet lord, you play me false...And I would call it fair play". Language probably will not turn out for her an instrument for evil purpose, but it is likely that it can no longer be for her merely a tool for innocent communication. As Kott puts it, "Miranda has not yet become the wife of a ruler, has not yet left the 'uninhabited island,' and already she has agreed to *'foul play'*" (*Translation* 94), even her use of language in verbal communication seems somehow finally associated with "foulness" by the end of this play.

The Tempest thus differs considerably from the previous romances in its presentation of the power and possibilities of language. The preceding last plays do not conceal language's dangerous potential for evil, but by the end of the story, language would nevertheless have redeemed itself by functioning as the key restorative force which enables reunion and reconciliation. In *The Tempest*, however, the portrayal of language remains problematic to the end. A universal communication which involves all the onstage characters is not achieved. Antonio remains unresponsive to Prospero's verbally expressed forgiveness. Prospero's promised tales, as we have seen, will conceal more than they can reveal. And even Ferdinand and Miranda, who might be looked on as the play's only couple to have achieved true communication, are now using language in rather an alarming manner.

The Tempest starts in a tumult of non-verbal noises and ends with another, the clapping of an audience. That in itself is not unusual, as all plays can be said to start and end with noise: the indistinguishable babel as the audience chat and await the opening of the drama, the trumpet blasts heralding the start of the performance, and the sound of clapping as the actors take their bows. However, what is significant about this play is that such noises are *built into* it. Unlike the preceding last plays—indeed, unlike most of the plays in the Shakespearean canon, apart from the few histories which open with a flourish—where the performance plunges almost directly into a scene of verbal communication, "*A tempestuous noise of thunder and lightning*" (Stage Direction 1.1) formally opens this one, probably also accompanied by distant and unintelligible shouts before they are finally transformed into the comprehensible verbal utterance "Boatswain!" (1.1.1). Similarly, although every play, as long as it does not displease, by convention would end in applause, *The Tempest* stands out in specifically stating that it is the sound of the audience's clapping that completes its action: "release me from my bands / With the help of your good hands" (Epilogue 9-10).

The Tempest thus has an overall "acoustic" structure, which the playwright appears to have taken pains to direct his audience's attention to, of "Noise—Verbal Communication—Noise". In showing that the worded play collapses back into noises in the end and Prospero asking to be set free with the din of clapping instead of for a verbal release, this "soundscape" can be looked on as a metaphor which reiterates what the plot says about language (and art): that it is ineffective and in the end not the preferred, or trusted, medium of communication. Such a structure also points out the essence of all plays: they are efforts to give order to confusion through art and language, but the ordered verbal picture they establish would inevitably crumble away as they draw to a close. This acoustic structure makes the audience *experience*, in addition to what they *witness* in the plot, the play's point about the limitations and unreliability of art and, particularly, language.

This method of using media other than the dramatic episodes themselves to complement and enhance what the action of the plot demonstrates is also found employed in between the two "noises", in the worded part of the play. Here Shakespeare, as he has done in the three earlier plays, uses linguistic style to augment the effect of the story. In this respect his practice in *The Tempest* is, for once, fully consistent with his previous efforts of linguistically recapitulating the action and thematic concern of the plot.

Of all the linguistic features of Shakespeare's late style, the one which particularly stands out in *The Tempest* is clearly repetition. McDonald remarks that "[r]epetition—of vowels and consonants, words, phrases, syntactical forms, and other verbal effects—is a fundamental stylistic turn in *The Tempest*" ("Reading" 17). The play's linguistic tendency to repeat is established almost as soon as the mariners' conversation becomes distinguishable above the roar of the sea and the thunderstorm:

(In the following examples, lexical and syntactic repetitions are marked out in bold, while additional phonetic duplications are underlined.)

> MASTER **Bestir, bestir.**
> BOATSWAIN H̲eigh, **my** h̲e̲a̲r̲t̲s̲! **Cheerl̲y, cheerl̲y, my** h̲e̲a̲r̲t̲s̲! **Yare,**
> **yare!** T̲ake in the t̲opsai̲l! T̲end t̲o th'Mas̲t̲er's whis̲tl̲e! (1.1.4-6)

Indeed, much of the mariners' speech in the first scene is spoken in the same repetitive manner:

Lay her **a-hold, a-hold**! (1.1.44)

All lost! To prayers, to prayers! All lost! (1.1.46)

We split, we split! Farewell, my wife and children!
Farewell, brother! **We split, we split, we split!** (1.1.55-6)

This impression of the play's repetitive style created by the first scene is immediately consolidated by Prospero's narrative in the next, which is also of a noticeably repetitive turn:

There is **no harm** done.
...**No harm**.
I have done nothing but in care **of thee**,
Of thee, my dear one, **thee**, my daughter. (1.2.15-7)

Twelve year since, Miranda, **twelve year since**. (1.2.53)

Both, both, my girl. (1.2.61)

Being once perfected **how to** grant suits,
How to deny them, **who t'**advance and **who
To** trash for over-topping, new created
The creatures that were mine, I say—or changed **'em**
Or else new formed **'em**; having both the key
Of **officer** and **office**. (1.2.79-84)

But such repetitive style is not limited to the language of the mariners and Prospero, but can be found throughout the play, spoken by all characters:

FERDINAND **He does** hear me,
And that **he does** I weep. (1.2.437-8)

ANTONIO O, out of that "**no hope**"
What great **hope** have you! **No hope** that **way** is
Another **way** so high a **hope** that even
Ambition cannot pierce a wink beyond,
But doubt discovery there. (2.1.235-9)

ANTONIO **She that** is Queen of Tunis; **she that** dwells
Ten leagues beyond man's life; **she that** from Naples
Can have no note...
she that from whom
We are all sea-swallowed. (2.1.242-44, 246-7)

STEFANO Come on **your** ways. **Open your mouth**. Here is that which
will give language to **you**, cat. **Open your mouth**. This is will shake
your shaking. I can tell **you**, and that soundly. **You** cannot tell who's
your friend. **Open your** chaps again.

(2.2.78-81)

ARIEL   **I go, I go.**
PROSPERO A **devil**, a born **devil**, **on whose** nature
Nurture can never stick; **on whom** my pains,
Humanely taken, **all**, **all lost**, quite lost. (4.1.187-90)

It appears that in *The Tempest*, while such repetitions have their
various specific functions under different circumstances, on the whole a
speaker employs lexical and syntactic repetitions either to express an
emotional state (usually of panic or distress) or for the purpose of
enhancing rhetorical forcefulness. Of course, often these two function
together. The mariners' phrasal repetitions, for example, are, in most cases,
repeated commands (increasing rhetorical strength by placing added
emphasis on an instruction just given) which express both the panic and
the despair of the speaker.

The close association of verbal repetition with emotional distress, often
out of a sense of one's helplessness to effect any change, captures on a
syntactic level the distress, both for the characters and the audience, of
experiencing the episodic repetitions throughout the play, as they too
demonstrate man's helplessness against the courses of nature and history.
In terms of plot, this piece is famously repetitive: "*The Tempest* is famous
for the density and congruity of its mirrored actions" as well as for being
"flagrantly intertextual" (McDonald, *Late* 196). The major episodic
repetition is the usurpation and regicide motif, which is presented no fewer
than three times—four, if one counts in the final chess scene, which, as
Kott points out in his suggestively titled essay "*The Tempest*, or
Repetition", is "the last regicide in *The Tempest*", for "[c]hess, the royal
game…ends with a checkmate, the surrender of a king" (*Translation* 94).
Similarly, more than once Prospero has suffered (or nearly suffered) from
his prioritising Artistic pursuit over "politics", as his devotion to "library
research" back in Milan led to his exile to the island, while his pageant in
4.1 makes him almost forget about Caliban's plot. The repeated
presentations of attempts of regicide reflect humankind's tenacious hunger
for power. Prospero's experience, on the other hand, reveals that as a
species, rather than learning from past errors, human beings are wont to
repeat their follies. As a result, human history, with such "perpetual,
unchanging mechanism" (Kott, *Contemporary* 301), like the play itself, is

repetitive, with the same pieces of folly and wickedness continually reoccurring, which also explains *The Tempest*'s "intertexuality", for in representing regicide and usurpation, it not only repeats itself, but a good many of the other plays in the canon as well. It is this unchanging and unchangeable course of history that eventually evokes from Prospero his resigned comment that the world is not going to be new.

Verbal repetitions of instructions or commands, on the other hand, can be looked on as linguistic consolidations of the point about language's lack of power. The ultimate cause, as well as direct manifestation of language's ineffectiveness, is, after all, the listener's refusal to act as he or she is told. Repeated instructions imply that saying them only once will not get the job done, indeed, might not even be enough to bring the listener to attention. The play is full of instances of refusal to follow instructions: the courtiers pay little attention to the Boatswain's command to stay below decks; Caliban is slow at fulfilling Prospero's order to collect firewood; and Stefano and Trinculo completely ignore Caliban's entreaty that they should finish off Prospero before spending time on selecting from the fancy garments hanging in the woods.

But more importantly, lexical and syntactic repetitions demonstrate that there is a gap between "speaking" and "meaning", for there is clearly a discernible dislocation between the quantity of words said and the amount of information passed on. Verbal repetitions simultaneously reveal that repeated statements communicate less than what is uttered, for a repeated message is but one piece of information, and that they communicate more than what is uttered, as repetition signals an emphasis, and an emphasis bespeaks an extra purpose, for example to express an emotion, to call attention to the urgency of the business discussed, or to impress upon the listener the absolute necessity of following the instructions given. Furthermore, as certain words or expressions are being repeated, their meaning may be subtly transformed to suit the purpose of its speaker, while its listener might lag behind in catching up with the different shades of meaning which switch from one repetition to another. The repetitions of "no hope" or the "sleep" metaphor in Antonio's speech in 2.1, as we have seen, are cases in point.

This dislocation, created through verbal repetitions, between language and meaning is part of the reason why the play, in Barton's words, "gives the impression of its being bigger than it is" (Introduction 14). Thus while members of the onstage audience are seduced by language, their offstage counterparts are also "fooled around" by the playwright's use of repetition, perhaps reading more meaning from a line or phrase than it actually contains. McDonald, for example, contends that Gonzalo's "Widow Dido" speech is perhaps less fraught with significance than scholars believe, and that its phonetic reverberations do much in creating this (probably) false impression: "Is it perhaps just another case of internal rhyme that sounds as if it ought to mean more than it does?" ("Reading" 22). The incantatory quality of phonetic, lexical and syntactic repetitions thus bespeaks language's power to bewitch, to seduce and to confuse. The audience experience firsthand what Caliban describes he does on the island. As "the isle is full of noises", so the play is also full of "noises" which seem to communicate something but remain ambiguous and imperfect, thwarting its listeners' confidence in language as a trusty medium of communication.

Other features of Shakespeare's late style also work together to enhance this feeling of imperfect communication and ineffective language. The play, rather paradoxically, apart from being a particularly repetitive piece of work, is also at the same time one of the most condensed in the canon, not only in terms of its strict observance of the unities, but also in terms of its length, it being one of the shortest of Shakespeare's plays. It would thus seem that considerable elisions and ellipsis have been employed in order to "make room" for the repetitions in the extremely limited space of *The Tempest*. Apart from the usual omission of sounds and conjunctions, the play is famous for the number of compounds which are formed by thrusting a noun and an adjective or another noun together, "spontaneous compounds", as McDonald terms them ("Reading" 19), such as "sea-change", "spell-stopped", "cloud-capped", "sea-sorrow" and "man-monster". Once more, language offers not the comforting sense of order and clarification but discomforting ambiguity, as the listeners are left to work out for themselves the "complex and unstable union" (Barton, Introduction 13) of the elements within such compounds. Furthermore, such formations, according to Barton,

> seem to be driving towards some ultimate reduction of language, a mode of expression more meaningful in its very bareness than anything a more elaborate and conventional rhetoric could devise. (14)

They therefore might be looked on as a linguistic anticipation of Prospero's eventual abandonment of his book (which is the collection of language) and his final appeal for release by the audience's applause (which might be considered as "a mode of expression more meaningful" than a verbal release).

And thus, with portrayals of language through episodes in the plot and the linguistic style of the play itself, *The Tempest* questions its own medium of existence—language—pointing out that often it is exactly language itself that frustrates communication or/and threatens its stability and reliability, dislocating as it does meaning and words, confusing wishes and realities, and failing to deliver neatness and unequivocality. By the end of *The Tempest*, Prospero has abandoned his art through the drowning of his book. It is a gesture that marks the end of his career as a magician and of his time on the magical island. Is it possible to read it also as a gesture of release from language, that problematic medium of communication?

The Complete Picture

In discussing the topic of dramatic art and language, *The Tempest* presents the audience with a paradox: the doubt and scepticism about art's effectiveness and language's reliability are demonstrated through art and language. Thus, when an audience perceives art *in* the play as ultimately ineffective and language treacherous, the art *of* the play has been effective and the language trusted. Even if one decides to distrust the art and language of the play itself and not jump to any hasty conclusions about art and language in the play, it would still mean that the former has been effective in persuading its receivers about the unreliability of the two. In other words, any intellectual conclusion a member of the audience might draw about the problems of art and language is provoked by the play's art and language.

Of course, one way to evade this dilemma might be for the audience to be aware of the difference between "Prospero's play" and "Shakespeare's play". The former is ineffective in changing the world according to plan. The latter, in contrast, is effective in demonstrating the former's ineffectiveness through art and language. In order to know how to handle one's own reaction to the play, there seems to be a need for constant awareness of the distinction between *The Tempest* as *Prospero's* play and *Shakespeare's*.

But *The Tempest* does little to help its audience keep up this alertness. If anything, it seems to have deliberately set out to blur any distinction between fiction and reality, the island and the theatre, or the romance world and the real world.

Prospero's "Our revels now are ended" speech directly informs the audience that illusion and reality are essentially one and the same. The "life as a play" metaphor in itself is no great innovation. It is, indeed, a theatrical commonplace which Shakespeare himself has used before, most memorably, of course, in Jacques's "All the world's a stage" speech in *As You Like It*, but also in Lear's "When we are born, we cry that we are come / To this great stage of fools" (*Lear* 4.6.176-7), and Macbeth's

Life's but a walking shadow, a poor player
That struts and frets his hour upon the stage,
And then is heard no more. It is a tale
Told by an idiot, full of sound and fury,
Signifying nothing. (*Macbeth* 5.5.23-7)

However, the way it is put forward in *The Tempest* makes it very different from these previous examples. First of all, in the case of *The Tempest*, there is a parallelism between the setting of the action on stage and the situation off stage, which the other instances do not have. Prospero's conclusion arises out of the experience of watching a performance, while watching a performance is exactly what the audience are doing at that moment. Consequently there is arguably greater sympathy between the audience and the onstage employer of the "play-life" metaphor in the case of *The Tempest* than that of *As You Like It*, *King Lear* or *Macbeth*. Listening to Jacques, Lear or Macbeth, one still feels more or less like a member of the audience—that is, a fairly detached looker-on who may assent to the justness of the metaphor intellectually, but without engaging with it emotionally. The mirroring contexts in *The Tempest*, on the other hand, put the audience more squarely under the influence of the metaphor.

Prospero, unlike Lear, Macbeth or Jacques, who, as it were, jump straight into the metaphor, leads his speech gradually towards it. In other words, the metaphor for Lear, Macbeth and particularly Jacques is a point of departure, a cliché to be elaborated upon, whereas in Prospero's case it is the conclusion of a meditation which starts out as a comment on an actual play but gradually and subtly extends to the solid "facts" of life—towers, palaces, temples, the globe—and then finally encompasses "we" and "our little life". The comparison between reality and illusion for Prospero is not a commonplace, but a personal revelation, which renders the cliché sincere and gives it pathos, in contrast to Jacques's version, which smells slightly of witticism. Moreover, Prospero does not start his speech bitter about the world, as Jacques and Lear are. He may be in a "passion" about Caliban's assassination plan, but at this point in the play he is not yet a disillusioned or bitter man. It is also worth remembering that his initial purpose is not to comment on the illusory nature of life, but in fact to reassure Ferdinand and persuade him to be "cheerful" (4.1.147). That he, who seems to be in control of his world and more or less sure of this control at this point, should eventually reach a conclusion so contrary to his purpose adds conviction to the theatrical commonplace, making it seem a sort of inescapable truth.

This speech also makes the "life-stage" metaphor disturbing to a degree unprecedented in the other versions. Where previous elaborations more or less concentrate on the "in real life we each play our parts" aspect of the comparison and might draw a conclusion to the effect of "like a play, a life must end", *The Tempest*'s "life-stage" comparison reaches to the root, so to speak, of the metaphor and asserts that both play and life are illusions, founded upon insubstantial fabric which eventually dissolves, leaving nothing behind. When Jacques, Lear and Macbeth employ the metaphor, they may be pointing out the deceptions in life, remarking on the pointlessness of personal struggle, or even questioning the purpose of life, but such a comment does not question the fact of life itself. Prospero's speech, on the other hand, denies the fact of existence, completely equating it with illusions. Consequently, it is as Barton observes, "[a]s Prospero's explanation reaches its end, the audience in the theatre seems to lose its identity. Life has been engulfed by illusion" (*Play* 203). The security of feeling that they can distinguish fiction from reality has been pulled from under their feet.

The play does not, however, content itself with only telling the audience that there is no great distinction between fictional drama and the real world. It makes them experience that erosion of the boundary between the two. *The Tempest*, it should be remembered, contains enough familiar motifs of romance to qualify as a romance. And in watching a play of this description, the audience in general would almost instinctively suspend disbelief to take illusions for real. Few critics, for example, experience surprise upon learning by the end of the play that Alonso's ship is "tight and yare and bravely rigged, as when…first put out to sea" (5.1.227-8), even though at the beginning of the play they are specifically told that the ship has split—"We split, we split, we split" (1.1.56). It is worth taking note that although the opening tempest is often referred to as an illusion, this description applies to its artificial cause rather than its real effect. The tempest is real for those on board the ship and for Miranda who has witnessed it from afar. That the ship does split, therefore, should be, within the context of the plot, a fact rather than an illusion. That it is whole and ready to sail in the last act is also a fact. But nothing is said during the play about Prospero or Ariel mending it. Thus the audience is in fact faced with the problem of resolving the two conflicting "facts". The solution is either to take it for granted that magic has been involved in the restoration, or that the breaking of the ship has indeed been an illusion. Either way, the audience are accepting the possibility of something contrary to their experience and reason. This they are in fact made to do throughout the entire play, accepting as solid facts Prospero's omnipotent magic, the existence of supernatural beings, and Ariel's invisibility, despite the fact that they can see the spirit perfectly with their eyes.

Apart from making use of the genre's inherent and compelling power for mixing up fiction and reality, *The Tempest* also has its own particular dramatic arrangements for this purpose. It first of all offers the audience a protagonist who bears close identification with his author. It is indeed difficult to resist identifying Prospero with Shakespeare—that is, Shakespeare in his capacity as a playwright, though some find it hard to resist associating Prospero with the private Shakespeare as well. Prospero's status as the master engineer behind the events of the afternoon makes him a sort of playwright/director figure, arranging the actions of the island party with a firm hand, not unlike, one might argue, what Shakespeare does with his own characters. But Prospero is not the only Shakespearean character who manipulates others. Duke Vincentio in *Measure for Measure*, for example, has often been compared with Prospero as an engineer of plots. What makes the mage, and not the others, the one whom commentators cannot resist associating with Shakespeare himself is that he, "[u]nlike other 'manipulating' characters in Shakespeare's plays…seems larger than the action, larger than the audience" (Mowat 80). Prospero has all the goings-on on the island tightly in his control, whereas the audience, for once, is not allowed the superiority of knowing more than any character in the play. "[L]ike Miranda, we must be told what is happening, and our innocent bewilderment is often much like hers" (ibid.). This arrangement elevates Prospero above the likes of Vincentio and indeed almost to the same rank as Shakespeare, the manipulator of the manipulators.

Prospero's special status as "playwright" is enough to provoke a close identification with Shakespeare. Consequently, the former's dramatic arrangements on the island is identified with Shakespeare's own play. But *The Tempest* takes the correspondence a step further. The unusual observation of the classical unities and, more importantly, the fact that the fictional time *in* the play is almost the same as the real time *of* the performance mean that the boundary between fiction and reality becomes significantly blurred. Prospero's plot *is* Shakespeare's plot. *The Tempest* is as much Prospero's play as Shakespeare's.

A third, and probably the most significant dramatic arrangement which obscures the line between fiction and reality comes in the epilogue. It is striking that in this particular epilogue Prospero asks for the audience's applause *as Prospero*, instead of as the *actor* of Prospero. This arrangement of keeping the mage in character right through to the epilogue creates a situation in which a character still standing in the illusion of the play addresses a theatre full of audience who have, supposedly, their feet securely in reality. Or does it suddenly feel not so secure after all? Which is which, then, at this particular moment? Are the audience now part of the illusion, or the fictional character part of reality? And if the audience clap—as they would; and whether they are clapping according to theatrical conventions or out of heartfelt appreciation of the performance, coming after the epilogue, that applause would in effect function as a response to the fictional Prospero's appeal—does it mean that illusion is now directing reality, or that reality has finally burst in upon illusion?

When one remembers that this applause is also a crucial element in *The Tempest*, not only incorporated into its acoustic structure, but also a vital device in completing the forgiveness motif in the plot, it would seem that Shakespeare—or Prospero—has actually assigned the audience a role in the story. This audience participation in the play further entangles the relationship between fiction and reality. Barbara Mowat writes that "Shakespeare has somehow turned us into the Theseus and Hippolyta-like audience of *A Midsummer Night's Dream*" (104). We are the audience of one play: Prospero and Shakespeare's play.

Mowat's remark points out another of *The Tempest*'s paradoxes. The audience watching the play are, she observes, "Theseus and Hippolyta-like". Indeed, like the onstage audience watching Peter Quince's production of *Pyramus and Thisbe* in *A Midsummer Night's Dream*, the offstage audience of *The Tempest* are also made continually aware of the illusory nature of the events they are witnessing—though, of course, with Shakespeare instead of the amateur thespians in charge, the reminding is done subtly and with great skill. Prospero's Act 4 speech discussed earlier is, for example, such a device, for it starts out as a reminder to Ferdinand, as well as the offstage audience, of the fictive nature of a play. In a manner of speaking, Prospero's "These our actors…were all spirits" (4.1.148-9), a reiteration of his earlier explanation that the betrothal masque is performed by

> Spirits, which by mine art
> I have from their confines called to enact
> My present fancies, (4.1.120-2)

is in effect not unlike Snout's "In this same interlude it doth befall / That I, one Snout by name, present a wall" (*Midsummer* 5.1.154-5) or Snug's "know that I as Snug the joiner am / A lion's fell, nor else no lion's dam" (5.1.218-9), which pulls the audience out of the fictive world.

The frequent employment of spectacles in Prospero's/Shakespeare's play also continually and frankly admits the artificiality and illusory nature of drama. Each of these spectacles—the tempest, the banquet, the wedding masque, the hounds—breaks into the action and disappears as abruptly as it comes, reminding the audience that they are only watching a performance as fleeting as these sudden spectacles. The wedding masque, in particular, by using a linguistic style distinctly different from normal everyday speech (rhymed throughout, with few enjambments, and made to stand out from the poetic style of the rest of the play), distances the stage and the audience still further.

Elements of reality also intrude upon the world of the romance in *The Tempest*. Antonio and Sebastian's *Realpolitik*, Caliban's (albeit clumsy) *coup d'état*, Stefano and Trinculo's drunkenness, and, most importantly, Prospero's reluctant forgiveness, Antonio's silence, and Sebastian's unchanged flippancy by the end of the play are destroyers of the romance vision. They are doing to *The Tempest* what Antonio and Sebastian's constant interruptions do to Gonzalo's description of his commonwealth: raising unpleasant but practical criticism to an idealistic vision of the world offered by the genre. This strain of the "antiromance" becomes almost unmistakable in the final scene, where reunions, reconciliations, restorations, and above all, forgiveness are almost mechanically delivered. Tony Tanner remarks that "[i]t is as if Shakespeare through Prospero is saying—these are the familiar conventions of the genre; let's just quickly run through them" (823). The reunions and reconciliations here lack the sincerity and warmth of the reunion scenes of *Pericles* and *The Winter's Tale*. Indeed, it cannot even match the dizzying dénouement of *Cymbeline*, which offers the audience the joy of relief and contains at least one particularly heart-warming line, "Hang there like fruit, my soul / Till the tree die" (5.6.263-4). In contrast, *The Tempest* has a most troubling scene of forgiveness and a disillusioned "'Tis new to thee" which shatters any idealism the audience may have had. Seen in this light, this play is, as Stanley Wells puts it, "a romance containing a built-in criticism of romance" (76) and one which, contrary to the demands of the genre, prevents the audience from fully immersing themselves in the fictional world.

It is by no means the first time that Shakespeare has used dramatic elements to pull his audience out of the world of the romance in a romance. Similar functions have been performed by Gower in *Pericles*, Time and the bear in *The Winter's Tale*, and Cloten's headless corpse in *Cymbeline*. But it is the first time that he has done so while simultaneously plunging his audience into an unprecedented degree of confusion of the distinction between the fictive and the real through various careful arrangements. As a result, the audience are made to be intellectually aware of the idea that there is supposed to be a demarcation line between illusion and reality, while experiencing that demarcation line as "blurring and blurred" (Tanner 793).

Such arrangements offer the audience a double perspective on their dramatic experience: an awareness of the separate existence of "the romance world" and "the real world" and at the same time of the great similarities between the two. They are both worlds in which tragedy and comedy coexist, or, indeed, exist *in* each other. Human actions in both worlds are frequently irrational. The strongest and sincerest human feelings in both are often provoked by illusions. In both exist things beyond reasonable explanations. And one cannot always be certain as to how one should react to one's world.

These are not new lessons. They are in fact the "moral" of all of Shakespeare's late romances where tragedy goes hand in hand with comedy, man acts upon impulse, characters' most intense emotional reactions are provoked by false impressions, and supernatural interventions direct human affairs. But it can be said that it is in *The Tempest*, where the audience are made to fully experience all of the above through being treated by the playwright as the characters are treated by the higher powers in the play that the "lesson" is most subtly and effectively incorporated.

To see *The Tempest* as presenting, or mirroring, the complete picture of the world would explain the prevailing sense of self-contradiction in the play, created not only by its habit of pulling the audience in and out of the romance world, but also by a number of other paradoxes which exist on all levels of the play: characterisation (Caliban the beast with music in his soul, Prospero the tyrannical forgiver, Miranda the obedient rebel), plot arrangements (Caliban's rebellion for freedom takes the form of swearing servitude to another; Prospero's recovery of his ducal authority is founded on the loss of his omnipotent power, the abandonment of which, according to Harold Bloom, "constitute[s] diminishments to the self" (*Invention* 667)), and literary practice (the play is a romance which breaks the conventions of romance). It also helps the audience to come to terms with perhaps the greatest paradox of all: the inevitable medium for the demonstration of one's scepticism of art and language is art and language. Mark Van Doran writes:

> It may well be that Shakespeare in "The Tempest" is telling us…about the world. But what he is telling us cannot be simple, or we could agree that it is this or that. Perhaps it is this: that the world is not simple. (139)

As the world is often paradoxical and seldom clear-cut, so is the case with *The Tempest*.

Because *The Tempest* is telling the audience about a paradoxical world, and because "the world" has a tendency to "[contrive] to confirm whatever idea of it we conceive it under" (Goddard 185), the play has given rise to a variety of readings, all of which make some sense. Receptions of the play's mood and philosophy, for example, in the four hundred years following its birth have been varied, with some regarding it as ultimately forgiving and tranquil and others seeing it as turbulent and melancholic. What is consistent about these varied views, however, is that all tend to consider that in the play a certain attitude has been carried to an extreme to reach an unprecedented and unsurpassed height. Edward Dowden in the nineteenth century, for example, wrote of Prospero that he

> has entered into complete possession of himself...Prospero has not only the higher levels of moral attainment; he has also reached an altitude of thought from which he can survey the whole of human life, and see how small yet how great it is. (418)

In contrast, more modern critics not infrequently reach an almost opposite conclusion about Prospero's philosophy. Bloom writes that

> [w]hat might vex the audience is the final realization that this powerful wizard pragmatically is a nihilist...whose project of necessity must end in his despair. (*Invention* 681)

It is a view that coincides with A. D. Nuttall's conclusion that in 4.1.146-58, Prospero "comes very close to nihilism" (*Thinker* 374). Similarly, Kott professes that *The Tempest* as a whole "has always seemed to me the saddest of Shakespeare's plays", which "[n]o one can avoid reading...as the story of his own defeat" (*Translation* 84). But merry or sad, tranquil or turbulent, triumphant or defeated, full of hope or nihilistic, *The Tempest*, on the extreme end of either spectrum, seems the perfect point, in terms of ideology, where the playwright should stop—indeed can only stop.

This tendency of seeing *The Tempest* as obtaining an extreme height is also evident in discussions of its demonstration of Shakespeare's technical skills and theatrical development. The play has often been regarded as representing the "limit", up to the time of its composition, in theatrical possibilities, a work of "perfection", if perfection is ever attainable in a work of art. Again, the superlative form of adjectives appears with steady consistency in relevant criticism. As early as 1667, Samuel Pepys put in his diary that *The Tempest* is "the most innocent play that ever I saw" (45). Nicholas Rowe in 1709 wrote of the play that "[i]t seems to me as perfect in its kind" (57). William Hazlitt wrote in 1817 that "*The Tempest* is one of the most original and perfect of Shakespeare's productions" (83). Henry James in 1907 commented that the "value of *The Tempest* is, exquisitely, in…its mark as of a distinction unequalled, on the whole, in any predecessor" (128). Other scholars are more specific. H. C. Goddard comments on the creation of Ariel that "Shakespeare could have bidden farewell to the theatre in no better way than through Ariel, for no figure he ever created more utterly transcends the stage" (181). For Nuttall, the play presents a degree of uncertainty unreached before: "[w]e have reached a pitch of uncertainty more radical than anything we have seen before" (*Thinker* 369). And Barton, in analysing the epilogue's unique way of transcending the formal limits of a five-act play and running straight into reality, considers it as "stand[ing] on a frontier for what is possible in the theatre" and so it is that in the play "even [Shakespeare] had reached the point beyond which there could be no further dramatic development" (Introduction 51).

Of course, not everyone is charmed by *The Tempest*. Although many scholars lavish on the play the epithet "perfect", others are more sceptical. But again, as is the case with the reception of the play's philosophy, scepticism of its quality tends to go to an extreme. Lytton Strachey in the early twentieth century famously—or infamously, for Bardolators—suggested that Shakespeare in his final period was bored with almost everything and that

> such is the conclusion which is particularly forced upon us by a consideration of the play which is in many ways most typical of Shakespeare's later work…—*The Tempest*. ("Final")

Anthony Dawson considers it to be the playwright's most consistently overrated work. He also suggests that it might not be too scandalous to imagine "Shakespeare's career trailing off, from bad to worse…before being judiciously terminated by his worried partners in The King's Men" (63). These sceptics of *The Tempest* would agree with Barton that Shakespeare in the play has reached a point beyond which he can "have no dramatic development", except that for Barton it is a point of ultimate triumph, while for them it is more likely a point of defeat, the ultimate proof of loss of sound dramatic instinct and artistic zeal.

And thus, whether *The Tempest* is indeed a perfect or a sorry play, a tranquil or a bitter play, an optimistic or a nihilistic play, there seems to be "an unmistakeable sense of finality that permeates" (Egan 171) it and an inescapable "feeling that this is a final mood…a sense that the end of the road has been reached" (Evans 213). And there is of course the leave-taking of Prospero, a character who almost compels the audience to identify him with Shakespeare. As Prospero, who has abjured his Arts, steps forward in the reality-illusion blurred and blurring epilogue to ask to be set free, it is difficult for critics to resist seeing it as the author's own farewell to his career. Prospero is looked upon as speaking on Shakespeare's behalf, abjuring his Art—triumphantly as his project is done or in despair as he discovers the powerlessness of Art and the illusory nature of reality—and begging the audience to set him free, either confident in the knowledge that he has pleased in the most spectacular manner, or apologetic with the awareness that he has lost his grip and should better be stepping down. "[I]ncreasingly I find in *The Tempest* one of the forms of farewell" (Introduction xiii), observes Bloom.

This sense of farewell is further consolidated by the play's incorporations of dramatic motifs which seem to have been gathered from across the whole span of the playwright's career. Stephen Greenblatt terms the play "a kind of echo chamber of Shakespearean motifs" not only linking it closely to the previous three romances, but also "resonat[ing]…with issues that haunted Shakespeare's imagination throughout his career" ("*Tempest*" 3055). Apart from a close examination of language and theatrical art, the play concerns itself with, according to Greenblatt's identification, no fewer than ten familiar Shakespearean motifs:

> the story of loss and recovery and…wonder…[;] the painful necessity of a father to let his daughter go (*Othello, King Lear*); the treacherous betrayal of a legitimate ruler (*Richard II, Julius Caesar, Hamlet, Macbeth*); the murderous hatred of one brother for another (*Richard III, As You Like It, Hamlet, King Lear*); the passage from court society to the wilderness and the promise of a return (*A Midsummer Night's Dream, As You Like It*); the young heiress, torn from her place in the social hierarchy (*Twelfth Night, Pericles, The Winter's Tale*); the dream of manipulating others by means of art, especially staging miniature plays within plays (*1 Henry IV, Much Ado About Nothing, Hamlet*); the threat of radical loss of identity (*The Comedy of Errors, Richard II, King Lear*); the relationship between nature and nurture (*Pericles, The Winter's Tale*); the harnessing of magical powers (*The First Part of the Contention [2 Henry VI], A Midsummer Night's Dream, Macbeth*). (ibid.)

Although by now one is thoroughly used to the idea of the last plays being distinguished by a set of recurrent motifs and of Shakespeare, throughout his career, frequently revisiting and re-elaborating upon old themes, this list of motifs echoed—indeed, almost crammed—in his fourth-shortest play is nevertheless impressive enough to make one wonder if this is indeed a summary of his career.

But the establishment in the canon of *Henry VIII* and *The Two Noble Kinsmen* (some also count in the lost *Cardenio*), which date later than 1611, means that *The Tempest* is not Shakespeare's last work and consequently Prospero's abjuration of his "rough magic" not the dramatic manifestation of his last bow. Moreover, despite the fact that it still holds the distinction of being the playwright's last single-authored play, biographical evidence seems to suggest that a semi-retirement to Stratford was probably not on Shakespeare's mind as he worked on it. At forty-six or -seven, he was far from the official Jacobean age of retirement of sixty.[4] As a matter fact, records appear to show a continued interest in London and the theatres on the part of the playwright. Jonathan Bate points out that in March 1613 Shakespeare, for the first time, bought instead of rented a property in London, "a substantial gatehouse close to the Blackfriars theatre" (*Soul* 353). The date of its purchase, it is suggested, reveals "Shakespeare's continuing commitment to London in the final years", "[e]ven if this was primarily an investment property" (354). Bate, surveying the contours of the playwright's career, also suggests that he "may never have fully retired, but he may well have semi-retired much earlier than we suppose" (359), meaning that he had probably retired to Stratford during the plague outbreak of 1603-4 and might have remained consistently absent from London from then on, as "we cannot formally prove that Shakespeare was in London between autumn 1604 and early summer 1612" (358). In other words, he did not, as most biographers believe, semi-quit the city only after the completion of *The Tempest*. If so, retirement for Shakespeare as he was penning the speeches of Prospero was no new arrangement at all. Thus it would seem that he had no cause to suddenly write it into his work in 1611, either because he was not contemplating it at all, or because by now it was not a new working arrangement that might affect his composition.

So *The Tempest* is not a farewell to the stage. But it is possible to see it as a farewell to a certain stage in Shakespeare's career. The biographical evidence just quoted, taken in conjunction with the sense of finality which most scholars see existing in the play, appears to suggest that he may have been ready to quit the dramatic patterns he had so far explored in the four last plays to try something new. And, as his "romance period" was ushered

---

[4] Jacobeans looked on the age of "sixty… [as] the age of incipient decrepitude" (Thomas 237). It was the age when a man was "relieved of civic obligations and thus officially considered old" (McMullan, "What" 12).

in by a collaboration, could it have been that collaboration with Fletcher, which was to follow, in some ways prompted the beginning of a new period in his professional career? All this is supposition, of course. But it is true that of all the four romances discussed so far, it is in *The Tempest* that he has challenged the conventions of the genre most violently by sticking to the classical unities, installing a protagonist who is in control— at least superficially—instead of being "chased around" by fate, and planting an ending which seems a parody of previous romance endings and which, moreover, is finally melancholic instead of happy, all of which visibly defy the requirements of the genre. In terms of linguistic style there is also a slight but significant shift as the "elliptical, roundabout, crowded, and extravagant" (McDonald, *Late* 254) verse begins to make the listener more uncertain rather than reassured about authorial artistic control. It is also in this play that Shakespeare supplants his ultimately positive presentation of the effects of language and art with doubts and scepticism. This is probably the last of *The Tempest*'s paradoxes: that it is simultaneously a farewell and a greeting, a farewell to the "romantic" way of looking at life, and a greeting to a new way of examining the world which is complicated enough to encourage wildly different interpretations in quest of the complete picture.

CHAPTER FIVE

HENRY VIII (ALL IS TRUE)

Words and Truth

Most scholars now tend to accept *Henry VIII* and *The Two Noble Kinsmen* as collaborations between Shakespeare and Fletcher. And they will be treated as such in this and the next chapter.

This theory of collaboration is mainly substantiated by the results of a series of independent language tests, conducted over the course of a century and a half.[1] But while the plays seem to be "established as such a case ever can be on purely internal evidence" (Maxwell xvi) as collaborations, as is the case with *Pericles*'s co-authorship, not everyone is convinced. Scholars suspicious of the theory question the reliability of language tests and offer in their own defence the plays' dramatic unity as evidence of single authorship. These dissenting voices prevent *Henry VIII* and *The Two Noble Kinsmen*'s authorship from finally being considered settled.

It can be argued that a judicious and, at times, sceptical approach to "what others say" lies at the heart of this prolonged authorship investigation and debate. The initial suggestion (made by James Spedding in 1850) that *Henry VIII* might have been a collaboration means that the First Folio's claim of its single authorship was not taken for granted. Similarly, it can be argued that the driving force behind every new linguistic test devised to pin down the Shakespearean or Fletcherian style is the uneasy suspicion that the results of previous tests are inadequate and therefore need to be checked, supplemented and strengthened by further research. And finally, that collaboration is treated still as a hypothesis—however probable—rather than a confirmed fact demonstrates a scholarly unwillingness to commit oneself to a final judgement merely on the

---

[1] For a detailed survey of the methods and results of the linguistic tests, see Vickers, Brian. *Shakespeare, Co-Author: A Historical Study of Five Collaborative Plays*. Oxford: Oxford University Press, 2002. 333-402. Print.

evidence of "words": the verse in the plays, the reports of the linguistic tests, and the interpretations of those results.

It seems appropriate that such cautious treatment of language as a medium for the transmission of facts should be partly inspired by the language of *Henry VIII*, for the play takes a particular interest in, amongst other things, the relationship between words and truth. In this respect, it, though in terms of its subject matter a seeming departure from the previous romances, inherits the four preceding plays' concern with the power of language.

Henry VIII clearly signals that the question of language's reliability for transmitting truth is at the heart of its dramatic concern. After all, it was probably once performed under the provocative title of *All Is True*, or thus subtitled. The self-irony is hard to miss, for the "truth" presented in *All Is True* is at best third-hand information, since a play is but a verbal reworking of historical records, which are verbal reworkings of historical facts in the first place. Even if a history play intends to follow its sources faithfully, how much truth can remain after two rounds of verbal transmission is highly questionable. And in the case of *All Is True*, the situation is worsened by the fact that the playwrights do *not* keep to their sources. They reshuffle the order of historical events and compress the time span between them. For example, Henry's marriage to Anne in 1533 is placed before Wolsey's fall, which in fact began in 1529 (Wolsey himself died the following year). Katherine's death in 1536 is presented as occurring before the birth of Elizabeth, which historically fell in 1533. And Buckingham's downfall, which actually occurred four years before the 1525 "Amicable Grant" episode, in the play takes place immediately after Henry learns of the Grant. Such liberal rearrangements and compressions of chronology forge new cause-and-effect relationships between events, which serve the internal logic of the play but do not always reflect the actual historical causality. While the play might claim to have unearthed hidden truths through its new interpretations, it cannot deny that it is grossly untrue to historical chronology. Therefore, for such a work to unashamedly call itself the representation of all truth is in fact to draw attention to the falsehood of the claim and the impossibility of finding that all is true in this dramatic narrative.

This play which cannot be all true not only announces its truthfulness in the title (or subtitle), but, as if fearful lest the audience should forget this claim, keeps reminding them of its concern with truth. By Gordon McMullan's calculation, "the word 'truth' itself turns up no fewer than twenty-five times, and there are six occurrences of 'truly', one of 'true-hearted' and eighteen of 'true'" (Introduction 2-3). "The play doth protest too much" seems an appropriate comment on the frequent appearance of the various forms of the word "truth" in *All Is True*.

The prologue alone contains two occurrences of "truth" and one of "true". It assures the audience that

> Such as give
> Their money out of hope that they may believe,
> May here find truth; (7-9)

that it presents "our chosen truth" (18); and that ranking the play with others less serious will

> [forfeit]
> Our own brains, and the opinion that we bring
> To make that only true we now intend. (19-21)

Like the ironic (sub)title, the prologue, in declaring itself to be true, in fact implies that it is futile to hope for an accurate reproduction of historical events in this dramatic presentation, for the way in which it protests truthfulness disqualifies its assurance. The promise that the production will satisfy the audience's "hope that they may believe" is in fact ambivalent about the play's commitment to truth, for the wording makes it easy for the playwrights to wriggle out of the contract: the prologue does not promise the truth, it only promises to meet with the audience's hope to believe. There is thus a subtle suggestion that the "truth" presented may turn out more consistent with popular belief than with historical facts. While lines 7 to 9 deftly shift from the speaker to the listener the responsibility of recognising truth, and thus with it, the blame for taking untruths for the truth, lines 18 to 21 further explain what kind of truth one will encounter. The play, the prologue makes it clear, shall offer its audience "chosen" truths, whose presentation involves "our own brains". In other words, the history presented is selected according to the playwrights' personal interpretations of events, and embellished, if not distorted, by their creative powers to meet with their artistic intention, which, as their unhesitant rearrangement of Tudor chronology reveals, is most certainly not to faithfully reproduce the history of Henry's reign. Thus the prologue, in about twenty lines, has made it clear that narrative history, filtered through the choices of generations of authors and presented through such an unreliable medium as language, should not be mistaken for historical truth. And by the same logic, any fact, conveyed through language, should not be taken for granted but rather viewed with suspicion.

Henry VIII dramatises the idea that known facts, historical or otherwise, are usually only second-, third- or even fourth-hand information through its numerous scenes of political news exchange and gossip. The thematic point that "we apprehend history largely through other people's interpretations of it" (Dean 177) thus becomes for the audience a sustained experience. Compared with Shakespeare's previous histories, there are fewer direct dramatisations of historical events here. Instead, much is told through the many exchanges between named noblemen or unnamed gentlemen. Almost every scene contains a conversation of this sort, sometimes working independently as a substitute for direct dramatisation (e.g. Norfolk, Buckingham and Abergavenny's discussion of the Field of the Cloth of Gold in 1.1), sometimes as a complement to a direct dramatisation which presents only part of an event (e.g. the Gentlemen's exchange about Anne's coronation in Westminster in 4.1), occasionally as prelude to an upcoming event (e.g. Norfolk, Suffolk, Surrey and the Chamberlain's anticipation of Wolsey's downfall in 3.2), and at times as commentaries accompanying an event which is being presented on stage (e.g. Norfolk, Suffolk, and Surrey's descriptions of Wolsey's movements in 3.2). Thus, while as a history play, in presenting "the very persons of our noble story / As they were living" (Prologue 26-7), *Henry VIII* brings the audience back in time and creates for them an illusion of immediacy of, and intimacy to, historical figures and events, at the same time, with these report scenes, it makes them personally experience the distance between themselves and those events which, even if very recent, are available to them only through report and opinion.

Some of these report scenes directly stage the process through which fact becomes distorted in verbal transmission. In 3.2, Norfolk, Suffolk and Surrey are shown to be observing and remarking on Wolsey's behaviour:

NORFOLK He's discontented.
SUFFOLK   Maybe he hears the King
   Does whet his anger to him.
SURREY   Sharp enough,
   Lord, for thy justice. (3.2.92-4)

A few moments later Henry comes in and asks them if they have seen the cardinal. Thereupon Norfolk enters into a detailed description of what they have seen of Wolsey:

                          My lord, we have
   Stood here observing him. Some strange commotion
   Is in his brain. He bites his lip, and starts,

Stops on a sudden, looks upon the ground,
Then lays his finger on his temple, straight
Springs out into fast gait, then stops again,
Strikes his breast hard, and anon he casts
His eye against the moon. In most strange postures
We have seen him set himself. (3.2.112-120)

In a performance, whether the actor playing Wolsey should take these lines as instructions on how he should act during 3.2.85-136 is his and the director's choice, but I suspect that this kind of performance is not what the playwrights would have wished for. After all, it is exactly the sort of exaggerated acting that Shakespeare repeatedly mocks and warns against, most famously in Hamlet's instructions to the players:

[D]o not saw the air too much with your hand...O, it offends me to the soul
to hear a robustious, periwig-pated fellow tear a passion to tatters, to very
rags, (3.2.4, 7-9)

but also in Ulysses' mockery of "the strutting player, whose conceit / Lies in his hamstring" (1.3.153-4) in *Troilus and Cressida*, as well as much earlier in *Richard III*, in Buckingham's contemptuous summary of over-acting:

Tut, I can counterfeit the deep tragedian,
Tremble and start at the wagging of a straw,
Speak, and look back, and pry on every side,
Intending deep suspicion; ghastly looks
Are at my service, like enforcèd smiles,
And both are ready in their offices
At any time to grace my stratagems. (3.5.5-11)

Moreover, Norfolk's description portrays a Wolsey who is more frightened or worried than angry. Although we are not sure what Jacobeans would have perceived as gestures of anger, Norfolk's account does not feel right, for it brings to mind similar descriptions of behaviour behind which pain or terror rather than anger is the dominant emotion. In *Much Ado About Nothing*, the love-sick Beatrice in Claudio's description, for example, "beats her heart" (2.3.134). And Gloucester in *Richard III* asks Buckingham if he can manage to

quake and change colour?
Murder thy breath in middle of a word?
And then begin again, and stop again,

As if thou wert distraught and mad with terror? (3.5.1-4, italics mine)

Wolsey's musings preceding Norfolk's report, however, have already revealed to the audience that what is on his mind is not the king's anger but the problem posed by Anne Boleyn. Although he is distressed, from the content of his speech one can deduce that it is an anger mingled with confident determination ("This candle burns not clear; 'tis I must snuff it, / Then out it goes" (3.2.97-8)) instead of fear. In short, the Wolsey in Norfolk's account acts in accordance with the reporter's mistaken belief that the cause of his distress is his fear of the king's wrath, rather than with Wolsey's real present state of mind. It therefore seems reasonable to conclude that the playwrights probably did not intend that the actor should behave in this exaggerated and "distraught with terror" manner constructed, even if only unconsciously, by Norfolk. The audience is thus witness to a report scene where the verbal description shows considerable discrepancy with the actual event—an event, moreover, which took place only moments before and is still fresh in the reporter's memory. If something that just happened cannot be accurately described, then absolute faithfulness to facts in narrative histories, where there is a considerable temporal gap between the occurrence and the report of an event, must be hard to come by.

In a manner of speaking, Norfolk, however intentionally or unintentionally, in reporting Wolsey's movements, has staged, or evoked, a play starring the cardinal. Thus in this instance, the audience can be said to be watching Norfolk's *All Is True*. It is a miniature version of the experience of watching Shakespeare and Fletcher's *All Is True*, except that with Norfolk's production, they are given the opportunity to witness the "historical original", and thus to see clearly that the verbal reconstruction gives Wolsey another style of performance as well as a different state of mind. For them, the scene becomes an occasion where truth is falsified during its transmission right before their eyes. In other words, they are watching the very process of events becoming "history". This should heighten their awareness of the problematic nature of this process, as well as the idea that *Henry VIII* is participating in this process by its reproduction and dramatisation of history.

In Act 1, Wolsey himself remarks on the distortion of facts which may result from an inadequate understanding of circumstances. He protests that he is

Traduced by ignorant tongues, which neither know
My faculties nor person yet will be
The chronicles of my doing, (1.2.73-5)

which seems to describe what Norfolk does in 3.2 rather neatly. Ironically, Norfolk himself is also heard to observe on language's inadequacy as a medium for recounting an event. In the middle of his extravagant report of the French and English encounter at the Field of the Cloth of Gold, he is interrupted by Buckingham's disbelieving "O, you go far" (1.1.38), to which he answers

> As I belong to worship, and affect
> In honour honesty, the tract of ev'rything
> Would by a good discourser lose some life
> Which the action's self was tongue to. (1.1.39-42)

Although Norfolk intends with this explanation to show that he has not exaggerated in his descriptions of royal splendour, he also admits that not only his report of the French and English encounter, but in fact any verbal account of any event, is incapable of faithful reconstruction, as "some life" would inevitably get lost in the process.

Taken together, the three comments summarise the reasons why verbally transmitted facts should be viewed with suspicion. Buckingham's "O, you go far" points out that a verbal account may contain the reporter's own embellishments. Norfolk's observation reminds the listener of the inevitable loss of facts which occurs in any report. And Wolsey's comment exposes the distortion of facts which a verbal report, made by "sick interpreters, once weak ones" (1.2.83), may result in.

It is worth noticing that Buckingham, Norfolk and Wolsey's comments all occur in scenes where reports take centre stage. Norfolk is verbally sketching out a picture of the sights at the Field of the Cloth of Gold. Wolsey is defending himself in answer to Queen Katherine's report about grievances caused by taxation. In effect, these comments, in openly questioning the accuracy of verbal reports, undermine the credibility of the scenes in which they appear. And since, as I have suggested, even scenes which directly dramatise history in *Henry VIII* contain verbal reports as substitutes for historical facts, the audience are prevented from fully participating in the "history", being continually reminded of the critical distance between narrative and fact.

This sense of distance from historical truth is further consolidated by the play's presentation of how crucial political decisions are made almost entirely on the evidence of verbal reports. Most characters in *Henry VIII* seem to take it for granted that that which is spoken by all must be the truth: "'Tis most true— / These news are everywhere, every tongue speaks 'em" (2.2.36-7). As a result, verbal testimonies become the base upon which important decisions are made. Even Buckingham and Wolsey, who have demonstrated an awareness of the possible inaccuracy of verbal reports, not infrequently depend on words. The cardinal, in 3.2, is himself soliciting from Cromwell a report of the king's reaction to some letters. And Buckingham actually intends to "cry down / This Ipswich fellow's insolence"(1.1.137-8) with

> intelligence
> And proofs as clear as founts in July when
> We see each grain of gravel. (1.1.153-5)

In other words, he is confident that on the evidence of secret reports ("intelligence"), he will be able to uproot Wolsey.

The play's most thorough and direct dramatisation of statesmen's dependence on verbal reports is the king's interview with Buckingham's surveyor, whose words are pivotal in deciding the duke's fate. Buckingham's guilt is constructed entirely on the "examinations, proofs, confessions, / Of diverse witnesses" (2.1.17-8)—verbal reports, in short. Of these, only the interview with the surveyor is directly dramatised, showing him reporting words and actions which are allegedly Buckingham's. Even third-hand information is made use of: "words used by his ex-master quoting his chaplain as the latter was repeating the confidence of a 'holy monk'" (Sahel 149). These are enough to draw from Henry the conclusion that "[b]y day and night, / He's traitor to th'height!" (1.2.214-5). Although, as Katherine cautions, there is the possibility of the surveyor, despite his vow to "speak but the truth" (1.2.178), conveying false information due to personal resentment of Buckingham, that consideration (if taken into account at all) is eventually outweighed during the trial by the fact that all witnesses speak against the duke. Thus on the strength that "every tongue speaks" of his guilt, Buckingham is finally found guilty of high treason.

While the surveyor's reports and the witnesses' testimonies are enough to satisfy the king and the jury, they may leave the audience with the uncomfortable suspicion that justice might not have been done. This doubt extends from the immediate, whether the play's Buckingham is really guilty, to the historical, whether the real Buckingham was really treasonous in the first place. It is as Pierre Sahel remarks, that through the intervention of oral reports, "[i]t even seems that the images of the dramatised events themselves have deliberately been put slightly out of focus" (145-6). Thus, in inviting scepticism, oral reports render not only narratives of history but history itself unreliable and ambivalent.

The play persists in denying its audience the satisfaction of insight into the truth about Buckingham's case. Even at his last moments, in his speech before execution, where "traditionally, convicted criminals would confess their crimes and ask the King's forgiveness" (McMullan, Introduction 99), little is revealed. Buckingham acknowledges the justness of the procedures of the law, but also says that "those that sought it I could wish more Christians" (2.1.65). Rather than asking for forgiveness, he forgives his enemies, yet at the same time looks forward to haunting them:

> Yet let 'em look they glory not in mischief,
> Nor build their evils on the graves of great men,
> For then my guiltless blood must cry against 'em. (2.1.67-9)

Such contradictory statements, spoken in a grand and heroic manner, not only confuse the listener as to his guilt or innocence, but also make it uncertain whether he is really as he says, reconciled to his fate and by now "half in heaven" (2.1.89), or whether he is striking up a pose and merely conforming outwardly to the Christian spirit of forgiveness and reconciliation.

Buckingham's ambiguous farewell is consistent with the play's general practice of denying its audience access to truth even when a character is seemingly confessing, in public or in private, true feelings or opinions. In *Henry VIII*, confessions generally hide more than they reveal. Sometimes they are immediately exposed as insincere, as is the case with Anne's declaration that she would not be queen. In the course of the relatively short and private conversation with the Old Lady, Anne swears six times (by her troth and maidenhead, in truth, and not for all the riches under heaven) that she would not be queen. But—if the Old Lady's taunting remarks are not enough to alert one to her "hypocrisy" (2.3.26)—her willing acceptance of the title of Marchioness of Pembroke and the accompanying annuity dispels any suspicion that her later ascent to queenship is made against her will.

Other times, though not explicitly exposed, the sincerity of a confession is nevertheless thrown into suspicion by the circumstances under which it is spoken. Henry's praise of Katherine and subsequent explanations about his conscience, for example, invite doubt, for they are wedged between scenes showing Anne Boleyn receiving favours from him and his obvious impatience with the cardinals for not reaching a verdict during the trial.

Sometimes the sincerity of a confessional speech is jeopardised by the style of language in which it is spoken. This is most evident in the case of Wolsey's farewell. Unlike Buckingham's last speech, Anne's declaration or Henry's explanation, which all have an onstage audience and therefore a cause to be disingenuous, Wolsey's farewell starts out as a private meditation. In 3.2, after the king and Norfolk's party have exited and before Cromwell's entrance, Wolsey is alone, making the first 23 lines of his farewell the closest the play offers to a soliloquy. But this is not a truth-revealing soliloquy. Both in content and in tone it feels remarkably similar to Buckingham's public speech. Like him, Wolsey locates his downfall in the caprices of uncontrollable external circumstances, portraying himself as the victim of forces largely external to himself. His style is one of declamation, "closely resembl[ing] a rhetorical exercise" (Waith 122), spoken as if he is conscious of being listened to. As a result, he seems

> to be assuming a role, and an unexpected one. The part of the tragic hero, noble and pathetic victim, awaits Wolsey as it does Buckingham. It is fully prepared, they need only speak the lines. (ibid.)

How much or whether at all he has, as he claims later to Cromwell, become better acquainted with himself and is

> feel[ing] within me
> A peace above all earthly dignities,
> A still and quiet conscience (3.2.379-81)

is doubtful, as his style of speaking makes it difficult for one to tell whether he is merely "whitewashing" himself with the speech of a heroic martyr or whether he is truly transformed.

That the language in which one speaks, even when without a conscious intention of altering the truth, may change the nature of the facts has been pointed out earlier by Katherine. In 3.1, in refusing to communicate with Wolsey in Latin, she comments that "[a] strange tongue makes my cause more strange suspicious" (3.1.44). Her comment applies equally well to Buckingham and Wolsey's farewells, which are both cases where a noble and heroic "tongue" makes their speakers' causes, whatever their original nature, noble and heroic. Both farewells, incidentally, are now usually ascribed to Fletcher. More will be said about his contribution to their collaboration in the next chapter, but this seems an appropriate place to mention that the declamatory style, which is Fletcher's hallmark and often frowned upon by critics when compared with Shakespearean lines, is well suited to reinforce this play's cultivation of scepticism about language. Like the various verbal reports which prevent the audience from seeing historical facts clearly, the rhetorical grandeur of the Fletcherian speeches makes it impossible to tell whether the speakers mean what they say. Thus, whether in the form of historical narratives or personal statements, words smother truth, "fall[ing] upon the facts like soft snow" (Orwell 166), covering and hiding them from view.

Katherine's last speech (also generally ascribed to Fletcher) in 4.2, this time spoken to an onstage audience, shares many of the stylistic properties of both Buckingham and Wolsey's farewells. It is again a speech of magnanimous forgiveness and of calm reconciliation with oneself, spoken in the declamatory style conventionally associated with large-than-life nobility. Although in this case, the consistency of the speech with characterisation makes it more convincingly sincere, to an audience which have by now been made almost hyper-sensitive to the unreliability of words, the close resemblance between the three farewell speeches has the unfortunate effect of cancelling out one another's trustworthiness.

Language does not redeem its reliability even by the end of the play, despite the final scene being dominated by the speech of a man who has just been vigorously praised for his integrity. One's knowledge of Elizabeth and James's reigns—which was the lived experience of most members of the original audience—will inform one that Cranmer's description of a golden future is at variance with historical facts:

> His paean to Elizabeth and James I cannot be confined to the literally "true" predictions of their actual reigns (already belied by the sublunar world of the original audience). (Bliss 20)

While this less-than-accurate prophecy may indeed serve a more profound purpose,[2] it cannot be denied that an audience's primary experience of, or first reaction to, it is very likely an awareness of the discrepancy between Cranmer's words and the truths of reality.

The epilogue presents the final blow to language's reputation with the lines

> I fear,
> All the expected good we're like to hear
> For this play at this time is only in
> The merciful construction of good women,
> For such a one we showed 'em. (7-11)

---

[2] For example, as Jay L. Halio suggests, a didactic function which "exhort[s] to the reigning monarch, James I (we recall that the play may have been designed for performance at court)" as "a mirror held up to him of what a great king should be" (37).

The reference of "such a one" is ambivalent. The listeners cannot know for certain whether it is speaking about Katherine, Anne, Elizabeth, the qualities of all three ladies, or the whole play (as one "merciful construction of good women"). Three lines later they are bid to clap, and it is likely that they clap in some confusion about how far what they have seen clears through the thick miasma of words to what is true in *All Is True*.

In recreating history, *Henry VIII* offers an experience resulting in scepticism about everything said, be it the assurances the play offers, or the oral reports, facts, public speeches of self-revelation or private confessional speeches it presents, or the historical narratives upon which it is based. Almost every speech in it is marked by a discrepancy, or at least a strong suspicion of one, between words and events, which is sometimes unintentionally caused by the speaker's insufficient grasp of the facts, sometimes intentionally brought about by a deliberate ill-interpretation of the truth, and sometimes further consolidated by its style. In this respect, *Henry VIII* takes *The Tempest*'s scepticism about the power of language even further. For while the earlier play's suspicion is cast on the use of language as an extension of the capacity for ill will, the present work is sceptical of all language, regardless of the speaker's intention, whether it is spoken with or without deliberate or unconscious manipulation of vocabulary, syntax or logic.

History and Performance

Through its dramatisation of the unreliable process of transmitting facts through language, *Henry VIII* offers its audience a history which ultimately destabilises existent notions of history. With its displayed scepticism towards language, not only does it throw suspicion over its own dramatised version of events, but also on its historical sources, which are themselves often narratives of history based on second-, third- or fourth-hand accounts.

This experience of history, at least for those who come to the play "out of hope they may believe", frustrates an audience's expectations of a work advertised as the dramatisation of the *famous history* of Henry VIII and promising "all is true". Coming to the theatre to find out what happened, or to have their knowledge of what happened either confirmed or decidedly contradicted, they leave it instead with the uncertain feeling that the truth of history might not ever be learnt, be it through the medium of a staged performance or written chronicles. This might not be to them an unpleasant feeling, but it is very likely an unexpected one.

Henry VIII, as a matter of fact, is a play which frustrates expectation in many respects. For example, as we have seen, speeches spoken on occasions where one would expect confessions seldom give their listener the satisfaction of knowing for certain what the speakers really think or believe. Buckingham's public farewell leaves one still uncertain about whether he is guilty or innocent of the treason for which he is executed, while Wolsey's more private account equally denies one an insight into his true state of mind when facing downfall.

Although both farewells are scenes where spoken language dominates the stage, the circumstances under which and/or the style in which they are spoken imbue(s) them with the qualities of a public, and fairly visual, spectacle. As mentioned earlier, Buckingham's farewell is spoken to an onstage audience. Wolsey's, or at least the first part of it, is indeed personal, but Fletcher's signature declamatory style, in freezing its speaker in a conventional heroic posture, somehow glosses the scene with a tableau-like quality, transforming the essentially auditory nature of the episode into a visual one. Hence this comparatively modestly-set scene, even in the absence of lavish stage props or an onstage crowd, becomes in effect a public display.

Both scenes are thus part of the play's general scheme of installing visual splendour in places where the audience would expect the revelation of truth, or, as Barton puts it, "[c]onsistently, where analysis or personal revelation might be expected, the play offers spectacles instead" ("Realism" 185). Apart from the two farewells, such moments include the party at York House (1.4), Katherine's state trial (2.4), Anne's coronation procession (4.1), Katherine's vision (4.2) and finally, Elizabeth's christening (5.4). The party in 1.4 is placed between the king's preliminary interview with the surveyor (1.2) and the formal condemnation of Buckingham (2.1). It thus forestalls the expected revelations about the duke's case. Katherine's trial, though presented in detail, fails to resolve the question of the marriage's legitimacy. Anne's coronation procession comes directly after Wolsey's farewell (3.2), so that it might be said that spectacle has been piled upon spectacle to deny the audience direct access to Wolsey's true response to his downfall. Katherine's vision by its nature becomes more puzzling than revealing, as it is impossible to tell whether it is only something dreamt up by the queen, or a real epiphany in the same league with Pericles' or Posthumus' vision. And the christening, though it does analyse Elizabeth's reign in the guise of Cranmer's prophecy, is again an occasion where rhetoric brings visual splendour to an auditory experience but stifles the complete revelation of the facts.

But it is not only expectations of analyses or revelations that the spectacles frustrate. These visually splendid scenes, carefully planned under "stage directions so elaborate that they might almost belong to a film script" (Barton, "Realism" 185), also defy expectations (the critics', if not the audience's) about the use of visual impact in a Shakespearean drama, especially one chronologically close to the romances. Unlike its counterparts in the four previous plays, spectacle here apparently accomplishes very little. In contrast to the statue scene in *The Winter's Tale*, the battle scenes in *Cymbeline* or the epiphany scene in *Pericles*, its presentation is not necessary for the unfolding of the story, nor does it serve any apparently didactic function like Prospero's drama in *The Tempest*. Indeed, it does not even fulfil its own significance as a public function, for the "functional" part of a ceremony is never directly dramatised. 4.1's presentation of Anne's coronation, for example, only shows the procession. The actual service in Westminster is not shown, merely reported. Likewise, during the scene of Elizabeth's christening, the action that achieves something, namely the christening itself, takes place offstage. Similarly, in the case of Buckingham's trial, the judicial proceedings which decide his fate are only presented by report. When he next appears, "[a]ll's done but the ceremony / Of bringing back the prisoner" (2.1.3-4). The same can be said of Katherine's state trial. For one thing, it is interrupted, since she storms out of the court in the middle of it. And, as in the previous three examples, the functional part of the procedure, in this case the debating process through which "the late marriage [is] made of none effect" (4.1.33) is not dramatised, but again reported. Indeed, it is four scenes after the trial at Blackfriars before we hear of the final verdict. For another, what is presented during the trial is, technically speaking, not relevant to its purpose. To put it in another way, Katherine's defence of herself, compelling though it is, is completely off the mark, for the tenor of her defence is that the king has no cause to divorce her since her conduct as a wife has always been beyond reproach, yet the trial's agenda is to debate whether the marriage has legal existence at all, in other words, whether Katherine has ever, in a legal sense, been a "wife" to Henry.[3] Katherine's straying defence thus reduces her grand trial

---

[3] The closeness of Katherine's defence to Hermione's in *The Winter's Tale* has been frequently remarked on.* However, this comparison in fact further reveals the ineffectiveness of Katherine's speeches at the trial, for their situations are actually widely different. While Hermione is defending herself against a husband's false accusation of infidelity, what the English queen is faced with is not the accusation of misbehaviour, but of the invalidity of her marriage in a legal sense.

scene, even if she had not walked out of the room, to a theatrical pose rather than a practical process. It is such arrangements in the play that have caused scholars to remark that "the spectacle of *Henry VIII* is a display of cost more than a use of symbolic language; it is not spectacle of the theatre, but spectacle in the theatre" (Leggatt 223), or that "[t]he tableaux of *Henry VIII*...appear to be there purely for their own sake" (Barton, "Realism" 185). They contradict existing understandings and expectations about Shakespeare's use of visual extravaganza in his last plays.

Henry VIII's treatment of extravagant theatrical displays also confuses critics as to what the play actually is. Its excessive use of courtly splendour and its general tendency to move "not through plot...but...through the dynamics of poetry and spectacle" (Berry 231) have led some scholars to the conclusion that it is in fact a masque. Yet the essential "emptiness" of the spectacles implies a sceptical attitude towards royalty's use of performance. The superficial quality of the visual experience may be looked upon as suggesting that, as truth in speech is stifled by language, facts of history are suffocated, and often deliberately so, by pomp and circumstance. In other words, the use of visual splendour here contradicts generic expectations of the masque, for, as F. Schreiber-McGee observes,

> [i]f a masque is defined by its appropriateness to the nobility it is fashioned to honor...then *Henry VIII* as a masque fails—mostly through its irrepressible sensitivity to the political ambiguities that shadow the theatrical spectacles. (193)

The play equally refuses to conform to the respective generic expectations of history and romance. Although its subject is the history of an English king's reign, it differs from Shakespeare's other English histories in containing, as Tanner puts it,

> [n]o rebellions, no usurpations, no invasions, no wars; no serious plotting, no really profound contestations, no irresolvable antagonisms—and no humour. (469)

The play, although named after Henry VIII, has no easily identifiable protagonist and no clearly discernible centre of conflict or plot line. It

---

*See, for example, note to 2.4.11-55 in the Arden Third edition of *Henry VIII*, edited by Gordon McMullan: "Katherine's speech here...bears close comparison with that of Hermione at *WT* 3.2, especially 21-53" (301). See also Vanita, Ruth. "Mariological Memory in *The Winter's Tale* and *Henry VIII*." *Studies in English Literature, 1500-1900* 40 (2000): 311-37. Print.

imposes a pattern on history by putting a series of rises and falls in close juxtaposition, and leaves its viewers with the impression that history proceeds on its own course regardless of human intervention, which is a view of history noticeably different from that of the other histories in the canon.

This sense of a higher force in control of human affairs gives a feeling of the romance to the work. Yet *Henry VIII* is also resistant to identification with Shakespeare's other romances. Its setting is distant neither in time nor in place. There is no travelling into foreign countries, no young daughter on the threshold of making a dynastic marriage, no reconciliation between families felicitated through the agency of the children, and no supernatural or exotic occurrences.[4]

In offering its audience an experience of history and language which results in uncertainty and scepticism, providing them with confessions which do not confess, substituting moments of revelation with sumptuous display, turning such shows-within-shows into mere "spectacle in the theatre" rather than "spectacle of the theatre", and resisting generic conventions of at least three types of literature, *Henry VIII* has demonstrated a general tendency towards frustrating expectations about itself. However, one should, perhaps, not feel too surprised at its refusal to meet with expectations. After all, right from the start it has warned its viewers against coming to the show with certain anticipations. The very first line of the prologue declares that one expectation at least the play shall not satisfy: "I come no more to make you laugh" (1), which is later expanded into

> they
> That come to hear a merry, bawdy play,
> A noise of targets, or to see a fellow
> In a long motley coat guarded with yellow,
> Will be deceived. (13-7)

The "merry, bawdy play" is generally believed to refer to other plays about Henry VIII, in particular Samuel Rowley's *When You See Me, You Know Me*, which is a comic rendition with a strong Protestant bias with considerable talk (if not play) of targets and a conspicuous fool in motley. As it was reprinted and very likely revived in 1613, the same year in

---

[4] Katherine's vision might be explained away as only a figment of her imagination or as a "real" (if distinctively Catholic) religious experience, while Prospero's magic, Apollo's oracle, Jupiter's tablet and Diana's epiphany take the audience unequivocally into the realm of the exotic.

which the King's Men's *Henry VIII* was probably first put on, presumably some, if not most, of the first audience at the Globe or Blackfriars would have been familiar with, or at least known of, Rowley's version. The prologue makes it clear from the start that if they come with the hope of seeing a similarly frivolous production, this play shall disappoint. Although here it is refusing one specific expectation, after watching the performance, one seems to be able to read in it the underlying message that other expectations about history, theatrical performance and/or literary genres ought also to be abandoned before the first act commences, and that the audience should respond to the play as it would make them, instead of according to their own preformed opinions about it: "Be sad *as we would make ye*" (Prologue 25, italics mine).

The problem with approaching a show—or anything, for that matter—with expectations is that, in most cases, such expectations stem from preformed opinions, which tend to greatly influence, if not determine, one's auditory or visual experience, further complicating the already hazardous process of communicating "truths". The section "Words and Truth" has quoted Wolsey's protest against "sick interpreters, once weak ones". He could be distinguishing between two kinds of interpreters here: the "sick" ones who deliberately distort facts to their advantage and the "weak" ones who do it unconsciously because they have not a sufficient grasp of the truth themselves. But although differing in intention, it might be said that both proceed by the same "method", which is to adapt facts to preconceived conclusions, rather than doing it the other way around, namely, judiciously reaching a conclusion on the evidence of the facts.

In the play, this threat to the smooth communication of truth is dramatised through a number of characters' questionable interpretations or accounts of their various experiences. Such episodes make the audience aware that there is often a difference between what one sees and what one thinks one sees, as what is happening on stage might be at variance with what a character says he/she believes to be happening. Again, it is the scene where Norfolk describes Wolsey's movements in 3.2 that provides the most striking demonstration of this discrepancy and its cause. As we have seen, it is very likely that Wolsey behaves in a way manifestly different from that which Norfolk describes. And in this case the cause of the deviation from fact is fairly evident: Norfolk's perception of the cardinal's movements is clearly influenced by his preconceived and misconceived opinion concerning the reason for the cardinal's apparent distress.

Theoretically, visual experience, because it is direct communication between a scene/object and its viewer, is subject to fewer rounds of information-sifting than verbal reports. Therefore the dramatisation of a character's reaction to visual information, compared with that of verbal communication, narrows down for the offstage audience the "suspects" responsible for the distortion of facts to three: it can be the creator of the scene, or the witness to the scene, or both. Wolsey's protest and Norfolk's description reveal that often, if distortion occurs at the "receiving end", preformed opinion concerning events related to the present sight is often the cause. If, on the other hand, it is deliberate manipulation of a tableau by the presenter that brings about the disparity between scene and interpretation, it might be argued that such deliberate manipulation succeeds because it feeds into conventional or pre-existing notions about movements, gestures or other forms of visual information. Therefore it seems reasonable to suppose that ultimately it is still preconceived opinions, expectations or conclusions about visual experience that bring about the failure of the communication of facts.

The scene of the three gentlemen commenting on Anne's coronation procession dramatises this point. Compared with the case in 3.2, it is a less straightforward example, for the discrepancy between sight and interpretation is not directly presented, nor is its cause simple and evident. In other words, on this occasion there is no immediate and definite contradiction to the gentlemen's remarks, nor does the play make it plain that they are under the influence of any preconceived opinion concerning the event or the new queen. Nevertheless, it is possible to see this episode as an illustration of the gap between interpretation of sight and sight itself, and, furthermore, between sight and truth. And it is possible to argue that preformed notions, if not entirely responsible, have their part to play in bringing about the discrepancies.

In contrast to their earlier commentary on political events, the gentlemen's observations in this scene are relatively objective, in that they tend to keep to "the pedantic reporting of details of protocol" (Leggatt 223), especially who is who in the procession. There are, nevertheless, a couple of comments on the new queen which are more than objectively descriptive. The Second Gentleman declares his gushing admiration on beholding Anne's beauty: "Thou hast the sweetest face I ever looked on. / Sir, as I have a soul, she is an *angel*" (4.1.43-4, italics mine). And the Third Gentleman is equally enthusiastic: "Believe me, sir, she is the *goodliest* woman" (4.1.71, italics mine).

Although the "angel" and the "goodliest" here describe more her physical beauty than her moral integrity, that the gentlemen should choose words which have moralistic connotations over the perhaps more superficial descriptors like "fair" or "beautiful" suggest that they may have formed a belief in, or at least an unconscious expectation of, Anne's moral righteousness. Yet history's verdict on this same woman was, as Shakespeare and his audience knew all too well, fiercely contested. Even if the allegations of adultery and immorality made against her at her trial and by Catholic polemicists thereafter are unjust, as they probably are, within the context of the play at least, morally Anne is represented as not entirely as angelic and "goodly" as the gentlemen take her appearance to reflect (her conversation with the Old Lady seems to be hinting at at least a degree of hypocrisy and calculation incompatible with angelic conduct). Of the three gentlemen, only the First displays an awareness of a possible mismatch between physical appearance and moral character, or between present fortune and future prospects. His observation, immediately snubbed by the Second, that some of the magnificently bejewelled countesses may in fact be falling stars might perhaps be looked on as the playwrights' footnote to the case of Anne.

Within the play there is no specific reference to any cause for this possible difference between the gentlemen's perception of Anne and her "real" character. These gentlemen, unlike Norfolk in 3.2, are not shown to have been equipped with extra-information concerning the new queen. What they have is the sight of Anne. It might thus be said that amongst other possible reasons for the Second and Third Gentlemen's unconscious choice of the words "angel" and "goodliest" in describing her is an almost intuitive association of outer beauty with inner grace, a fallacy which most, if not all, human beings are prone to, especially at first sight. In other words, the gentlemen's visual experience is formed under the influence of a notion which has existed before they are presented with the sight of Anne, resulting in the failure of the faithful transmission of the truth through visual display.

In not specifying that it is the Gentlemen, the "receiving end" of the scene, that are entirely responsible for the misinterpretation, the playwrights make it possible to approach the cause from the "issuing end" of the spectacle, namely, Anne herself. She may have deliberately exploited the impact of her beauty and gracefulness in order to generate exactly the sort of opinion voiced by the Second and Third Gentlemen. We are told that during the service in Westminster, Anne

> sat down
> To rest a while—some half an hour or so—
> In a rich chair of state, *opposing freely*
> *The beauty of her person to the people*. (4.1.67-70, italics mine)

The "freely" here is suggestive of her inviting the public gaze and also of her confidence in "the beauty of her person", no doubt improved by careful makeup and rich attire, in drawing admiration and approval which, as the gentlemen's comments show, may extend from her physical grace to her moral integrity. It is also worth noticing that the italicised lines are not information from the original sources. Holinshed's chronicles make no mention of Anne displaying herself to the spectators, only that she sat down in a stately chair. Another such improvised detail is the account of her "bow[ing]...to the people" (4.1.87), which seems a further revelation of purposeful manipulation of her spectators' visual experience, which again, as the Third Gentleman's choice of adjectives with moralistic connotations in describing the scene shows, has succeeded:

> At length her grace rose, and with *modest* paces
> Came to the altar, where she kneeled, and *saint-like*
> Cast her fair eyes to heaven, and prayed *devoutly*,
> Then rose again. (4.1.84-7, italics mine)

Again, it is possible to see that at the heart of all this lies the power of pre-existing views over the interpretation of visual information. A public ceremony, by its nature, derives its significance as a confirmation of power, legitimacy, etc. by feeding into preformed views on the manifestation of these abstract notions through strictly proceeding under the direction of established guidelines which prescribe forms, procedures, attires and movements. Anne's coronation is such an occasion in itself, while her attention to the display of her personal appeal on the occasion further exploits the psychology of the spectators. While the ceremony as a whole seeks to confirm royal splendour and her queenship, Anne, by deliberately conforming her appearance and movements to pre-existing views on the manifestation of virtue and grace, seeks to establish in her people a favourable first impression of her qualifications as a good queen.

Thus in the play, the scene of Norfolk misinterpreting Wolsey's movements provides a clear case of preformed judgement influencing one's visual experience. The royal procession and the reported coronation ceremony, on the other hand, offer a slightly more complex dramatisation of both the kind of subtle discrepancy which may exist between sight and perception of what one sees, and its possible causes. Ultimately, though, what lies at the root of the mis-transmission is, again, the problematic method of approaching a piece of visual information with a preformed or pre-informed mind. Through dramatising the mishaps which occur between what Anita Sherman terms "the activity of seeing and the activity of making sense of what one has seen" (126), the play demonstrates that visual experience, like verbal reports, can be subject to deliberate or unconscious manipulation that results in the imperfect communication of "truths".

The play's scepticism towards visual experience not only parallels its displayed suspicion of language, but also reinforces the general sense of distrust of historical process as well as of history itself, which its use and portrayal of verbal communication have raised. In the latter half of the drama, it is possible to detect in the characters a gradual, though slight, shift from almost complete dependence on verbal report to increased reliance on visual information as the basis upon which to make decisions. However, although the play offers no direct contradiction to the rationality of these decisions, their reliance on the problematic evidence of visual experience for authentication nevertheless raises a degree of doubt about their judiciousness, which might also extend to the historical personages who form them.

This shift towards greater demand for visual authentication becomes particularly noticeable during and after 3.2, the scene of Wolsey's fall from power. It is possible to detect from 3.2 onwards, and especially in Henry, an increased awareness of the need for first-hand verification in making political assessments, an awareness also reflected by his awakened suspicion of verbal communication. This is most manifest in the episode of Wolsey's fall, where during his "interrogation" of the cardinal, the king clearly distinguishes between words and truth, emphasising all the way through that Wolsey has *said* well and thus implying that he has not *done* well:

> You have said well.
> ...'Tis well said again,
> And 'tis a kind of good deed to say well—
> And yet words are no deeds. (3.2.150, 153-5)

> Fairly answered.
> A loyal and obedient subject is
> Therein illustrated. (3.2.180-2)

> 'Tis nobly spoken. (3.2.200)

That Wolsey's fall should become a dividing point in the play in terms of Henry's attitude towards verbal communication is not surprising. After all, in a court where information transmitted through language is the basis upon which important political decisions are made, Wolsey's crime is the first which is exposed and pinned down by direct physical evidence—his letter to Rome and inventory of wealth—rather than second-hand oral testimonies. Moreover, in *Henry VIII*, Wolsey stands for, amongst other things, skilful manipulation of language. His mastery with words has been remarked on by several characters. Norfolk, apart from describing the bewitching quality of his rhetoric as "[t]he honey of his language" (3.2.22), accuses him of

> div[ing] into the King's soul and there scatter[ing]
> Dangers, doubts, wringing of the conscience,
> Fears and despairs. (2.2.25-7)

Katherine says that his "words, / Domestics to [him], serve [his] will as't please" (2.4.111-2) and pronounces him "ever double / Both in his words and meaning" (4.2.38-9). It therefore has to be on the strength of solid visual evidence that Wolsey's guilt can be brought to light and confirmed, or else he, no doubt, would have been able to talk his way out of the situation, as he does when confronted on the matter of taxation. And the fall of Wolsey, who epitomises the height to which the power of language has attained, is thus symbolic of the start of the fall of language's power over the Henrician court.

It has to be pointed out that this is not to say that from 3.2 on Henry completely converts from reliance on verbal reports to confirmed scepticism of words. As we have seen, oral reports remain the major source of political information throughout. And Henry is, even until the end of the play, susceptible to the charm of language, taking great pleasure in Cranmer's prophecy of the future:

> Thou speakest wonders...
> O lord Archbishop,
> Thou hast made me now a man, (5.4.55, 63-4)

apparently not remembering his own verdict that "words are no deeds" this time. Nevertheless, one is able to detect in him, and those around him an increased emphasis, after the fall of Wolsey, on the visual rather than auditory experience as proof of fact.

It should also be noted that this emphasis on the visual after 3.2 does not mean that the characters have hitherto been overlooking visual information as an authentication. Indeed, in the first half, on several occasions descriptions of visual experience have been the key component of scenes of verbal exchange. The opening scene presents Norfolk in an attempt to verbally reconstruct the sight at the Field of the Cloth of Gold.

The court gentlemen's commentary on Buckingham's case consists of a careful description of the gradual changes of the duke's countenance during the trial. Wolsey listens to Cromwell's account of the king's physical reaction to the packet of letters sent to him. Henry himself is given a description of Wolsey's movements. It therefore might be said that visual experience has always been an element in the transmission of facts in the Henrician court.

Indeed, there is reason to believe that, much as the political figures rely on verbal information, the visual has always been looked upon as the preferred form of proof. This is most evident in Henry's interview with Buckingham's surveyor, where though the latter has quoted, seemingly verbatim, the duke's supposed words, what finally convinces the king of his crime is the account, not of Buckingham's words, but of his murderous posture:

> After "the Duke his father", with "the knife",
> He stretched him, and with one hand on his dagger,
> Another spread on's breast, mounting his eyes,
> He did discharge a horrible oath whose tenor
> Was, were he evil used, he would outgo
> His father by as much as a performance
> Does an irresolute purpose. (1.2.204-10)

The gist of this speech is in fact no different from what the surveyor has been saying all along: that Buckingham has his eye on the throne. What is different, and apparently looked upon by Henry as conclusive proof of treason, is that a vivid picture of that "treason" is sketched out. As Anston Bosman writes:

> Buckingham's knife is most fearsome when incorporated into the physical enactment of a regicide pledge. The sight of a body is assumed to reveal a truth that the sound of words cannot. (466)

what is finally damning in this piece of verbal evidence is the visual experience it offers.

Therefore, what becomes different after Wolsey's fall is not that visual proof is finally demanded, but that the definition of what counts as visual authentication is narrowed down. Previously, as the case of 1.2.204-10 demonstrates, visual experience in the mind's eye induced by oral sketch is valued as an embodiment of fact. In the latter half of the play, however, a suspicion of verbally-produced images is beginning to manifest. Direct visual experience becomes the only kind of evidence to be trusted when dealing with facts about the present and the past.

It is Wolsey himself who is the first to ask for solid visual information as an authentication of reported fact. He demands a written commission before he is willing to hand over the great seal: "Where's your commission, lords? Words cannot carry / Authority so weighty" (3.2.234-5). This forms a sharp contrast to Buckingham and Abergavenny's reaction to their arrest in 1.2. Both lords give themselves up without demanding to see the warrant. It is actually the arresting officer who later voluntarily produces one.

This emphasis on direct visual proof is also reflected in the decrease in subjective remarks without visual support in the nameless gentlemen's verbal exchanges. In both halves of the play there is one scene showing them engaged in political gossip, in the first half on the occasion of Buckingham's trial and in the second during Anne's coronation. The first contains a number of fairly subjective comments on the motive, character or personal qualities of political figures founded on hearsay or speculation, as for example when they judge that "[c]ertainly / The Cardinal is at the end of" (2.1.40-1) Buckingham's ruin, or that, again, it is because "the Cardinal" (2.1.161) wishes

> to revenge him on the Emperor
> For not bestowing on him at his asking
> The Archbishopric of Toledo (2.1.162-4)

that plans for the royal divorce are set. However, such comments are reduced to a minimum when they meet again. This time their conversation consists mainly of oral description of what they are witnessing or have witnessed, concentrating on the "technical" aspects of the occasion, such as the identity of the various royal personages in the procession or the coronation procedures in Westminster, generally refraining from drawing judgemental conclusions. They do, as we have seen, occasionally voice their opinion, but while such comments are perhaps unconsciously and almost unavoidably subjective, it has to be said that their initial concern is with what they are looking at, namely, Anne's appearance, rather than the cause or motive behind an event.[5] Indeed, these gentlemen seem not

---

[5] The one comment on the ceremony which clearly goes beyond the immediately visual is the First Gentleman's observation that the coroneted ladies in the procession are "sometime falling ones" (4.1.56). It is cut short by the Second's "No more of that" (ibid.). Of course, one should not over-interpret and conclude that the time between Buckingham's fall and Anne's rise has changed the Second

particularly interested in "the inner significance of the occasion itself" (Leggatt 223).

But the most obvious manifestation of this shift towards dependence on visual authentication is found in Henry. That it should be the king who has changed the most as a result of the exposure of Wolsey's crime is, again, not surprising. When Henry first appears, he enters *"leaning on Cardinal [Wolsey]'s shoulder"* (Stage Direction 2.1). If Wolsey can be looked on as the personification of the skilful manipulation of language, then Henry's posture here is symbolic of his blind faith in manipulated verbal communication. Wolsey's undoing, signalling the exposure and fall of the power of language, severely undermines that faith, resulting in a discernible change of the monarch's relied form of evidence.

Before 3.2, the three most climatic political decisions in the first half are made on the basis of oral reports. Henry rescinds the tax upon hearing Katherine's report of its terms and the grievances it caused. He and the law accept the verdict of Buckingham's guilt on the strength of the witnesses' oral testimonies. Even his decision to divorce Katherine, at least according to his account of the struggle of his conscience, is initially triggered by "certain speeches uttered / By th' Bishop of Bayonne" (2.4.168-9).

In contrast, in the latter half, attention is focused on visual authentication during the only directly-dramatised political manoeuvre in which Henry is involved, that of the prevention of Cranmer's ruination. In contrast to his attitude the Buckingham case, the king does not hurry to the verdict that Cranmer is "traitor to th'height" upon receiving "many grievous—I do say, my lord, / Grievous—complaints" (5.1.99-100) of him, but instead confirms that he is honest at the sight of his tears. Granted, other considerations may have contributed to this conclusion, but

---

Gentleman from the less-than-cautious commentator in Act 2 to the now reticent reporter of only visually-verifiable information. After all, the same gentleman, toward the end of the same scene, falls back into passing on judgements formed on second-hand information:

He of Winchester
Is held no great good lover of the Archbishop's,
The virtuous Cranmer. (4.1.105-7)

Possibly, he resists joining the First's speculation because he considers it not the best of occasions for the discussion. Nevertheless, if one looks beyond characterisation and compares the more descriptive nature of the exchanges in this scene in general with the more commentative streak in those of the earlier one, it seems not unreasonable to conclude that the gentlemen's behaviour is consistent with the second half's slightly increased emphasis on visually presented rather than verbally transmitted information as authentication of facts.

the way in which the play places Henry's verdict directly after Cranmer begins to weep leaves one with the impression that *the* finally conclusive piece of evidence for him is the visual impact of the archbishop's tears:

> Look, the good man weeps.
> He's honest, on mine honour. God's blest mother,
> I swear he is true-hearted, and a soul
> None better in my kingdom.
>   ...He has strangled
> His language in his tears. (5.1.153-6, 157-8)

Similarly, during the next scene's "trial", Henry's visual experience of the lords' slight of Cranmer at the door becomes his main argument for the archbishop's innocence:

> Was it discretion, lords, to let this man,
> This good man—few of you deserve that title—
> This honest man, wait like a lousy footboy
> At chamber door?
>   ... There's some of ye, I see,
> More out of malice than integrity,
> Would try him to the utmost, had ye mean;
> Which ye shall never have while I live. (5.2.171-4, 178-81)

Careful examination of Henry's speeches in this scene will reveal that he in fact offers no solid proof of Cranmer's integrity, nor does he directly rebut the charges made against the archbishop. But witnessing the lords' treatment of Cranmer provides him with a firmer ground for overruling the council's decision to try the archbishop as a traitor, for this visual information allows him to conclude with confidence that some of the lords' intention is malicious and their accusations thus invalid.

Doubt is, however, cast on the king's prudence in handling the case. The play does not plainly contradict his interpretation of these two sights, but it does make it abundantly clear that he approaches both scenes with firmly-held preformed convictions of their respective meanings. Quite a while before Cranmer starts to weep, Henry has voiced his opinion that

>   good Canterbury
> Thy truth and thy integrity is rooted
> In us, thy friend. (5.1.114-6)

It is also in the same scene—in other words, about half a scene ahead of the lords' contemptuous treatment of the archbishop—that he makes known his opinion concerning Cranmer's persecutors:

> Your enemies are many, and not small; their practices
> Must bear the same proportion, and not ever
> The justice and the truth o'th'question carries
> The due o'th'verdict with it. At what ease
> Might corrupt minds procure knaves as corrupt
> To swear against you? Such things have been done.
> You are potently opposed, and with a malice
> Of as great size. (5.1.129-36)

The same judgement is echoed in the next scene:

> There's some of ye, I see,
> More out of malice than integrity
> Would try him to the utmost, had ye mean. (5.2.178-80)

For someone approaching the sights with an unbiased mind, however, neither piece of evidence is enough to establish Cranmer's innocence. Cranmer may be, although granted it seems unlikely, feigning his tears. And even if they are sincere, they are most likely tears of, amongst other emotions, relief and gratitude. Yet there is no inherent connection between relief for one's escape from impending doom or gratitude for the prevention of this catastrophe and one's guiltlessness. Similarly, the lords' incivility to Cranmer, even if indeed done out of malice rather than, as the lords claim it, with the purpose of making it possible to try someone who, by his status as "a Councillor...no man dare accuse" (5.2.83-4), is still no proof of Cranmer's integrity and innocence. Viewed in this light, visual experience, for Henry, becomes rather a confirmation of his version of the truth rather than a reflection of the truth itself.

Norfolk and Suffolk, in discussing the king's contemplation of divorce, conclude that it is all Wolsey's doing and hope that "[t]he King will know him one day", or else "[h]e'll never know himself" (2.2.20, 21). Wolsey's fall has indeed made the king aware of the cardinal's true nature. And in becoming less dependent on verbally-transmitted intelligence and more demanding of immediate visual authentication, he is shown to have become more actively and directly involved in political manoeuvres. However, it remains questionable if this may count as "knowing oneself", or, indeed, knowing anything. Although the Henry of the second half certainly contrasts sharply with his former self, his approach to visual experience in the case of Cranmer still leaves one with doubts about his competence as a just ruler. Although his admonition in 5.1.129-36 in particular reveals a depth of political insight and wisdom unthinkable in the Henry interviewing Buckingham's surveyor, his approach to the sight of Cranmer's tears and the lords' incivility gives one the uneasy suspicion that he has simply gone from one undesirable extreme to another equally undesirable: from complete dependence on others' words to complete confidence in his own judgement, neither of which seems the best kind of government for the kingdom.

The volatility of visual experience means dependence on it makes the workings of history no less opaque. The sense of doubt and uncertainty clouding historical decisions and verdicts in *Henry VIII* brought about by the play's language, instead of being dispelled by the more frequent reliance on visual "evidence" in political assessments after Wolsey's fall, is in fact further consolidated. As long as one approaches a piece of visual information with a mind already more or less made up, it would seem that distortion of truth, to a greater or lesser degree, would inevitably occur.

As a matter of fact, my own reading of the gentlemen's comments on Anne's beauty, Henry's reaction to Cranmer's tears, or the play's use of visual experience can be easily accused of committing exactly what I am claiming the playwrights to be sceptical of: approaching the play with a preformed mind about its theme and significance, as well as fitting facts to opinion rather than the other way around. And it will not be easy for me to defend myself against such criticism, for although in coming to my conclusions, I have made an effort to be judicious, to extract meaning from the plot and dramatic arrangements instead of moulding them to my personal opinions about visual experience, I cannot deny that I am influenced by my sense of the play's general doubt about historical facts, a sense gained from its use and portrayal of verbal communication and my reading of previous scholarly opinions.

The catch here is that it is almost inconceivable that anyone can approach a piece of information, visual or verbal, without a degree of pre-existent background knowledge or opinion, for not only is it difficult for one's own mind to resist the influence of one's own mind, it would also be quite impossible to make sense of anything one is seeing without such stored knowledge. The gentlemen's "pedantic reporting of the details of protocol" concerning the coronation reflects a need for necessary background information of a ceremony to ensure a spectator's comprehension, and consequently full enjoyment, of the significance of the sight, which would otherwise merely be to the watchers one of gaily-clad people walking stiffly down the street. Similarly, an audience coming to the theatre to watch a play would need "certain skills in [them], as an audience, as to how to respond, appreciate and judge the performance" (Sutherland 34), gained through former personal or book-learnt experience about drama, in order to make sense of the sight of an actor on stage pretending to be someone else. It is therefore impossible to ask anyone in the position of a spectator to entirely suspend former knowledge when faced with a piece of visual or verbal information.

Ideally, of course, one would allow one's pre-gained knowledge to aid rather than manipulate interpretation and judgement, and be willing to adjust opinions to facts. While the latter can be achieved, the former is easier said than done, for in practice it is difficult to mark and observe the distinction between "aiding" and "manipulating". So in the end, it is possible to claim that an objective view of history is almost impossible. If *Henry VIII*'s use and portrayal of language demonstrate that our knowledge of history is problematic because we comprehend it largely through others' interpretations, its dramatisation of the nature and use of visual information in history shows that history is equally unsafe from our own interpretations.

The matter of preformed convictions influencing one's perception of facts thus seems to be a common factor which strings history and performance together in the dramatic experience of *Henry VIII*. History, as in the context of the plot, suffers from and exposes its influence, while performance sets out to challenge it by deliberately not meeting with spectators' likely expectations about genre, soliloquies and confessions, or the use of lavish theatrical display. But history and performance in the play are linked together by more than this. Indeed, it would not be too much to claim that the concepts of history and performance are more or less interchangeable here.

Henry VIII erodes the distinction between history and performance further than any other history play in the canon. The prologue, in fact, demands that the audience

> Think ye see
> The very persons of our noble story
> As they were living, (25-7)

in other words, to take the present performance of history as history itself, rather than as a performance. If one compares this prologue with that of *Henry V*, one can see that in *Henry VIII* the playwrights offer no apology, as Shakespeare does fully in the earlier play, for the insufficiencies of drama:

> But pardon, gentles all,
> The flat unraisèd spirits that hath dared
> On this unworthy scaffold to bring forth
> So great an object. (*Henry V*, Prologue 8-11)

Such apology—and there are at least ten more such lines in *Henry V*'s prologue—for the limitations of the stage draws attention to the distinction between history and the performance of history. *Henry VIII*, in contrast, "conflates 'true things' with their representation" (Kezar 16). The audience are asked to take history and performance as one and the same in the present case.

The play's extensive use of theatrical display is another way of blurring this line. In the first place, its many in-play performances and spectacles *are* history, in that they are resplendent events which did take place in history: the French and English encounter at the Field of the Cloth of Gold, Katherine's state trial, Anne's coronation procession and Elizabeth's christening. But in not dramatising their historically functional part, the play puts emphasis more on the events' nature as splendid dramatic displays rather than as historically significant moments. It is also worth noticing that the very first visual splendour which the play offers is Norfolk's rich verbal reconstruction of the sumptuous display of "earthly glory" (1.1.14) during the meeting between the English and French kings, which, as it turns out, is a "costly treaty" which "swallowed so much treasure and, like a glass / Did break i'th'rinsing" (1.1.165, 166-7), as "France hath flawed the league" (1.1.95). Not only is this (verbally reconstructed) sight the first of the dramatic spectacles the play offers, it is also the first subject it discusses. Thus in a way 1.1 sets the tone for the play's attitude towards history and dramatic performance, which is that often history is but a costly performance.

This sense of history as no more than a series of dramatic performances is also evident in the case of Katherine's trial, which, as Henry has taken pains to inform his councillors, should take place in Blackfriars, "[t]he most convenient place that I can think of / For such receipt of learning" (2.2.138-9). For Shakespeare and Fletcher's original audience, Blackfriars was both the historical location of the trial and the indoor theatre which the King's Men had recently begun to use. And for some of them, it was probably *the* theatre they were sitting in as the actor playing Henry announced where the trial would be held. What members of this first audience would be experiencing, then, was sitting in the historical site of the trial which was now a theatre, watching a performance of the trial, which the playwrights had asked them to take as real. History and performance meet and merge inside Blackfriars, as the audience, in following the prologue's advice to "think ye see the very persons of our noble story as they were living", became witnesses to both a dramatic performance and a historical moment.

Of course, this particular experience of history as performance and vice versa is rather exclusive to the Blackfriars audience. However, although the audience at the Globe—and we know for certain that *Henry VIII* was performed there—or modern readers and audiences cannot personally experience such a bizarre moment, their knowledge that the Blackfriars was a theatre at the time would have offered some semblance of that experience. Moreover, apart from the Blackfriars reference, the play blurs the line between past history and present performance in other ways which are not theatre-house-specific. Throughout, the audience are continually put in the same position as the historical characters in the plot. They are in the same position as Buckingham when Norfolk recounts the kings' meeting; as the onstage court gentlemen when Buckingham makes his last public speech, or when Anne passes by in regal splendour; or as Katherine when the dream vision occurs. In short, the play's many offerings of public ceremonies make the audience part of the crowd that gathers to watch these sights. On these occasions, the distinction between the onstage crowd and the offstage audience is minimum.

This similarity in situation between historical onlookers and present spectators is further enhanced by the fact that the latter are denied the privilege of hindsight, or, to be more accurate, although they know the verdicts of history, that knowledge is destabilised by the play's use of language and visual experience, so that they, like most of the onstage characters, are never sure of the facts and can only learn of political events and current affairs through the medium of verbal exchange. In this way, "[t]he play rewinds the clock to the moment before judgement has weighed in", transferring the audience from the present to the moment when "events feel new" (Sherman 126), thus making the experience of a performance of history the same as that of history itself.

As a result of such special treatment of history and performance, the two concepts become more or less interchangeable, so that in most cases what applies to history also applies to performance, and vice versa. Therefore, the play's defiance of generic or dramatic expectations might be looked on as suggesting that history may in fact vary greatly from one's interpretations of it or even from acknowledged conclusions about it. Similarly, the dramatisation of the mis-transmission of facts in history under the influence of preformed convictions may be taken as a way of demonstrating that experience of performance may suffer from the same, so that it is best to approach a play suspending previous knowledge or expectations about form, genre, dramatic arrangements and plot devices. Seen in this light, the purpose of the play's alternative title, *All Is True*, rather than to proclaim the truthfulness of this version of history, could be to signal the idea that all history is more or less constructed and that such construction problematizes the concept of historical truth.

In one respect at least, the playwrights seem to have succeeded—and succeeded within the space of the first act. *Henry VIII* appears to have successfully induced its first audience at the Globe to doubt their ability to perceive the distinction between reality and performance, so successfully in fact that it resulted in the burning down of the Globe. According to a contemporary account, during a performance there,

> King Henry making a masque at the Cardinal Wolsey's house, and certain chambers being shot off at his entry, some of the paper, or other stuff, wherewith one of them was stopped, did light on the thatch, where being thought at first but an idle smoke, and their eyes more attentive to the show, it kindled inwardly, and ran round like a train, consuming within less than an hour the whole house to the very grounds. (Wotton, qtd. in Chambers 344)

The fire was not immediately put out but allowed to kindle because it was first taken to be an idle smoke, or, even possibly some stage effect to boost the visual impact of the masque at York Place. For a while then, reality was taken to be performance. And for those who remember Prospero's "Our revels now are ended" speech in *The Tempest*, it is also a moment when reality conforms to performance. Prospero says solemnly in the production of a work of fiction that

> The cloud-capped towers, the gorgeous palaces,
> The solemn temples, *the great globe itself*,
> Yea, all which it inherit, shall dissolve, (4.1.152-4, italics mine)

—and the great Globe did dissolve. As it burnt down, then, acknowledged distinctions between the present and the past, history and performance, and reality and illusion seemed to be burning down as well.

The Globe fire, although an unfortunate incident in itself and for the audience on that day—one is glad to report, however, that two other contemporary accounts confirm that no one was seriously injured—as well as for the King's Men, seems somehow an appropriate result of a performance of *Henry VIII*, a play which sets out to challenge, if not destroy, established convictions about history, uproot confidence in language, and break out from the literary traditions of mode and genre, including Shakespeare's own pattern in his late plays. Now, with the Globe and all it stood for gone, there would be a new theatre, a new working routine and a new kind of play.

CHAPTER SIX

THE TWO NOBLE KINSMEN

Breaking the Form

Upon first inspection, *The Two Noble Kinsmen*, instead of a new sort of play, seems quite the reverse. It has, first of all, an old theme for a plot, the theme of the "ethics of friendship", which not only had countless authors worked on before, but Shakespeare himself had elaborated upon in several of his own plays, including his earliest work, *The Two Gentlemen of Verona*, whose title the present work seems to re-invoke. Moreover, this ancient theme is embodied in an ancient and familiar story, that of the Theban kinsmen Palamon and Arcite, which both Boccaccio and Chaucer had already presented in the form of narrative poetry. The latter's version is a canonical piece in Renaissance England and appears to have been the main source of the present play. As *The Knight's Tale* was "one of Chaucer's most popular poems" (Teramura 557) in Shakespeare and Fletcher's day, the original audience's familiarity with the cousins' story was probably the norm rather than the exception. Indeed, the play, rather unusual for a Renaissance drama and only the second time in the Shakespearean canon, explicitly foregrounds the source-text author himself, acknowledging Chaucer as the "noble breeder" (Prologue 10) of the story, and therefore, in a way, confirms that the tale is old.

Yet *The Two Noble Kinsmen* is not only old in the sense that its main plot is built on a medieval poem, but also in that it contains echoes of Shakespeare's own earlier works. In terms of genre, the authors, instead of following in the footsteps of *Henry VIII* and departing further from romance, seem to have gone back (with the play's "medieval source, pseudo-historical ancient Greek settings, emphasis on spectacle and ceremony" (Cohen 3204)) to the pattern used from *Pericles* to *The Tempest*. Similarly, in terms of dramatic arrangements, this play, particularly in the parts identified as Fletcher's, rather like *The Tempest*, continually recalls scenes or characters from Shakespeare's earlier works.

Adding to this feeling of "oldness" is the linguistic style of the Shakespearean parts. The verse seems frequently to arrest movement, "manifest[ing] little action and minimal character portrayal" (Bloom, *Invention* 694), so that it often creates two-dimensional tableaux rather than three-dimensional performances. This language also strikes some critics as being "fatigued" and in "the style of old age" with "an old man's imagery" (Spencer 257). It is the poetry of "a man who has come out on the other side of human experience" (264). In other words, Shakespeare's language here is doubly "old", for it appears both to make "[d]rama...[return] to its womb, and...once more become ritual" (263) and to reflect the weariness of old age. To sum up, then: in *The Two Noble Kinsmen*, the authors have apparently committed themselves to an old theme, an old plot, an old pattern, old dramatic sequences, and, on the part of the older playwright at least, a linguistic style which seems to be both old and of the old.

Closer examination, however, reveals that the "oldness" of *The Two Noble Kinsmen* is in fact the premise, as it were, of its "newness", for it is a play that, by deliberately situating itself within the confines of established forms, undermines and criticises from within the folly of an excessive adherence to the orthodox, and thus seeks to break away from its dictates. In terms of the plot, this version of the two noble kinsmen's conflict questions the rationality of organising one's life according to standard ways of behaviour. The linguistic style—the older playwright's "static" poetry and the younger's declamatory rhetoric—which results in the often criticised two-dimensional quality of the action and characterisation, is in fact an integral part of the construction and presentation of this critique. Furthermore, paralleling the plot's problematization of the idea of established authority, the play as a whole, despite its displayed deference to Chaucer and its professed fear of "let[t]ing fall the nobleness" (Prologue 15) of his poem, through subtle but daring deviation from *The Knight's Tale* in several crucial points, presents an adaptation so significantly different from its source text in tone and outlook that it can be looked on as a challenge to the literary authority of both Chaucer's original narrative and existent readings of it, which up until this time had without exception regarded the piece as "a 'noble tale'", with "virtually nobody consider[ing] Chaucer subversive or contestatory" (Herman 1). It is also these changes made to the original that mark the departure of this work, despite its outward commitment to the late Shakespearean dramatic pattern and its ample inclusion of romance elements, from the earlier last plays in the canon. Indeed, it seems to have gone so far that it has been "sometimes viewed as an antiromance" (Cohen 3204). The combined effort of the plot manoeuvres, the linguistic style and the dramatic arrangements of this version of the story of Palamon and Arcite thus makes *The Two Noble Kinsmen* a distinctly new play.

The play's concern with the authority of form and its tendency to break and challenge it are established as early as in the first scene. The centrality of form becomes clear as soon as the prologue ends, for the play proper opens with a splendid marriage procession. This arrangement is significant, for frequently though masque elements are employed in late Shakespeare, "in no other play does spectacle make such a bold statement before words are spoken" (Magnusson 376). The opening thus prepares the audience for a world of ceremonies and formalised actions. At the same time, however, the first scene also foregrounds the breaking of form, as "a pattern of disrupted rituals that continues through the play" (Potter, Introduction 2) is established when three queens in mourning waylay Theseus on his way to his wedding to demand his immediate action in defending their right, denied by King Creon of Thebes, to bury their dead husbands. Theseus' wedding is the first of a series of interrupted ceremonies in the course of the play, which include Palamon and Arcite's interrupted duel in Act 3, Arcite's interrupted triumphal procession, and Palamon's interrupted execution in the last scene. Stretching the definition of "ritual" and "ceremony" a little to include any form which sets standards to and thus restricts movement to a certain degree, and taking into consideration the highly mannered way in which some of the characters speak, one might also add to this list Palamon and Arcite's interrupted vow of eternal friendship in 2.1, Arcite's release and Palamon's escape from prison in Act 2, and even Emilia's finally frustrated determination against matrimony. Procedures which formalise and constrain actions by a prescribed form are thus consistently subject to disruption, beginning as early as in the very first scene of the play.

The first scene, while setting off the chain of disruptions to formalised procedures, at the same time establishes the primary importance of coded behaviour and the observance of established forms in the lives of the characters. Both the queens' request and Theseus' initial reluctance to grant their wish stem from their belief in the necessity of completing "the formalities". The queens' urgent appeal is that they be "give[n]...the bones / Of our dead kings that we may chapel them" (1.1.49-50). The emphasis of their speeches, as well as the elaboration of their grief, always falls on unobserved funeral rites. Of course, since the object of their speeches is to persuade Theseus to defend their right to "burn their bones, / To urn their ashes" (1.1.43-4), it is natural that they should stress "[w]hat griefs our beds, / That our dear lords have none" (1.1.140-1). Nevertheless, it is curious and worth noticing that little is said about their sentiments towards the loss of their husbands itself, as if their grief arises more from their inability to bury the dead than the fact of the deaths. The queens' emotions, it seems, are invested more in established forms than in individual persons. This is a tendency shared by many of the major characters. Indeed, the queens' apparent lack of emotional investment in individuals anticipates the "inadequacy of [Palamon and Arcite's] romantic response to Emilia" (Lief and Radel 412).

Theseus, like the queens, is equally insistent that social customs be observed. He considers the "sacred ceremony" to which he is going the "grand act of our life", "a service...[g]reater than any war" (1.1.131, 163, 170-1). At the same time, he professes that "[t]roubled I am" (1.1.76) to learn that Creon has forbidden the burial of the kings and promises that he will "give you comfort to give your dead lords graves" (1.1.148) after the marriage service has been performed. The arrangement, however, fails to satisfy the queens.

This conflict in 1.1 between the queens' demand for immediate action and Theseus' wish to complete the wedding ceremony first has often been interpreted by scholars—indeed, by the queens and Theseus themselves by the end of 1.1—as embodying "a conflict between duty and sexual temptation" (Hillman 72). At the same time, however, and perhaps primarily, considering that in this play the only person who can be said to have convincingly demonstrated a real sexual desire is the subplot's Jailer's Daughter, 1.1 presents a conflict between the observance of different sets of established (and therefore "right and proper") procedures, in this case between granting the dead a funeral and offering the betrothed a wedding (the conflict between the queens and Theseus), as well as between fulfilling the obligations of a bridegroom and those of a nobleman (Theseus' own internal conflict). And as each of these sets of procedures denotes a different aspect of the code of chivalrous conduct, or, as Theseus himself puts it, actions worthy of the "human title" (1.1.232), their untimely confrontation results in the dilemma of choice on the part of Theseus, whose own behaviour is governed by the code. It is a dilemma that will be repeated in Act 3, when Theseus becomes once more "frustrated, indeed all but helpless, in the face of absurdly conflicting noble gestures and motives" (Hillman 72).

Theseus' dilemma in 1.1 further reflects the primary importance which the characters attach to the observance of social customs, which in turn reflects, amongst other things, a self-consciousness of "living up to the occasion" (Potter, Introduction 2). By "living up to the occasion", Lois Potter here is referring to the queens' apparently uncanny awareness that "they [are] taking part in a tragedy" (ibid), reflected by their often grotesque language and melodramatic gestures. But "living up to the occasion" can also mean a general effort to construct and preserve a self-image that conforms to the standards of rigid ideals, which prescribe forms of behaviour to different occasions. 1.1, in fact, reveals and establishes that the society in the main plot is one dictated by such self-awareness of and attention to self-image. In most cases, a character is both acutely conscious of his or her own self-image and aware of the others' consciousness of their own respective self-images. Thus the queens, in their endeavours to persuade Theseus, apart from emphasising the indecency of unburied bodies, also approach him from the angle of his image as a man of action in the eyes of the world:

> Remember that your fame
> Knolls in the ear o'th'world: what you do quickly
> Is not done rashly; your first thought is more
> Than others' laboured meditance; your premeditating
> More than their actions. But, O Jove, your actions,
> Soon as they move, as ospreys do the fish,
> Subdue before they touch. (1.1.133-9)

Once he has given in, the queens express their gratitude again from the flattering perspective of how the world esteems, or shall esteem, him:

> FIRST QUEEN Thus dost thou still make good the tongue o'th' world.
> SECOND QUEEN And earn'st a deity equal with Mars—
> THIRD QUEEN If not above him, for
>   Thou being but mortal mak'st affections bend
>   To godlike honours; they themselves, some say,
>   Groan under such a mast'ry (1.1.225-30)

Theseus' response, which is also the conclusion of this scene, that

> As we are men,
> Thus should we do; being sensually subdued
> We lose our human title, (1.1.230-3)

reveals a regard for his reputation as one who lives up to his human title. It also "graciously absorbs the 'deity' thus earned into his humanity" (Hillman 72). This attention to self-image is also evident in the words of Hippolyta, who, when speaking for the queens' cause, impresses upon Theseus that her own reputation is at stake should he fail to grant the mourning widows their wish:

Did I not by th'abstaining of my joy,
Which breeds a deeper longing, cure their surfeit
That craves a present medicine, I should pluck
All ladies' scandal on me. (1.1.188-91)

Of all the characters who speak in the first scene (with the exception of Pirithous, who has fewer than three lines), only Emilia does not directly mention the subject of her or anyone else's reputation. But she does, in joining her sister and the queens in kneeling to Theseus, "threaten" him with "If you grant not [m]y sister her petition...henceforth I'll not...be so hardy [e]ver to take a husband" (1.1.199-200, 202-4). In declaring that should he refuse the request, she would then not consider marriage—an established social institution then regarded as the customary state of existence for women who had reached a certain age—Emilia is threatening not to live up to the orthodox social form, which is a gesture that would, one imagines, result in a certain degree of damage to her own reputation as well as that of Theseus, who, through marriage to Hippolyta, is related to Emilia. Thus, in short, 1.1 demonstrates the almost manipulative power which the concern for a self-image that conforms to social protocol has over the characters.

Such close adherence to form- and occasion-fitting behaviour and attention to self-image often result in a role-playing-like quality in the actions and words of the characters. In 1.1, as elsewhere, this is particularly manifested in the style of the language in which they, the queens especially, speak. These ladies, suiting the solemnity and formality of their tone to what they perceive as their tragic role, speak in a manner "curiously stylized, both strange and over-ornate" (Magnusson 377). Yet the very elaborateness of their speeches speaks against the sincerity of the grief they express, for in real life, grief tends, it would seem, to make a person taciturn. Whether this applies to all is of course hard to say. And as Shakespeare's *is* a rhetorical theatre reliant upon a language that is generally "artificial" in structure, lexis and tone, certain allowances must be made for a considerable lack of naturalism, as it were, in a character's expressed reaction to any situation. Indeed, the young Shakespeare was quite prepared to offer highly formal, artificial expressions of grief in his early works. Titus' speech (3.1.91-113, "It was my dear, and he that wounded her / Hath hurt me more than had he killed me dead...") upon the discovery of the maimed Lavinia in *Titus Andronicus* is markedly formal and rhetorical, as is that of the solider who discovers that he has killed his father in *3 Henry VI* (2.5.61-72, "It is my father's face / Whom in this conflict I, unawares, have killed..."). However, as his technique matured, Shakespeare moved towards a sparer style in the tragedies, in which the majority of his most heart-rendering lines at grievous moments, such as Lear's "Never, never, never, never, never!" (*Lear* 5.3.307) in reaction to Cordelia's death, or Macduff's "All my pretty ones?" (*Macbeth* 4.3.217) on hearing of the murder of his wife and children, are marked by, as Maurice Charney puts it, "an avoidance of eloquence at heightened moments" (332). This toning down of oratory in the face of woe his late style has inherited, despite the fact that in other respects it shows a general tendency towards a return to the early plays' "flaunting" of technique. Leontes, upon receiving the news of Mamillius' death, can only manage "Apollo's angry, and the heavens themselves / Do strike at my injustice" (*Winter's* 3.2.144-5), while Hermione faints straightaway. Alonso's despair for the loss of his son is manifested in his "Prithee, peace"s. He hardly says anything else in the entire scene (*The Tempest* 2.1). And Pericles abandons speech altogether after learning about the "death" of Marina. Thus, the three queens' eloquently expressed grief here stands out from the late-play group, arousing a listener's suspicion over how much true sorrow it contains.

The Second Queen's plea to Hippolyta provides an illustrative example of the queens' style:

> Honoured Hippolyta,
> Most dreaded Amazonian, that hast slain
> The scythe-tusked boar, that with thy arm, as strong
> As it is white, wast near to make the male
> To thy sex captive, but that this, thy lord—
> Born to uphold creation in the honour
> First nature styled it in—shrunk thee into
> The bound thou wast o'erflowing, at once subduing
> Thy force and thy affection; soldieress,
> That equally canst poise sternness with pity,
> Whom now I know hast much more power on him
> Than ever he had on thee, who ow'st his strength,
> And his love too, who is a servant for
> The tenor of thy speech; dear glass of ladies,
> Bid him that we, whom flaming war doth scorch,
> Under the shadow of his sword may cool us.
> Require him he advance it o'er our heads.
> Speak't in a woman's key, like such a woman
> As any of us three. Weep ere you fail.
> Lend us a knee:
> But touch the ground for us no longer time
> Than a dove's motion when the head's plucked off.
> Tell him, if he i'th'blood-sized field lay swoll'n,
> Showing the sun his teeth, grinning at the moon,
> What you would do. (1.1.77-101)

This "outlandish" (McDonald, *Late* 154) passage starts with a breathtaking first sentence which stretches across sixteen lines (ll. 77-92). Indeed, in some editions, *The Riverside Shakespeare* for instance, the whole passage is presented as one single sentence. The actual request— "Bid him...Require him...Speak't...Lend us a knee...Tell him...what you would do"—is delayed as long as possible as the speech meanders through "that" and "who" and "whom" clauses. However, although the first sixteen lines invariably run over and the passage is abound with digressions, repetitions, ellipses and parentheses, all of which seem to suggest disorder of thought, the Second Queen's speech is in fact well controlled, the grammar never astray, the semantic unit always completed, and the request, though delayed, forcibly uttered. Moreover, the force of the request is built upon the strength of the apparently digressive argument about Hippolyta's power over the male sex in general and Theseus in particular. In other words, the passage, though outlandish in its daunting sixteen-line first sentence, is in fact a tightly organised and logical unit.

The complexity of the syntax and the articulacy of the passage combine to make the speech more like a rehearsed performance. As it is a petition to a duchess, it is of course possible that the argument has been planned beforehand and deliberately formalised. Nevertheless, it is striking that coming from a widow, the ultimate strength of whose request rests upon her proclaimed injury and grief, the passage seems peculiarly untinged with personal feelings. It bespeaks a coolly logical mind and strategic rhetorical skills rather than deep-felt grief or outrage, for few in the throes of passions are capable of manoeuvring smoothly back to the main argument after drifting through a profusion of digressive subordinate clauses, let alone organising such clauses to add force to his or her point. One would only need to contrast this passage with Leontes' "Affection" speech or even Queen Katherine's trial speeches in *Henry VIII*, to perceive its lack of spontaneity and relative freedom from the interference of personal feelings. Rather than strangling her language with her tears, as Cranmer does in *Henry VIII* when he gets emotional, the Second Queen seems to have strangled her tears with her language to coolly give

> a performance, a structural tour-de-force, a kind of litany unresolved until the long-delayed arrival of the final noun clause that serves as the direct object. (McDonald, *Late* 155)

This speech is also typical of the "clotted rhetoric" (Spencer 257) of Shakespeare's poetry in *The Two Noble Kinsmen*—clotted not merely in the sense that he employs convoluted syntax or complicated expressions which are a mouthful, but more in that action or thought is stayed, instead of advanced, over the length of lines. In the passage above, it is not until fifteen lines into the speech that the subject finally begins to move from the description of Hippolyta's power to the suggestion that she use it in aid of the queens. The subordinate clauses led by "that", "who" and "whom" thus elaborate repeatedly and continuously upon the same point, with the result that they come across as piled upon one another instead of developed from one to another, finally building up a sentence that feels stagnant and over-ornate, "finished with action" (ibid.), as Theodore Spencer puts it.

It should perhaps be mentioned here that in the Fletcherian parts, particularly when he is having the kinsmen utter lofty ideals, this kind of repeated elaboration on the same idea also exists in profusion. Indeed, as repetition is "[t]he chief element in the rhetorical style of John Fletcher's plays" (Hoy 99), it seems not surprising that re-elaboration of thought should also frequently appear in his verses. Arcite's prison speech in 2.2, for example, amply contains such re-embellishments:

> Let's think this prison holy sanctuary,
> To keep us from corruption of worse men.
> ...And here being thus together
> We are an endless mine to one another:
> We are one another's wife, ever begetting
> New births of love; we are father, friends, acquaintances;
> We are in one another, families—
> I am your heir, and you are mine; this place
> Is our inheritance: no hard oppressor
> Dare take this from us. (2.2.71-2, 78-85)

Like the Second Queen's elaboration on Hippolyta's power, Arcite's lines here are essentially different ways of saying the same thing (that we are blessed to be locked up here together). But unlike Shakespeare's Queen, Fletcher's Arcite makes his point at the beginning of the speech instead of delaying it until the end. In other words, Arcite comes up with an idea and then develops it, while the Queen first develops a line of thought that seems to sidetrack but in fact prepares the way for and adds strength to the main argument of her speech. Thus compared, Fletcher's Arcite's language leaves less of an impression of pre-meditated rhetorical control—thus less of a sense of rehearsed role-playing—and more of thoughts being developed on the spot. Moreover, with the main argument presented at the beginning, the sense of stagnancy which infuses the poetry in the Shakespearean parts is greatly reduced, for the arrangement leaves the listener with the impression that the main argument is being further modified and qualified, while with Shakespeare, before the final clause is uttered, one often dreads that the speaker is going nowhere.

Compared with Fletcher's mostly end-stopped, easy-flowing sentences, Shakespeare's often develop with, to quote Spencer, an "adagio rhythm, haunting, invocatory, spoken, as it were, behind a veil" (260). This elaborate, digressive yet controlled style which makes the speaker sound a bit removed from his or her expected emotional response to a situation is found throughout the Shakespearean parts, as for example when Pirithous recounts Arcite's riding accident or when Palamon prays to Venus. While Spencer believes that this poetic style reflects its writer's old age, in which he, losing interest, "half automatically" (263) puts brilliant but tired and hardly emotional poetry into the mouths of his characters, I am more inclined to see it as a strategic stylistic contribution to the illustration of how consideration of form-fitting behaviour has manipulated the characters to the extent that when they speak and act, they sound and look as if they are giving a performance according to what they believe form expects from them on the occasion. Their language, often having "the tone of a looker-on, not a participant" (260), bespeaks not only a self-suppression of personal feelings, but also perhaps a total absence of unregulated feelings in the first place, which further reflects the horrific power which form has over them.

But, to return to the queens in 1.1: the other two queens, though their sentences are perhaps less convoluted in syntax, communicate in the same well-controlled and statically formal speeches as the Second. Moreover, their speeches contain a profusion of imagery which, though at first glance it seems to hark back to the linguistic method of Shakespeare's tragedies, upon closer inspection demonstrates greater adherence to "the far-fetched conceits that occasionally decorate the courtier language in *Cymbeline* and *The Winter's Tale*" (Magnusson 377). For example, the Third Queen's "strained expression", writes A. Lynne Magnusson,

> of her "heart-deep" sorrow—"he that will fish / For my least minnow, let him lead his line / To catch one at my heart" (I.i.115-17)—recalls the odd contrivance of a courtier's pretty sentiment in *The Winter's Tale*: Perdita's woe "angled for [his] eyes, caught the water though not the fish". (ibid.)

As a result of this laboured use of imagery, and together with their often tortuous but articulate sentences, despite the repeated declarations of their "hot grief" (1.1.107), the three queens' eloquently expressed sorrow has a suspicious taste of play-acting. It is as if they, recognising that their role in the first scene is that of the helpless victims of tyranny, have duly put up a self-conscious performance as such. The antiphonal pattern of the delivery of their plea, enhanced by the antiphonal (as it were) pattern of their kneeling and rising, adds to this sense of staged theatricality. The characters' tendency to "play the part" in a given situation will, as the play unfolds, and as I shall endeavour to demonstrate later, become the ultimate cause of the lamentable but at the same time ridiculous tragedy of the two noble kinsmen. The ridiculousness of the practice, indeed, has already begun to show in 1.1. For one thing, the scene has demonstrated that noble gestures and motives can become, as Richard Hillman puts it in the description quoted earlier, "absurdly conflicting", with the result that observance of one set of coded behaviour is achieved only by rudely disregarding another set. Stubbornly determined to fulfil their husbands' funeral rites, the queens break up a marriage service. Moreover, to make sure that the dead kings should have their proper burial, the widows urge Theseus—and he also considers it necessary—to go to war with Creon, which would, however, as none in the first scene seems to have considered, result in innocent deaths and, presumably, more bodies that will "i'th'blood-sized filed lay swollen / Showing the sun [their] teeth, grinning at the moon". Chaucer's Knight tells of how Theseus

> With Creon, which that was of Thebes kyng
> ...faught, and slough hym manly as a knyght
> In pleyn bataille, and putte the folk to flyght;
> And by assaut he wan the citee after,
> And rente adoun bothe wall and sparre and rafter. (986-90)

He also relates that

> To ransake in the taas of bodyes dede,
> Hem for to strepe of harneys and of wede,
> The pilours diden bisynesse and cure
> After the bataille and disconfiture. (1005-8)

And although the playwrights in their version do not directly dramatise the war, the Herald's description in 1.4 of Palamon and Arcite as "not dead...[n]or in a state of life" (1.4.24-5) allows a glimpse into the gory consequences of war as a destroyer rather than rectification of form, be it "wall", "sparre", "rafter" or human life. The ridiculousness of the situation lies not merely in the fact that in making sure that the dead are properly honoured, the queens completely overlook the living (including Theseus and Hippolyta, the Athenian soldiers, their Theban counterparts, and the citizens of Thebes), but more in the fact that their insistence on the observation of a set of protocols completely defeats the object of prescribing forms to actions in the first place, which is to ensure, through the regulation of individual behaviour in individual events, order in and stability of society. In 1.1, deference to form, instead of establishing order, generates disorder, while attentiveness to prescribed forms of action which in theory should reflect goodness of heart, nobility of mind and righteousness of cause only denotes selfishness and lack of human feeling.

1.1, apart from problematizing the idea of form and its observance, also presents a challenge to authority. In terms of storyline, it is a scene in which Theseus' authority as a man and as the head of state is challenged by women,[1] as his decision and command that the wedding be carried through, which is not wrong in principle, are resisted and eventually overturned by the queens and the Amazons. As mentioned earlier, this is not the only time in the play that Theseus' authority meets with (albeit gentle) confrontation. And it is through the dramatisation of these oppositions that his reliability as a ruler is put under suspicion.

More significantly, however, in terms of dramatic composition, 1.1 is a deviation from its source and thus presents a challenge to the authority of the original author and text. In *The Knight's Tale*, Theseus and Hippolyta have already been married when the queens approach them. Chaucer's Theseus has demonstrated none of the hesitation and reluctance that Theseus here has shown, but instead,

> right anoon, withouten moore abood
> His baner he desplayeth, and forth rood
> To Thebes-ward. (965-7)

While the later Theseus' reluctance is, in a way, the natural consequence of the ill timing of the queens' request, it is also an indication of the changes the playwrights have made to his character.[2]

---

[1] Two of whom, Hippolyta and Emilia, are in fact "less than subjects in Theseus's dukedom" but rather "captives...lives to be disposed of by decrees" (Shannon 666).
[2] It is perhaps worth recalling that the Theseus at the beginning of *A Midsummer Night's Dream* shares the same situation in being on the brink of marriage. In that play, he is outspoken about his frustrated sexual passion for Hippolyta, reproaching the moon for "linger[ing] my desires" (1.1.4). It is thus not unreasonable to believe that Theseus' sexual impatience has always been for Shakespeare an important part of his characterisation, a feature which *The Knight's Tale* does not portray. This apparent consistency of his characterisation between *A Midsummer Night's Dream* and *The Two Noble Kinsmen* is another instance of Shakespeare following his own designs rather than those of his source materials in adapting the old tale for the stage. Incidentally, this could also be a case of authorial cross-referencing: *A Midsummer Night's Dream*'s Theseus offers insight

These changes made to Chaucer's tale will have important and serious consequences for subsequent events in the play. In 1.1, the rearranged timing of the queens' approach and the changed character of Theseus mean that the dramatic sequence of women kneeling in plea to the duke, whose counterpart in this section of Chaucer's poem is only a brief sentence "ther kneled in the heighe weye / A compaignye of ladyes" (897-8), is greatly embellished and highlighted. These new arrangements heighten dramatic tension in the opening scene. Indeed, they have introduced into the old story new conflicts and, more importantly, signalled that the root of the tragedy of the two noble kinsmen is being relocated from the devastating power of love to the destructive power of strict observance of form. By thus considerably revising Chaucer's narrative right at the beginning of the play proper, the playwrights— perhaps Shakespeare in particular, as the first act is generally recognised as his—are posing themselves as challengers to the authority of the canonised text of a canonised author as well as that of conventional interpretations of a canonical piece, a gesture which is, in a manner of speaking, a kind of form-breaking as well.

Right from the start of *The Two Noble Kinsmen*, then, the playwrights have made their agenda clear: this is a play which problematizes the idea of form and authority through significantly rewriting Chaucer's *Knight's Tale*. The present play evolves around apparently momentous but at the same time ridiculous, even trivial, conflicts of form. The characters are excessively aware of their self-image, allowing their actions to be dictated by prescribed forms and forcing their language to rise to what they perceive as the formal demands of the occasion, so much so that what they speak and do often comes across as the outcome of compulsive role-playing rather than the expression of truly human feelings or desires. It is into such a world that the audience are led. And it is in such a world that they will meet with Palamon and Arcite, the two noble kinsmen in the title.

Unlike in *The Knight's Tale*, where the reader first makes the two noble kinsmen's acquaintance after Theseus' raid on Thebes, when they "[t]hurgh-girt with many a grevous blody wounde" are "liggynge by and by" (1010, 1011) in a pile of the dead and wounded, in the present version Palamon and Arcite make their first appearance before the news of the battle has reached Thebes. Moreover, they are assigned an extensive conversation before they are called to action. This scene establishes and

---

into *The Two Noble Kinsmen*'s less outspoken character's internal struggle, while the interrupted and delayed marriage in the later play adds a further cause for the earlier Theseus' eagerness for his nuptial.

makes clear that they are upholders of the code of chivalry. Again, like the characters in 1.1, through the affectedness of their conversation, which, as Potter observes, "keeps drifting away from its apparent subject into generalized and irrelevant social satire" (Introduction 3), they reveal a self-consciousness about living up to the expectations of their roles as virtuous knights in a corrupted world. Their discontent with Creon's regime is expressed in terms of its disruption of the laws of chivalry, in particular the martial aspects of the chivalric code:

> Scars and bare weeds
> The gain o'th'martialist who did propound
> To his bold ends honour and golden ingots,
> Which though he won, he had not; and now flirted
> By peace for whom he fought. (1.2.15-9)

> Yes, I pity
> Decays where'er I find them, but such most
> That, sweating in honourable toil,
> Are paid with ice to cool 'em. (1.2.31-4)

Their strict subscription to the rule of chivalry also means that, despite their expressed contempt for Creon and the condition in Thebes, when called on to defend the city they are equally ready to offer their service and lives: "let us follow / The beckoning of our chance" (1.2.115-6). They will, as Theseus' account later reveals, fight with all their might and "[l]ike to a pair of lions smeared with prey, / Make lanes in troops aghast" (1.4.18-9).

Thus in the space of 1.2 alone, the audience are witness to Palamon and Arcite in their roles first as discontented and critical young men and then as loyal soldiers, as they suit their actions and speeches to the formal requirements of the occasions. It is a pattern of behaviour that will be sustained throughout the play, as they switch from the role of forlorn prisoners—for whom, incidentally, Thebes is no longer the city of "strange ruins" (1.2.13) but their "noble country" (2.2.6)—to that of models of cheerful acceptance of fate and of male bonding, enraptured lovers, bitter enemies, good kinsmen, courteous opponents, merciless rivals, and finally, reconciled friends and cousins, all put on with an apparent chameleon-like swiftness which renders them slightly absurd.

It should be mentioned that Palamon and Arcite's excessive role-playing has often been put down by critics and scholars, rather disparagingly, as typical Fletcherian "fragmentation [of plot and characters] into self-contained effects...that characterizes many of his collaborations with Beaumont" (Magnusson 389). Fletcher's characters, as Eugene Waith identifies, are "[p]rotean characters...who belong to a world of theatrical contrivance...living in abstractions and combinations of irreconcilable extremes" (38). However, while the two knights in the Shakespearean scenes are perhaps not as manifestly volatile under the older playwright's subtler segueing as they are under Fletcher's treatment, they nevertheless show themselves to be equally capable of fairly different and rather contradictory modes of behaviour in the space of a single scene, as for example Arcite's switch from ecstatically singing Emilia's praises (3.1.1-16) to complacently congratulating his own good luck (3.1.16-23), gloating over Palamon's misfortune (3.1.23-31), warmly greeting him (3.1.44), indignantly declaring him an enemy (3.1.46-54), challenging him to a duel (3.1.54-8), nobly promising to bring him nourishment and clothing (3.1.82-90), and again, warmly encouraging him to "[t]ake comfort and be strong" (3.1.101). Moreover, the same self-centred streak in the cousins found in Fletcher's scenes is also evident in Shakespeare's parts, in particular the prayer scenes, which "become virtual emblems of narcissism" (Hillman 71). Thus, while one cannot know for certain whether Fletcher's portrayal of the two is the result of design or unconscious habit, it, like his inflated rhetoric in *Henry VIII*, incorporates well into the general pattern of characterisation and is integral to the play's central concern with form.

Like the queens and Theseus in 1.1, Palamon and Arcite's role-playing is driven by their excessive concern for the cultivation of self-image, which results in a self-centeredness clothed in chivalric pursuits but often betrayed by the note of self-love in their language. Their exchange in prison about the value of their friendship, for example, is spoken in a way "a bit too self-conscious (and absurd) to be seen as anything more than posturing" (Lief and Radel 411). Furthermore, for all its expressions of spiritual loftiness and nobility, the exchange concludes in an almost smugly self-congratulatory note:

> PALAMON Is there record of any two that loved
>   Better than we do, Arcite?
> ARCITE   Sure there cannot. (2.2.112-3)

Not giving the audience the chance to miss the smell of conceit, five lines later, when Emilia comes to the garden, Fletcher has her eyes fall first on a narcissus (or possibly a host of them), which leads to a comment on the flower's origin in Greek mythology:

> EMILIA What flower is this?
> WOMAN   'Tis called narcissus, madam.

EMILIA   That was a fair boy, certain, but a fool
         To love himself. Were there not maids enough? (2.2.119-21)

While part of the function of this exchange, to judge from the last sentence, is to bring out the irony of the situation in which two men who have just spoken eloquently on the benefits of not getting involved with women will be falling—indeed, are already falling—in love with a maid, it is worth remembering that Emilia has previously professed a firm preference for same-sex companionship, therefore her own censure probably falls not on the exclusion of the society of the other sex, but on self-love. It is also worth recalling that Narcissus' self-love is literally for his own image and that he dies for it. Excessive devotion to self-image is thus highlighted and criticised, directly after the kinsmen's self-image-conscious speech about their noble existence in their prison-cell sanctuary.

The self-centeredness of the cousins becomes even more manifest when they start to quarrel about their love for Emilia. Indeed—if one might digress a little here—saying that their argument is about their *love* for the lady is allowing them too much credit for an adequate emotional response to her. Their expression of love throughout the play is unconvincing, for neither in this nor in other scenes do they have much to say about Emilia that is not commonplace. Compared with the other young heroes in love—Posthumus, Florizel, Ferdinand, even Pericles in the Wilkinsian scenes—in the last-plays group, Palamon and Arcite's praises of their lady rarely go beyond her physical beauty and are mostly confined to clichéd generalities such as "a goddess", "a rare one" and "a matchless beauty" (2.2.134, 154, 155), which seem particularly limp coming from a pair who have fully demonstrated their rhetorical capacities in their former speeches on corruption and their visions of friendship. Their reticence, of course, could be the stunned reaction to the experience of love at first sight, except that praises for the woman they love are even rarer in subsequent scenes. Moreover, their lack of poetic invention on the subject is evident not only in the Fletcherian scenes, but in the Shakespearean parts as well. Indeed, in his scenes, except for one instance, 3.1.4-14 ("O, Queen Emilia, / Fresher than May...") when Arcite, alone, praises Emilia in a passage developed from Chaucer's Knight's description of Emelye (1035-9, "Emely, that fairer was to sene / Than is the lylie..."), which is, one must admit, rich in poetic imagery, there is hardly a complete line about Emilia from the two. This dramatic arrangement further reduces Chaucer's original design, where the cousins at least have slightly more elaborate things to say on first beholding Emelye's beauty: (Palamon) "But I was hurt right now thurghout myn ye / Into myn herte, that wol my bane be" (1096-7) and (Arcite) "The fresshe beautee sleeth me sodeynly / Of hire that rometh in the yonder place" (1118-9). Furthermore, in Chaucer, their deficiency in romantic verbal expression is made up by their constancy, as both pine away owing to their love for Emelye, Arcite in Thebes for two years and Palamon in prison for seven. In Fletcher and Shakespeare's version, however, there is no great span of time nor long sufferings to demonstrate the centrality of the love for Emilia in their lives.

Any hope, or suspicion, that under the cousins' clichéd praise of Emilia hides a passionate love which words are inadequate to express is dispelled once they begin to quarrel in 2.2. It quickly becomes clear that love for Emilia is in fact not the centre of their argument. The focus of their dispute, as of their lives, is always themselves. In quarrelling over the right to love, their emphasis falls not on love, but on the idea of personal right of possession.

> PALAMON   You shall not love at all.
> ARCITE Not love at all—who shall deny me?
> PALAMON I that first saw her, I that took possession
>   First with mine eye of all those beauties
>   In her revealed to mankind. If thou lov'st her,
>   Or entertain'st a hope to blast my wishes,
>   Thou art a traitor, Arcite, and a fellow
>   False as thy title to her...
> ARCITE I love her, and in loving her maintain
>   I am as worthy and as free a lover,
>   And have as just a title to her beauty,
>   As any Palamon, or any living
>   That is a man's son. (2.2.168-75, 182-6)

In this debate, the lady sounds more like a commodity than a living human being. The exchange reveals that both view love more in terms of an inviolable personal right than an emotional engagement with another person. In other words, self rather than the loved one is the dominant consideration, manifested in the reiterated "I"s and "my"s in their language. It is therefore not surprising that by the end of this quarrel, professions of love are dropped altogether, replaced by verbal abuse of each other:

> PALAMON Thou art baser in it than a cutpurse.
>   Put but thy head out of this window more
>   And, as I have a soul, I'll nail thy life to't.
> ARCITE Thou dar'st not, fool; thou canst not; thou art feeble.
>   Put my head out? I'll throw my body out
>   And leap the garden when I see her next,
>   And pitch between her arms to anger thee. (2.2.215-21)

Arcite's last remark also makes one suspect that the two are in fact rather enjoying this verbal combat and have put themselves in character, so to speak, for the parts of opponents in an argument. A few lines before, Arcite points out that Palamon is "play[ing] the child extremely" (2.2.208). While he probably does not use the word "play" in its theatrical sense, the manifest childishness of his own last remark seems to suggest that he has also fitted himself into the role which their immediate situation—the play *The Two Quarrelling Kinsmen*, as it were—demands: another unreasonable child. The object of this dispute has thus changed from claiming the right to love Emilia to inciting each other's anger, a switch of emphasis that would, unless one of the parties begins to act reasonably, in theory provoke an endless round of verbal and possibly even physical conflict, which is indeed what comes to pass in the rest of the play before the last-minute deathbed reconciliation in the final scene. Their claim of love for Emilia has become merely a topic that helps fuel their dispute. They seem to be disputing for the sake of disputing.

As in their initial stage appearance, during their second in 2.2, the cousins swiftly change from one role to another radically different, within the space of a single scene. They start out as "one another's wife, ever begetting / New births of love", then turn into infatuated lovers, and finally become bitter rivals and unyielding defenders of their own rights. Their actions can be said to fall within the prescribed form of behaviour of respective aspects of the code of chivalric honour: in respect to a knight's treatment of his friend, partner and equal, of his lady, and of his enemies. The cousins' subsequent actions—Arcite's service in Theseus' court, the cousins' encounter in the woods, their genial conversation and affectionate arming of each other before their duel, etc.—can also be said to fall roughly within these three categories of knightly conduct. However, their lack of emotional engagement with Emilia as a person rather than a concept and their brisk back-and-forth switch of role from friends to enemies in response to the demands of their situations bespeak a rigid subscription to the superficial forms of knightly conduct without a sufficient grasp of the chivalric spirit of "*prouess, loyauté, largesse... courtoise,* and *franchise*" (Keen 2). Instead, their actions throughout are essentially self-centeredness, albeit clothed in knightly actions, words and ceremonies.

I have repeatedly described the heart of the kinsmen's conduct as selfish or self-centred. Unlike the usual kind of selfishness, however, theirs is a self-centredness tied specifically to the idea of honour (or "self-image"), attained and preserved by conforming their actions to the rules of knightly conduct. It is a self-centredness underlined, paradoxically perhaps, by a lack of self-interest—or, to be more accurate, a lack of self-comprehension about desire, for Palamon and Arcite's role-playing leaves one with the suspicion that they probably do not, and do not know that they do not, care for each other as much as they profess, or hate each other as much as they vow, or love Emilia as much as they think they do. Their strict observance of the prescribed forms of conduct seems to have clouded their understanding of their own feelings or true wishes.

The story of the two kinsmen in this way becomes a story about "much ado about nothing", in the sense that it is a play whose protagonists abide by form without understanding its purpose. Furthermore, it is a tragedy in which, where the human feelings of the protagonists are concerned, there might in fact be no conflict at all. Thus, when by the end of the play, Palamon cries, as Arcite's dead body is being brought off the stage,

> O cousin,
> That we should things desire which do cost us
> The loss of our desire! (5.6.109-11)

besides referring to Emilia and heterosexual love by "things desire" and their friendship "the loss of our desire", it is possible to see the playwrights using the same lines to comment on the kinsmen's blindness to their true human desires, which they have neglected to pause and examine in their compulsive pursuit of self-satisfaction as the perfect form-abiding knights.

Most critics talk of Palamon and Arcite in *The Two Noble Kinsmen* in the same breath—as I have done in the last part—as though they are more or less indistinguishable from each other. It is true that as far as what they finally choose to do is concerned, the two are essentially the same. But despite this similarity of actions, there are indeed subtle differences between the personalities of the kinsmen. And more than contributing to the individuality of characterisation, these differences play an important part in helping to make this work "that most distressing of plays" (Donaldson 50). They also reinforce the playwrights' criticism of the manipulative power of form.

While the various descriptions of the kinsmen's physical appearance throughout the play are, especially in Emilia's speech in 4.2.1-54, fairly contradictory to one another, suggesting perhaps a likeness in appearance, that there must be something different either in looks or air is reflected by the Daughter's fervent preference for one over the other. There are, moreover, decided differences in their respective personalities, evident from their first appearance in 1.2.

Of the two, Palamon is the more straightforwardly chivalric, in that he thinks in the way of a martial knight and does not express any doubt as to the wisdom of the chivalric code. (Incidentally, about seventy percent of the "incriminating" quotations I have used in the last part of the discussion actually come from him.) It is he who, joining in Arcite's reflection on the corruption in Thebes, immediately narrows the discussion down to offences against the martial laws of chivalry, professing that his pity is mostly bestowed on the neglected soldiers. It is also he who responds with "Leave that unreasoned" (1.2.98) to Arcite's laments that a man's worth is greatly reduced when he knows the action he has to undertake to be unworthy. Palamon has the mind of a soldier and is the "more impetuous, the more excitable of the two knights, jumping at decisions and translating his ideas into action as soon as they come to him" (Donaldson 56). He initiates the dispute over the right to love Emilia, insisting that by daring to declare his love for her, Arcite commits treachery; renews their quarrel on re-encountering this cousin after his escape from prison; turns their friendly chat about the past back to bitter rivalry by accusing the other of sighing for Emilia; refuses Arcite's suggestion to halt their duel to hide from the approaching Theseus; and informs the duke who they are and asks him to put them both to death if he must. All these he does—and believes he does—in the name of chivalric honour. Except for his final cry of "That we should things desire which do cost us / The loss of our desire!", Palamon never once demonstrates any doubt as to the reasonableness of his actions or the worthiness of his undertakings.

Arcite, in contrast, seems the more philosophical—and in many cases the more sensible—of the two, whose ideas are not always confined to chivalric martial pursuits, despite the play's frequent references to his superior martial capabilities. Both in 1.2 and the opening of 2.2, it is he who elevates the kinsmen's conversation to a more spiritual and principled level. He reminds Palamon in 1.2 that in concentrating on the soldiers he is "out" (1.2.26) and that the greater ill is an environment where

> every evil
> Hath a good colour, and every seeming good's
> A certain evil. (1.2.38-40)

In 2.2 it is also he who suggests that there are spiritual comforts which may help them better endure imprisonment. It is therefore not surprising that the one sufficiently poetic tribute to Emilia in the whole play (3.1.4-14) should come from him rather than his cousin.

This philosophical touch in Arcite allows him to recognise the irrationality, even the subhuman quality, of Palamon's supposedly chivalric actions. Many a time during their quarrels he has pointed out the childishness of the other's behaviour, that "[y]ou are mad" (2.2.204) and "[y]ou are a beast now" (3.3.47). It is also he who observes that their "vain parleys" "[m]ake talk for fools and cowards" (3.3.10, 12).

Arcite also occasionally has his reservations about the wisdom of their observance of the chivalric code. One manifestation of this is his open expressions of doubt or regret, as for example in his lamentation over the unworthiness of their cause in fighting for Creon and Thebes. It is also he who describes their duel as "our folly" (3.6.107). Another manifestation is his relatively practical turn of mind. Upon hearing Theseus' party approach, he immediately suggests that Palamon

> retire,
> For honour's sake and *safety*, presently
> Into your bush again, (3.6.109-11, italics mine)

which presents a sharp contrast to the other's insistence that they fight on and risk direct confrontation with the duke. But the most frequent, though subtle, indication of Arcite's qualms is his persistent address to Palamon as "dear cousin", "my coz" or "my noble kinsmen" even after their breach. Set against the other's coldly formal "sir"s and accusatory "cozener Arcite", his terms of address seem less of an expression of formal courtesy than a reflection of his genuine regard for their family ties. It is as Peter Herman writes:

> Arcite will fight Palamon in the name of love and honor, but he always hesitates, always reminds Palamon of the unity they have lost on account of courtly love and honor. (10)

Arcite's problem, however, is that for all his philosophy, sense and good will, he is all too susceptible to influence by others' mode of behaviour. In this he is sharply contrasted to Palamon, who, though impetuous, is at the same time unswayable, disdainful of following the footsteps of others:

> Either I am
> The fore-horse in the team or I am none
> That draw i'th'sequent trace. (1.2.58-60)

This unfortunate weakness in Arcite's character is most evident during his quarrel with Palamon in prison, when, having accused the other of playing the child, he proceeds to speak and act in a manner that seems to "out-child" the childishness of his cousin. It is also part of the reason why the essentially stupid conflict between the cousins can be sustained, for Arcite's swaying reason will always be overcome by Palamon's firm unreason.

But most importantly, Arcite's susceptibility to the influence of others means that despite his occasional doubts about chivalric values, as long as he inhabits a world in which these values are respected and observed, he will be a faithful subscriber to them and to the forms of conduct they prescribe. He is himself possibly aware, whether consciously or unconsciously, of this weakness in his own character. When he first appears on the stage, he is shown to be remarking on the urgent need to "leave the city, / Thebes, and the temptings in't" (1.2.3-4). However, while he can flee from one city and its "temptings", he cannot escape the rule of chivalry in the world of *The Two Noble Kinsmen*, and therefore will continue to subscribe to the code to the point where, like his "out-childing" Palamon in prison, he will out-do his cousin in obeying the rules of the martial knight by choosing to pray to Mars before the final tournament.

The choice of Mars as his patron[3] is an indication of Arcite's being finally, as it were, driven to a firm observance of knightly conduct at its martial root: "in war, [the knight] fought on horseback where the Roman legions had fought on foot; in peace, he held his land because he was a skilled fighter" (Barber 17). Tragically, but also ironically, it is when he is

---

[3] At first glance, the cousins' respective choices of patron in Act 5's prayer scenes seem out of character. The usually martial-minded Palamon prays to Venus for strength, while Arcite, who impresses one as more capable of tender affections, turns to Mars. However, the scenes may in fact be a further demonstration of the subtle differences in the kinsmen's mentality and personality. In praying to Venus, Palamon, the straightforwardly chivalric, is guided by the emphasis on love's strength in the courtly love tradition: "the lady [is] the source of inspiration behind knightly deeds" and "the thought of his loved one will lend strength to a knight's arm, skill to his riding, and accuracy to his aim" (Barber 71). Arcite, however, ever practical, calls on Mars, the god of war, for support in what is essentially a mini-battle. And, as has been mentioned, when provoked, Arcite can be as martial-minded as Palamon. The prayers might also be looked on as a case of "for what we lack, we pray" (though most likely unconsciously on the part of the prayers). Palamon is assigned Venus because he lacks true appreciation of love as a human desire, which is also reflected by the content of his prayer, with its appalling imagery of the power of love, which can make "men wince" (Bloom, *Invention* 710), while Arcite, whose regard for his kinship with Palamon might impede a venture which must be "dragged out of blood" (5.1.43), needs hardening up, so to speak, with the aid of the brutal and merciless power of Mars.

at his most literally chivalric moment that he meets with his fatal accident. As his horse falls down, Arcite, rather than falling off the animal, has "kept him [the horse] 'tween his legs, on his hind hooves" (5.6.76)—the standard image of triumphant horsemanship, if one might add—so that he falls to the ground with it and is crushed by it, which proves fatal. Thus, where in Chaucer's Knight's account, he is immediately thrown off the startled horse:

> And er that Arcite may taken keep,
> He pighte hym on the pomel of his heed,
> That in the place he lay as he were deed, (2688-90)

the present rewriting of Arcite's accident highlights the responsibility of chivalry for his death by painting a picture of great horsemanship, the etymological root of the concept of chivalry. It is as Paula Breggren puts it, "Arcite's accident punishes him for being manly, responsible, and—literally—chivalric" (13) .

Thus, when one distinguishes between the characteristics of the two cousins, a further layer of tragedy in the story is revealed. While the conflict of the cousins (viewed together) demonstrates how blind observance of form distorts normal human relationship, the tragic story of Arcite tells of an otherwise sensible man's disastrous struggle—albeit a relatively unconscious and mild one in his case—against the manipulative power of form, disastrous both in the sense that he finally fails and gives in to form and that he is punished for his observance of form by death. Arcite himself, in his first speech in Act 1, remarks that

> not to swim
> I'th' aid o'th'current were almost to sink—
> At least to frustrate striving; and to follow
> The common stream 'twould bring us to an eddy
> Where we should turn or drown; if labour through,
> Our gain but life and weakness. (1.2.7-12)

This seems to have anticipated and summarised his own tragedy perfectly.

It is also worth noticing that the only other character in the main plot who has questioned the authority of form, Emilia, also fails in her struggle. She is married off to Palamon, and thus becomes, against her inclinations, a woman confined in the established social institution of marriage. Form thus triumphs in the end. Indeed, form triumphs all the way through to the end. The final sentence in the play proper is Theseus' "Let's go off, / And bear us like the time" (5.6.136-7)—let us go and act in accordance with the demands of the occasion, to play our assigned roles in Arcite's funeral and then Palamon's wedding. With this the play is brought back full circle to its beginning, where the three widows' insistence that they "bear" themselves "like the time" triggers the whole sequence of tragic events. The world of *The Two Noble Kinsmen* remains unchanged by the tragedy of the sundered cousins and the death of Arcite, and its highest human authority (Theseus) none the wiser—this is ultimately what is tragic about this play.

Before his concluding exhortation that the party go and bear themselves like the time, Theseus endeavours to summarise and rationalise the turn of events:

> O you heavenly charmers,
> What things you make of us! For what we lack
> We laugh, for what we have, are sorry; still
> Are children in some kind. Let us be thankful
> For that which is, and with you leave dispute
> That are above our question. (5.6.131-6)

This concluding speech has often been criticised as inadequate, one that "eva[des] underlying issues" (Hillman 69), including Theseus' own responsibility for the tragedy of the kinsmen.

Theseus' conclusion is indeed inadequate, for he lays the blame on the wrong quarter. The figure of authority responsible for the tragic turn of events in this version is not the "heavenly charmers". The role of divine intervention is actually minimised in the play. Unlike in *The Knight's Tale*, the gods, with the exception of Hymen in the opening, do not directly come to the human world. Saturn, as Ann Thompson puts it, is "reduce[d] to a simile" (207), while Mars, Venus and Diana make their appearance "by proxy". But, although the thunder, the doves and the rose tree which show up in the prayer scenes may suggest the involvement of the gods in the affair, unlike the direct narrative of their row in Chaucer, these signs cannot confirm that divine intervention in human affairs is merely a sort of irresponsible game among the "heavenly charmers".

The authorities which exert direct control over the lives of the characters are formalised codes of conduct, in particular the chivalric model. However, what is finally responsible for the death of Arcite and the misery of Palamon and Emilia is not, to be fair, the code itself, but their world's strict adherence to such forms in the absence of true understanding of the original moral considerations behind them. As we have seen, the queens and Theseus, in placing the preservation of self-image at the forefront of their considerations, defeat the purpose of chivalry and prescribed form by cruelly imposing injury on others (including those equal to them in class) and upsetting order. And the case of Palamon and Arcite is the same: chivalric conduct is merely a cover for self-centeredness. Devoid of true human sympathy, the chivalric code is but a hypocritical, inflexible and slightly ridiculous set form, in the same way that the characters' stylised rhetoric, rather than a medium for communication, is but strained and ridiculous set speeches which impede true communication.

If the ridiculousness and madness of the characters' practice are glossed over by their nobility, superior oratory and the solemnity of the atmosphere in the main plot, it is fully exposed in and by the subplot. It is Shakespeare's habit to "[use] subplots to comment on the main plot" (Herman 12). And although this subplot appears mainly to be Fletcher's, it seems that in this instance it does act in the Shakespearean tradition as a parody of the main plot. For example, Gerald the Schoolmaster's pedantic flaunting of his Latin and his strained effort for formalised speech, like the noble characters' rhetoric and courtesy, reflect his conscious effort to live up to what he believes is expected of a schoolmaster on encountering the nobility. In other words, in his effort to play his role, he is as self-conscious about his image as the queens, Theseus or the kinsmen, and seeks to construct and preserve it through observance of the relevant form of behaviour. The country setting renders his efforts out of place and his inferior talents make him ridiculous, a ridiculousness which reminds the audience that stripped of the tinsel of class and rhetoric, the main plot's protagonists are just as laughable as the schoolmaster.

If Gerald is a comment on the ridiculousness of role-playing, the Daughter is a reflection of the madness of what Palamon and Arcite are doing for "love". Herman observes that

> [t]he closer the Daughter comes to losing her sanity, the closer Palamon and Arcite come to fighting, thus ensuring that the audience (and the reader) perceives the mirroring between the Jailer's Daughter and the noble lovers. (13)

But it might be said that in this respect the noble kinsmen are even madder than the Daughter, for while her sanity is driven away by a genuine sexual desire for Palamon, the cousins' brawl, though they believe themselves to be fighting for love, is driven more by a desire to defend what they see as their rights as knights rather than a genuine love for Emilia.

The country dance which concludes the subplot represents a neat summary of the actions in the main plot. A performative dance is fundamentally a series of prescribed stylised movements which adhere to the demands of the occasion of the dance. Moreover, in the subplot, the dance performed is a morris dance, where the dancers, "*apparelled to the life*" (Stage Direction 3.5), all have a designated part to play, so that the role-playing quality of a dance becomes even more prominent. Gerald organises the dance. The Jailer's Daughter, in the absence of one of the original members of the side, is called on as a substitute. The final performance is prefaced by another of the schoolmaster's pedantically formal and laughable speeches. The elements of the main plot are thus all there: awareness of self-image, formalised language, organised movements, role-playing, obsessive madness. The eventual dance is essentially a series of formalised movements with madness at its centre, as is the series of events that constitute the main plot.

The plot of *The Two Noble Kinsmen*, then, tells of how strict observance of form in the absence of proper understanding of the moral considerations behind it can result in regulated actions that have the opposite effect to what is intended by the regulations. Paralleling this theme, the play as a whole demonstrates how, despite its careful inclusions of the elements of late Shakespearean romance, it, without the heart, as it were, of a romance, does not belong to the group.

Like its characters in their dogged practice of chivalry, the play consciously adheres to the romance model by incorporating almost all the elements of Shakespeare's late romances: noble protagonists, foreign land, remote age, span of time—though not as long as in Chaucer's original, at least much greater than that of *The Tempest*—movement from city to country, conflicts which occur in the name of love, acts of reconciliation and the prospect of a marriage. The play also shares many of the characteristics of the last-plays group: tortuous language, relatively simple characterisation, a linguistic experience complementing the experience of the plot.

However, although outwardly observing the romantic model, *The Two Noble Kinsmen* differs from the other last plays in precisely those points which make a Shakespearean romance a Shakespearean romance. A Shakespearean romance is first of all a tale in which society moves from order to disorder and back to order in the end, with the experience of the protagonists paralleling that movement. In the present piece, in contrast, not only is society's order never really disturbed, it is in fact jealousy guarded and faithfully upheld by the characters in the main plot, including Emilia, who, though expressing a preference for female society, never absolutely refuses the idea of marriage and therefore does not pose a substantial threat to the stability of the social fabric. The movement of the story, therefore, is a curious one in which the destruction of the protagonists' orderly existence arises out of the stability of the established rules. In this *The Two Noble Kinsmen* seems to be in a class of its own, for not even in the tragedies or histories is there such a paradoxical case of destruction resulting from the observation of an existing order.

In the romances, the movement from order to disorder is usually propelled by the destructive power of obsessive love (for a person, for power or for wealth), while the final re-establishment of order owes much to the healing power of unselfish love. In this play, however, love manifests itself in obsessive desires to the point where one is fairly uncertain whether there is love in the same sense as Florizel's feelings towards Perdita or Ferdinand's toward Miranda anywhere in the play. For all their declarations of love, Palamon and Arcite's feelings for Emilia, as we have seen, appear more a kind of possessiveness rather than an emotional response to the lady herself. The Jailer's Daughter's feelings for Palamon are driven by lust, which becomes particularly evident after she loses her sanity. Theseus' insistence that the marriage ceremony proceed as planned could reflect his regard for Hippolyta, but it may equally be merely a reflection of the almost exaggerated importance that he attaches to the completion of a ceremony. Similarly, the queens' insistence that their dead husbands be buried immediately may be driven more by a regard for proper form than for the lords themselves. Thus, although in most criticism, *The Two Noble Kinsmen* is looked upon as a piece which depicts the destructive rather than regenerative power of love, it is also possible to see it as one in which love as reciprocal emotional engagement, or at least as a longing for such engagement, is entirely absent. In this sense it again proves the odd-piece-out in the last plays canon, for instead of participating in its predecessors' dramatisation of both the ugliness and beauty of love, it constructs a society in which gestures of romantic and selfless love abound but where romantic heterosexual love itself does not seem to exist.

The most obvious deviation from the romance model is, of course, the play's problematic ending. It is problematic not because it juxtaposes the death of one cousin and the marriage of another, though admittedly the close proximity of the two events has its part to play in establishing the uncomfortableness of the conclusion, but because without the healing power of love—Emilia and Palamon do not talk to each other in the last scene—this ending, contrary to those of the other last plays, refuses to promise a hopeful future regenerated by happy marriage and/or new birth.

Furthermore, as has been discussed earlier, with Theseus' arrangement that

> A day or two
> Let us look sadly and give grace unto
> The funeral of Arcite, in whose end
> The visage of bridegrooms we'll put on
> And smile with Palamon, (5.6.124-8)

and his order that the party go and bear themselves "like the time", the ending denies the audience the satisfaction of feeling that things could be changing for the better, for the grip of form over the characters is as firm as ever, firmer perhaps, as by now it is not only ruling their actions, but declared to be the regulator over their feelings as well. Nothing changes by the end of *The Two Noble Kinsmen* except for the irretrievable loss of Arcite and the kinsmen's companionship, which, again, makes the play stand out not only in the last-plays group, but also in the whole Shakespearean canon, for it is the only piece in which change, whether for the better or the worse, is not even given a chance.

Up until the production of *The Two Noble Kinsmen*, Shakespeare's last plays (including *Henry VIII*) are works in which "nothing is ever abandoned beyond recovery; resurgence is always possible" (Beer 38). The four romances, in particular, are plays of "nobility and hope" (Hirst 34). This play, in contrast, is one in which what is lost is irreversibly gone and the hope of a change for the better faint in the extreme. Therefore, like its characters who, in strictly observing the codes of chivalry without bothering to comprehend the heart of its principle, turn it from a cult of generosity, kindness and courtesy to one of selfishness, cruelty and savagery, the play, confined to the form of romance without upholding the central romantic value, becomes in effect an antiromance in the sense that it actually breaks the form of Shakespearean romance. It not only stands out in the last-plays group, but is also like no other in the entire canon.

In making *The Two Noble Kinsmen* break out of Shakespeare's own romance pattern, the playwrights have introduced changes to their source text, an act which in itself constitutes another manifestation of the form-breaking quality of the play. As we have already begun to see, deviations from Chaucer's original are numerous. Apart from the obvious addition of the subplot of the Jailer's Daughter, dramatic arrangements in the main plot have introduced either subtle or radical changes to the original. In terms of characterisation, Shakespeare and Fletcher's portrayal of Theseus amplifies and makes explicit the frustrations, vanity, and cruelty which are only hinted at with subtle irony in *The Knight's Tale*, turning him more manifestly tyrannical and inflexible. The role of Emilia has been greatly enlarged as the playwrights rewrite Chaucer's Emelye, who is almost completely silent in the Knight's narrative, into a compassionate, outspoken young woman who, though finally overpowered by the currents of her adopted society, nevertheless puts up a (little) fight by speaking her mind. And in portraying Palamon and Arcite, as we have seen, Arcite's character and experience are made more complex, which adds weight to his role. Chaucer's portrayal of the kinsmen, on the other hand, is weighted towards Palamon.

The alterations to Theseus' character, in particular, have resulted in some rather large-scale changes to the details, though not the general development, of the plot. The encounter with the queens, originally a device to demonstrate his chivalry and to, as it were, get him to Thebes, develops into a conflict which takes up a whole (and long) scene. Later, in contrast to Chaucer's Theseus, who strives to minimise the death toll in the cousins' conflict, this one is unyielding in his insistence that the suitor who fails to win Emilia's hand must die and that his entourage be executed with him, thus in fact increasing the number of unnecessary deaths.

Other major changes to the original narrative include the radical shrinking of the time span, so that the whirlwind of events following the cousins' first sight of Emilia in effect increases the sense of madness surrounding their infatuation and introduces a great element of uncertainty about the nature of their feelings towards her. It also changes the quality of the ending, for, while in Chaucer's text, a sufficient length of time passes between Arcite's funeral and Palamon's marriage to make the latter less jarring, here only "one or two days" of mourning are allotted the memory of Arcite, so that Palamon's marriage comes across not as an occasion for healing the wounds of the past, but rather as a heartless gesture which prevents the final scene from being the hopeful ending of a romance or the comic ending of tragicomedy.

Another important deviation from *The Knight's Tale* is, as we have seen, that in *The Two Noble Kinsmen*, the gods, with the exception of the brief appearance of Hymen, are never directly presented on stage. In Chaucer's poem, a row between Venus and Mars, in which Saturn intervenes, is directly presented in the narrative. Earlier in the story Diana appears before Emelye, and, still earlier, Mercury before Arcite. More importantly, it is explicitly stated that the gods are directly responsible for Arcite's death: "[o]ut of the ground a furie infernal sterte, / From Pluto sent at requeste of Saturne" (2684-5) frightens Arcite's horse so that it throws its rider off. In contrast, in the play, the only god that appears on the stage, Hymen, can be said to have been interrupted in his function as god of marriage by the mourning queens. In other words, in *The Two Noble Kinsmen*, compared with the case in *The Knight's Tale* or Shakespeare's earlier romances, not only is the direct presentation of divine intervention greatly reduced, but the power of such intervention is also shown, right at the beginning of the play, to be susceptible to *human* action.

It is through these changes that *The Two Noble Kinsmen*, though at first glance rather a faithful adaptation of its source text, proves itself to be the "new play" that it announces itself to be in the first line of the prologue. The changes mentioned above are all manifestations of the playwrights' radical reinterpretation of Chaucer's tale. The expanded dramatisation of the encounter between the duke and the queens, in adding conflict where there is originally none, introduces into the story, as soon as the play proper starts, the theme of the problematic consequences of insistent observance of form. The authority ruling over man's fate is shifted from the heavenly powers to the human sphere. Form is the ultimate manipulator of fate in the present story, and the characters' blind observance of it without comprehending its purpose results in the final tragedy. It starts with the queens' insistence on the funeral rites of their lords, Theseus' final consent to wage war on Creon, and the cousins' chivalrous participation in the defence of a city which they loath, which together transfer the two from Thebes to a prison cell in Athens, where they fall in love with and fight over the claim to Emilia, performed in accordance with the code of knightly conduct. Theseus intervenes and, following the chivalric tradition, prescribes a tournament. Arcite wins but dies when his horse falls, his superior horsemanship proving to be the death of him. Of course, most of these arrangements are there in the original tale, but the removal of the onstage presence of the gods and the additional conflict in 1.1 highlight the rule of form, rather than divine powers, in the present plot.

The doggedness with which the characters pursue a form which they do not fully comprehend renders the excessive formality of their language, with its "stylized chivalric ethos...that go[es] beyond even what it found in Chaucer" (Cohen 3204), artificial and ridiculous. Together with Fletcher's less subtle portrayal of Gerald and the Daughter, the overall effect of *The Two Noble Kinsmen* changes Chaucer's "philosophical" (Benson 7) romance of chivalry which reflects on "human destiny, the inevitable alternation of joy and sorrow, and the divine order of the universe" (ibid.) to an antiromance that ironically portrays man's own folly.

Thus, despite the inclusion of the word "noble" in the title, any note of nobility or grandeur that Chaucer's original story may have evoked is removed from the present version, replaced by a sense of mockery, which, again, the play displays right at the beginning, through the prologue's rather flippant language, its provocative association of new plays and maidenheads, and the equally irreverent depiction of the rattling of Chaucer's bones. Indeed, for all the prologue's declaration of fear that the present effort may not do the original justice, many of the arrangements in the play seem calculated exactly to "shake the bones of that good man / And make him cry from under ground" (Prologue 17-8).

The Two Noble Kinsmen is thus a challenge to the authority of Chaucer's original text and to mainstream interpretation of the tale as a "noble story". Without altering the general development of the narrative, Shakespeare and Fletcher construct a version in which most of the main characters are only noble in birth and the outward form of their actions, which glosses over the absence of the nobility of their minds.

If one individualises, at this juncture, Shakespeare and Fletcher's contributions to the play, it is possible to discover a third layer of challenge to authority, that of Fletcher's engagement with the authority of the Shakespearean canon. It has often been pointed out that "Shakespearean 'allusions' throughout the play are myriad in the scenes commonly attributed to Fletcher" (Teramura 576). And, like the play's general response to Chaucer, Fletcher's engagement with the Shakespearean *oeuvre* is one of imitation and parody which results in a departure from the originals that, in Mira Teramura's words, "generates new literary birth" (ibid.).

It is hard to know whether this momentum to struggle against the burden of authority of a more established writer, detectable in the parts of both playwrights, comes at the instigation of Shakespeare or Fletcher. It may even have been a case of an idea occurring simultaneously to both, especially considering that the method of their collaboration was most probably of each undertaking their sections separately without much communication during the actual composition process.[4] Whatever the source of influence, however, that Shakespeare was doing something which a younger writer far from approaching the end of his career was also doing seems to suggest that he, rather than "despaired of all

---

[4] "The play's structure, with its almost complete separation of main plot and subplot and its large number of soliloquies, seems designed to facilitate collaboration between two people who did not expect to have much opportunity to talk about the work in progress" (Potter, Introduction 25).

audiences" (Bloom, *Invention* 710) or "tired" and having "come out on the other side of human experience" (Spencer 261, 264), as some critics take him to be, was still very much engaged with human experience, his art, and his career when he worked on *The Two Noble Kinsmen*.

Another manifestation of this sense of continued engagement with play-writing as an art and career may be the fact that, in the last plays in general and this one in particular, Shakespeare's writings are, as Bart Van Es puts it, "alive with the presence of other writers" (264). *The Two Noble Kinsmen* is indeed very much so. There is, first of all, the presence of Chaucer. Not only is his text the foundation upon which the play is built, his authority is also a central concern, as the prologue foregrounds. Another possible literary figure who may have had his influence on the composition of the play is Cervantes, as Palamon and Arcite's persistence in acting the knight in love and in combat does occasionally seem to have something of Don Quixote to it. The playwrights' practice of criticising form by taking up that form, too, shows an affinity to Cervantes's method of passing literary criticism on romance novels with the composition of the "romance" of *Don Quixote*.[5]

Cervantes was one of Fletcher's special interests. And the possible presence of the Spanish writer in the play reflects the presence of Fletcher in *The Two Noble Kinsmen*. Since Fletcher contributed more than a half of the entire play, his presence is a matter of course. What should not be taken for granted, however, and is worth noticing, is the way his characteristic style—inflated rhetoric, an interest in Cervantes, the sexuality motif, an emphasis on artifice and sudden dramatic revelations—is incorporated into the structure of the play to help illustrate its theme. Again, whether the dramatic unity of the collaboration reflects Shakespeare adapting his own writing to the influence of his co-author or cleverly putting the idiosyncrasies of his co-author to good use, it would seem that in this work he was still fully engaged with the literary world of his time in general and the art of play-writing in particular. In this the "old" Shakespeare is not unlike his younger self in his early and mature years, for it has been suggested that the playwright of the comedies and

---

[5] "Although we cannot know for certain how Cervantes finally felt about the Spanish books of chivalry, it is obvious that he knew them well. It would also seem clear that the full parodic effect of *Don Quijote* depends upon readers who will immediately recognize the chivalric material. Thus the fictional world of *Don Quijote*, full of readers of chivalric romances, was created for a public made up of readers of the same romances, by an author who was also a reader of the romances" (Whitenack 62).

tragedies "seems to have been unusually sensitive to what other dramatists were doing" (Charney 327).

Shakespeare's continued engagement with his career is also reflected in his development in *The Two Noble Kinsmen* of his ongoing analysis of the effects of art and language. The tragedy of the story, which, as we have seen, directly results from the characters' compulsive role-playing, carries his "study" one step further. It is a step which, in turning the discussion in a new direction, both shows the playwright's continued interest in art and language, and marks the possible start of a new line of thought.

Up until *The Two Noble Kinsmen*, theatrical performance—the combination of visual gestures and verbal expressions—however frequently made use of in the lives of the characters in the last plays, is still very much a separate event, differentiated from the normal routines of everyday life by visual magnificence and/or verbal grandiosity. In the present play, by contrast, performance is completely integrated into the realities of the play world to the extent that it cannot be distinguished from that reality. In other words, the characters' language and actions are self-conscious role-playing and un-self-conscious spontaneous actions at the same time. They are self-conscious because they are performed in strict accordance with the conventional demands of the occasion and the order of knightly conduct for the construction and preservation of self-image. Yet they are also un-self-conscious in that this role-playing has already become a habit with the characters. It is what the majority of people in that society have always been and will be doing. Theatrical role-playing is almost intuitive for them and thus, in a way, the natural mode of their existence.

When role-playing becomes a habit, it clouds self-recognition, as the tragedy of the kinsmen reveals. As we have seen, Palamon and Arcite's feelings for each other and for Emilia seem more the result of their declaration of such feelings than true attachment. Their role-play-like actions are not the expression of their beliefs and emotions, but what drive them towards their conviction that they are in the grips of certain emotions, while in fact there is a distinct possibility that they might not hold as strong a feeling as they are made to think by their own actions. In other words, compulsive acting blinds their recognition of their true feelings or desires.

That language and gesture actually bar their performer's experience of his or her true emotions is most clearly demonstrated in the queens' speeches about their grief in 1.1. In fact, there the Third Queen seems to have become briefly aware of the inadequacy of language to express her anguish when she remarks that her "sorrow, wanting form, / Is pressed with deeper matter" (1.1.108-9). However, even with this recognition, instead of keeping silent, she goes on, by bizarre imagery, to vividly illustrate how words and outward appearance cannot begin to express her grief, which impresses one as more a skilful rhetorical device which accompanies the posture of sorrow than a true reflection of a grief-stricken heart. In effect, the three queens' verbal demonstrations of grief generally drown out grief. The ultimate impression one receives seems to be that, temporarily at least, grief is expunged from them, for, to attain their level of rhetorical control over the "fine excess" (Magnusson 380) of their syntax and imagery, emotions have to give way to the intellect.

Gestures and language in this play are thus frequently dictators, in a fairly negative manner, of the heart and mind of their performers. This portrayal of the effect of visual and verbal expression is a great step away from the picture presented in *Pericles*, *Cymbeline* and *The Winter's Tale*, where language and performance's powers are ultimately restorative. It also departs from the position of *The Tempest* and *Henry VIII*. In these two earlier plays, the effects of language and performance are presented as problematic. And the problem lies in their susceptibility to the purposeful manipulation of individuals or to unconscious distortion under the influence of preformed opinions. In other words, the negative portrayal of the power of language and performance focuses on their negative power on the "receiving end" of information, to which truth is not faithfully transmitted. In *The Two Noble Kinsmen*, on the other hand, the emphasis falls on the power of words and gestures over their users, suppressing natural emotions and impeding true self-awareness. The victim of language and art in the last plays has, up until now, been the beholder— the listener and spectator. But it would seem that with this piece, Shakespeare is beginning to explore new territory by dramatising their manipulation over their performers as well.

The Two Noble Kinsmen and *Henry VIII*: Shakespeare's Lateness Revisited

The Two Noble Kinsmen is thus a work which makes new things out of old materials and styles. Its re-reading of Chaucer, its departure from Shakespeare's own romance model, its further development of the ongoing discussions of language and art, and its interaction with other writers, all taken in conjunction with its chronological position in the Shakespearean canon, prompt us to re-examine and reconsider the idea of Shakespeare's lateness.

Conventionally, scholars, probably taking the cue from Prospero's farewell speech in the epilogue of *The Tempest*, though admitting *Henry VIII* and *The Two Noble Kinsmen* into the canon, view them as exemplifying the half-mindedness or the deteriorating powers of a writer moving from semi-retirement towards complete retreat from his career. *Henry VIII* is often seen as "[a] dramatic poem of things-in-farewell...a performance piece, perhaps a last hurrah" (Bloom, *Invention* 686), while *The Two Noble Kinsmen* with its "old man's" poetry is looked on as the work of a brilliant writer who has lost interest in his art, though still capable of tossing out splendid poetry. In short, as Bloom puts it, "[t]he world seems very old in *Henry VIII*, and in the scenes Shakespeare wrote for *The Two Noble Kinsmen*" (692).

This sense of oldness and tiredness in style is often attributed to the "old" Shakespeare's developing personal despair about art, mankind and the order of the world. Here are three examples of concluding sentences from articles on *The Two Noble Kinsmen*. It is not difficult to realise that, although the authors have approached the play from different angles, they share a common conviction about Shakespeare's mood of disillusionment or despair at this stage in his career:

> To critique chivalry at this juncture suggests a profound skepticism of not only England's past, but of England's future as well. (Herman 24)

> Shakespeare had written dark comedies before, but none with so bleak an ending. It is no wonder that so many generations of Shakespeareans have preferred to regard Prospero's serene acceptance of the ending of the revels as Shakespeare's last words on his theatrical career. (Clark 138)

> No one should be sorry to have this play, but maybe we should laugh for what we lack: had Shakespeare told us everything he knew at the end of his career, it might have been too much to bear. (Breggren 15)

Even Bloom, who suggests that with *The Two Noble Kinsmen* Shakespeare is entering into a "strange new mode" (*Invention* 690), concludes that it is in the end a mode which the playwright "declined to develop", probably because it touches on an "all-but-universal guilt and shame" (710), most clearly manifested in Palamon's appalling description of Venus' powers.

Without definite information about Shakespeare's situation at this stage or about the extent to which he would allow his private emotions to influence his writing, it is hard to deny or confirm that the scepticism— over truth and history in *Henry VIII* and over strict observance of form in *The Two Noble Kinsmen*—displayed in the two plays is indeed a manifestation of the playwright's own sense of disillusionment or despair. However, there are signs in the plays which seem to indicate that he, rather than languid and in despair, was professionally quite robust. Charney writes of the mature Shakespeare that

> [a] typical Shakespearean posture is to imitate contemporary forms and models, if only to improve on them and to bring them, as it were, to their natural perfection. This suggests a highly competitive spirit in Shakespeare. (327)

The Two Noble Kinsmen, with its engagement with the romance/tragicomedy model, its re-interpretation of the canonical *Knight's Tale*, its challenges to the powers of Chaucer, Shakespeare himself and perhaps even Fletcher, seems to indicate that that "highly competitive spirit" in the younger Shakespeare was still working in the older.

In these two chapters, therefore, I have endeavoured to present an alternative interpretation of the style and theme of these two last of the last plays, which sees Shakespeare, whatever his private moods, as still taking considerable professional interest in his art and career. The poetic style of the plays works as an important linguistic support to the construction and presentation of their respective themes. The finished works not only integrate Shakespeare's own late style, but also neatly absorb the poetic style of his younger collaborator. The two plays contain new discussions and new experiments, and show their author still fully engaged with contemporary literary trends. This level of consideration, planning and interaction, to me at least, speaks of compositional vigour rather than tiredness, and professional interest instead of despair.

Therefore, instead of seeing Shakespeare in his last phase as tiredly writing out a few scenes in semi-retirement as a favour to the King's Men in aid of Fletcher, or, as some critics suggest, with the aid of Fletcher, it is perhaps possible to envision him as still accepting, indeed, setting up, the challenge of pushing himself towards new development. *Henry VIII*'s scepticism about language's reliability for the transmission of truth, rather than an indication of his profound disillusionment with the power of language, the attainability of truth, or the workings of history, might perhaps be regarded as an inevitable and necessary position taken when he took up the difficult, if not impossible, idea of reproducing the past—and the fairly sensitive recent past, moreover. The play's concern with the problematic transmission of historical truths and its ambiguity in presenting historical events, caused by the contradiction of voices in the plot, could be Shakespeare's way of resolving the problematic process of collaboration—two interpretations of materials which are interpretations of historical events in the first place—by incorporating the mechanics of collaborative composition into the play's presentation of history. And, in the case of *The Two Noble Kinsmen*, as we have seen, the oldness of its story, the frequent image of decay which appears in its language, the clotted rhetoric of the Shakespearean parts, and the distressing finale, all contribute to bringing out the theme of the destructive consequence of confinement to form, which, though the characters in the story fail to challenge, the play itself succeeds in breaking away from. It would thus seem that Shakespeare, at the very end of his career, was still striving for new challenges, new developments and new departures.

EPILOGUE

Despite the exciting prospect of new dramatic development which *The Two Noble Kinsmen* seems to open up, Shakespeare would write no more. And as the playwright went on to live for almost two more years, during which time he was apparently well enough to travel to London and be actively engaged in business, [1] one cannot very well attribute this discontinuation of dramatic output to disabling ill health or death's cruel intervention. The termination of his play-writing career was apparently a conscious choice on Shakespeare's part, the considerations behind which are still under investigation.

While it is not completely ruled out that Shakespeare could have experienced a growing disillusionment in dramatic art, mankind and/or the workings of justice, which might have led to a decision to give up writing altogether, recent scholarship tends to avoid speculating on the more or less impenetrable matter of his mood and to adopt instead a less, as it were, sentimental approach. It is argued that his decision to retire was formed mainly on financial considerations. The theory starts with Shakespeare's will. As this document contains no mention of his shares in

---

[1] "In November 1614 Shakespeare and John Hall went [to London] together" (Potter, *Life* 403). Whilst there, Thomas Greene, a cousin and former lodger, called on him on the 17th. During Greene's visit discussions about the crisis of Enclosure in Stratford, in which the properties of both were concerned, came up. Dealings about the Enclosure scheme were a major part of Shakespeare's business activities during 1614-1615, though he also had time to consider, amongst other things, the marriage arrangements for his younger daughter Judith. His London properties were also attended to, as, for example,

> [i]n the spring of 1615...Shakespeare joined several other property owners in the Blackfriars in petitioning the Court of Chancery to give...Mathias Bacon*...authority to surrender the "letters patents and other deeds" pertaining to the said "messuages, tenements and premises" (the documents in the case are dated 26 April (Complaint), 5 May (Answer), and 22 May (Decree). (Schoenbaum 274-5)

*Mathias Bacon was the son and executor of the recently deceased Anne Bacon, who had "boarded up on two sides" (272) a plot of ground on the west side of Shakespeare's Blackfriars gatehouse property.

the King's Men and the playhouses, "whereas shares do appear in the wills of many professional actors" (Van Es 301), the implication would seem to be that he had sold them. And although there is no document that can specify a date for the transaction, it is not unlikely that he sold them after the Globe fire in 1613, for he might have been unable to afford his share in the rebuilding of the theatre so soon after his investment in the Blackfriars gatehouse.[2] And since it is known that another shareholder, John Witter, who "could not put together his contribution", did indeed "[bow] out from the syndicate" at this point (Schoenbaum 277), it is not impossible that Shakespeare had chosen to do the same. As to his shares in Blackfriars, Peter Ackroyd believes that he might have sold them either when he gave up the Globe shares or slightly later. Bart Van Es, on the other hand, mentions that it is sometimes suggested that "the playwright dropped out of the [Blackfriars] syndicate within a year and half of the agreement [i.e. in 1610]", possibly having "made a substantial loss on the deal" (258). But whether he sold the shares in the Blackfriars theatre on an earlier or later date, by the time he drew up his will he was seemingly no longer a shareholder of the King's Men; and the decision to withdraw had probably been made on financial grounds. Shakespeare, one should remember, had always been "a keen businessman" (Honigmann 702), so that this was a move very much, so to speak, in character. And as he was already semi-retired in Stratford,[3] bowing out financially from the company may have been a catalyst for his full retirement from playwriting, "a practical end," as Ackroyd comments, "to a thoroughly pragmatic career" (472).

---

[2] Samuel Schoenbaum points out that

> the expenses fell upon the shareholders, required by the terms of their lease to maintain and repair the theatre. Each sharer was at first assessed £50 or £60 towards the charges, but ended up having to pay much more. (277)

Peter Ackroyd adds that at the time Shakespeare

> still owed £60 for the mortgage on the Blackfriars gatehouse, to be paid back within six months. Even for an affluent country landowner, these were large sums of ready money. (471)

[3] "The playwright's name appears near the top of a list of subscribers for a bill promoting highway maintenance [in Stratford] compiled in September 1611 (suggesting he was by then considered a resident) and in May the following year 'William Shakespeare' was recorded as 'of Stratford upon Avon' when he testified at the Court of Requests...[W]hen he bought the Blackfriars Gatehouse in 1613 it was again as a man 'of Stratford'" (Van Es 261).

See also Jonathan Bate's suggestion, quoted towards the end of Chapter 4, that Shakespeare may have had semi-retired to Stratford as early as 1603-4.

Shakespeare's final full retirement, its probable cause in the financial turmoil of his company, and Ackroyd's comment that his had always been a pragmatic career remind us, lest we are wont to forget, that late Shakespeare, apart from an "old" man and an artist, was also, and probably primarily, someone whose finances had been invested deeply in the welfare of one specific theatrical company since 1594 and whose literary output had a not inconsiderable influence on its fortunes. This realisation opens up another angle of approach to the last plays, namely that they could have been the result of, amongst other things, practical adaptation to changes which occurred or could have occurred in the King's Men, including the gradual changes in the composition of the company (the aging of former members and the incoming of a younger generation of actors), its change (or addition) of playhouse, and Shakespeare's own changing relationship with the company.

That Shakespeare did write with the company and its resources in mind has more or less been accepted as a fact. Quarto texts of his plays occasionally display speech-prefixes or stage directions which use the name of an actor rather than a character. For example, the second Quarto (1599) of *Romeo and Juliet*, generally believed to have been "set from the author's own rough draft, or 'foul papers'" (Greenblatt, "Textual" 903), contains a stage direction that announces "*Enter Will Kemp*" (Shakespeare, *Romeo*), from which one might infer that Shakespeare wrote with "specific *members* of his company in mind" (Mardock and Rasmussen 115). This close identification of characters with actors in the company during his creative process offers another possible explanation for the last plays' shift of focus from romantic love to familial turmoils and their emphasis on the older rather than the younger generation. As Shakespeare progressed towards his last period, the company was inevitably experiencing the aging of its leading actors (Burbage, for example) and the loss of senior members (Pope, Philips, Crowley and, of course, Shakespeare himself, all quit acting). Andrew Power suggests that this left a conspicuous age gap between the leading male actors and the boy actors who played the female parts, which made a focus on the romantic pairing of the protagonists slightly undesirable.[4] It therefore follows that the company needed to

---

[4] While an actor, especially a great one in the era before the arrival of close-up shots and the high-definition video, is of course capable of convincingly portraying ages other than his own, it is worth noticing that "Shakespeare does not write a part improbably younger than Burbage for him to play after Romeo" (Power 179). It is also significant, notes Power, that there is a corresponding progression of age of the female counterparts to the protagonists, as they move from the youth of Kate, Luciana and Adriana, Hermia and Helena, Juliet, Portia and Jessica, Rosalind and

recruit new talents to fill the void, but who were not yet ready to take up leading roles. Consequently the plots' focus begins to shift from love interest to other matters. By the time of *The Two Noble Kinsmen*, however, these apprentices were sufficiently trained and experienced to take up major roles, and "[i]t is easy to imagine the strength of the younger actors being capitalised on as a new phase of the company begins" (Power 185), with the play re-focusing, "for the first time in several years" (ibid.), on youth and the rough path of immature love.

As the company's "human resources" were very likely a consideration influencing the composition of the last plays, so probably was its playhouse(s). The impact of the purchase of the Blackfriars playhouse on Shakespeare's dramatic output has long been a point of discussion. Although with the exception of *The Tempest* and *The Two Noble Kinsmen*, all the last plays are known to have been performed at the Globe, it is believed that the purchase of the new theatre had nevertheless a certain degree of influence on their composition. G. E. Bentley suggests that although the Blackfriars was not put to use until 1610, discussions preceding the legal purchase in 1608 (he estimates that discussions could have started as early as March 1608) would have alerted the King's Men that "their plays needed to be changed to fit them to the theatre and its select audience" (42). Plans for the purchase may have prompted the company, Bentley suggests, to commission Jonson, who had "a following among the courtly audience (always prominent at the Blackfriars) by his great court masques" (43) and also a "great reputation among the literati and critics" (44), to write for them; to engage the service of Beaumont and Fletcher, who "had already displayed those talents which were to make their plays the stage favourites at Blackfriars for the next thirty-four years" (44-5); and to decide that "William Shakespeare should write henceforth with the Blackfriars in mind and not the Globe" (46). Whether Shakespeare did write the plays, apart from perhaps *The Two Noble Kinsmen* and *Henry VIII*, with Blackfriars primarily in mind one cannot know for certain, but Bentley's theory about the company's decision to engage Jonson and Fletcher for the new theatre is cogently argued. Moreover, it throws light on—and is at the same time supported by—some of the features of Shakespeare's last plays discussed in previous chapters. Their foregrounded examination of art, *The Winter's Tale*'s commitment to enacting every item on Sidney's list of abominable dramatic

---

Celia, Ophelia, Cressida, and Viola and Olivia to the maturity of Lady Macbeth and Cleopatra (she and Antony are the "last great lovers" (ibid.) in the canon). To Power's list of mature leading females one may also add the last plays' Hermione, Paulina and Katherine of Aragon.

arrangements, *The Tempest*'s close adherence to the classical unities, and, of course, the co-authoring of two plays with Fletcher all seem to suggest increasing interaction with his fellow playwrights, which could have been spurred on by the company's engagement of Jonson and Fletcher, whose contribution to the King's Men's repertoire may have inspired friendly rivalry in Shakespeare, stimulating him to new departures and new creative heights.

This picture of late Shakespeare tuned in to "the literary mainstream" (Van Es 276) in fact corroborates well the theory about the changed composition of the company affecting his writing. The last plays' literary turn, reflected by their linguistic style, embrace of artifice, participation in literary debates and the weakening of characterisation may have been partly the result of Shakespeare's gradual withdrawal from the company of actors. The departure of original members and the influx of new apprentices perhaps meant that he was becoming less familiar with the actors' idiosyncrasies and capabilities, an unfamiliarity perhaps increased by his semi-retirement to Stratford. More importantly, according to Van Es, "[t]he Blackfriars investment, in fact, crystallized a separation between housekeepers and mere actors that had been in progress for sometime" (258), with the new financial structure of the company breaking "the performers' majority stakeholding, which had been a foundation principle of the Chamberlain's Men" (259). Shakespeare's "practical engagement with the acting profession" must have thus been greatly lessened by

> [t]he low level of involvement of players in the Blackfriars syndicate; the 50 per cent dilution of the King's Men's acting shares; and the sustained period of pestilence, (260)

a distance which possibly resulted in, as Van Es puts it, a "return to the literary mainstream" in the last plays, reflected by "metaphors and allegories that represent the literary creator", an art that displays art which at the time was practiced by "the young, new dramatists, such as Marston and Fletcher" (276). This also sheds light on the last plays' displayed resemblance, in both their selection of dramatic motifs and their language's flaunting of artifice, to the playwright's earliest works, which were also written at a time when he had been comparatively distanced from the company of the actors.

The impression of late Shakespeare's increased interest in the activities and output of his literary contemporaries is strengthened, according to Van Es, by the publication in 1609 of his *Sonnets*. Although the sonnets were not his "late" work, and their publication was probably not exactly authorial, Shakespeare seemed not to have made an objection to the publication and by this silent consent was perhaps "making a statement", for "here was a collection that repeatedly alluded to rival poets and made its claim to originality through the imitation and twisting of existing forms" (277). This opinion coincides, in a way, with Potter's conjecture that Shakespeare may have planned to spend his retirement "revising his work for publication" (*Life* 402). Potter writes:

> He must have known of Ben Jonson's plans for what became the 1616 Folio. Jonson evidently saw it as a stopping point, since it was ten years before his next play was performed. The reluctance of the King's Men to publish Shakespeare's Jacobean plays may mean that he wanted to revise them with the care that he knew Jonson was giving to his own works. Neither dramatist wanted to leave behind the unfinished drafts or notes that fascinate the modern student...After years of working quickly, a quiet year or two at Stratford might allow him to decide his canon and polish his works to his own satisfaction. (ibid.)

Having his canon published would indeed have been the ultimate literary gesture, and perhaps again not untinged with a little professional rivalry with Jonson.

There is, of course, no documentary evidence at all to prove that Shakespeare had ever contemplated having his plays collected and published as his "canon". Indeed, this picture of him conscientiously revising and preparing his plays for publication somewhat contradicts the conventional impression of him having, in contrast to Jonson's self-conscious meticulousness, never blotted out a line and hardly involved in the publication of any of his dramatic works. But taking into consideration the last plays' "conspicuous literar[iness]" (Van Es 296), the ongoing debate (perhaps partly in response to Jonson's criticism) about art and language they present, the publication of his sonnets, and that he very probably did revise his previous works, [5] the idea of the retired Shakespeare planning for revision and publication is not entirely fantastical. If he indeed had revision in mind, then the endeavours towards new artistic development which went into the composition of *The Two Noble Kinsmen*, instead of being cut short by his retirement, might have been carried into the revision of his previous works. In a way, this would have been a continuation of what he had been doing all along (and most manifestly in the last plays): reacting to his own earlier works, though this

---

[5] About Shakespeare's revision of his works, see, for example: Wells, Stanley. "Pluralist Shakespeare." *Critical Survey* 1 (1989): 63-9. Print.; or, less academic in style: Greenblatt, Stephen. "Did Shakespeare Ever Think Twice?" *The Wall Street Journal*. 5 Mar. 2011. Web.

time it would have been a response directly applied to the old plays instead of generating a new one.

It could seem rather injudicious to introduce a new approach in the concluding chapter, for, apart from the dangerous possibility of insufficient exposition, one runs the risk of, if not overturning, at least undermining the argument which one has been developing so far. But in this case at least the second risk may be avoided. Interpreting Shakespeare's lateness in the light of his role as a commercial company's playwright seems in fact to add support to my argument against the idea of his last period being marked by artistic languor, for it shows him devising ways of maximising company resources for artistic expression, turning disadvantages (the company's lack of competent young leading actors and his own personal distance from the present generation of performers) into an opportunity for new explorations, which appears to suggest, despite his semi-retirement and his final decision to fully retire, active engagement with playwriting rather than professional and artistic torpidity.

Another theory which I have been trying to advance is that, in terms of his art and working method, late Shakespeare was doing what he had been doing throughout his career: reacting to his own previous works, experimenting and "trying out [the kinds] of play[s] that others had done before him" (Charney 326), and developing his lifelong fascination with the effects and possibilities of language and drama. Again, late Shakespeare's manoeuvres as a professional playwright lend credibility to the idea. Although his development in this period was marked by noticeable changes in dramaturgy and style, these changes were partly responses to the changes in the King's Men and reflect "a pragmatic utilisation of resources as a facet of the successful business of the theatre (or, indeed, the successful production of that art)" (Power 185), which had been a major part of his concern throughout his career. In other words, the changes in his dramatic output are the results of his unchanging working attitude and principles.

Shifting back from an emphasis on Shakespeare as a playwright tied to the fortunes of a company to an approach based on his capacities as an artist, an examination of his last works yields equally ample signs of his sustained creative energy. One manifestation is the plays' carefully controlled structures. As we have seen, in all the last plays, micro structures such as vocabulary (comprising of sounds) and syntax are designed to recapitulate and reinforce macro structures such as plot manoeuvres, enabling a parallelism between the audience's experience of listening to the lines and the characters' of living through the plot.

Moreover, the self-consciousness of the linguistic style foregrounds authorial control, which is also at work on other levels of the plays' dramatic arrangements. Together, this artistic self-consciousness displayed in language and in plot enhances the audience's experience of the metadramatic, which the plays' thematic preoccupation with language and art, as well as frequent use of theatrical spectacles and plays-within-plays, also calls attention to. Different components of drama are thus geared to the purpose of one another, with language reinforcing plot and dramatic arrangements, plot and dramatic arrangements highlighting theatrical art, and theatrical art advancing discussions about language and drama. In addition, not only are Shakespeare's own linguistic and dramaturgical styles thus built into the mechanism of the plays, but those of his co-authors (Fletcher's especially) are also turned into important devices for the advancement of plot, theme and argument. Such elaborate integration suggests a degree of meticulous planning and mental effort which seem the very opposite of boredom, depression or deterioration of artistic capabilities.

Another sign of Shakespeare's continued interest in his work is his changing and developing views on the same subjects, which, again, appear to suggest an active brain rather than a lethargic one. Re-thinking older ideas and hatching endeavours for new development, or, in Bloom's words, his taking "Shakespeare the playwright [as] the source of his own continued artistic struggle to break free of self-overdetermination" ("Who" viii), are characteristic of his artistic manoeuvres in general. And the last plays are no exception. They are a continual re-exploration and re-examination of certain recurrent themes: family, forgiveness, loss and restoration, breach and reconciliation, human struggle and the dictates of fate, art, and language. Of these, the concern which runs through all six plays and is the most evidently changing and developing is that with the power, effects and possibilities of language and art. In the great tragedies they are generally signs and forces of evil and misfortune, but by the end of *Antony and Cleopatra* there is a glimpse of their glorious ability to turn death into triumph through their power of re-creation, which in *Pericles* grows into a major restorative force. In *Cymbeline* there is a balanced representation of both the good and ill which language can do, though the extraordinary dénouement, where tangles in the past are unravelled by acts of storytelling coming forth in a steady stream, seems finally to tip the balance in language's favour. *The Winter's Tale* discusses narrative and performative art. Again, there is a dramatisation of both its negative and positive effects. But once more, as in *Cymbeline*, a breathtaking final scene ultimately puts the emphasis on art as a positive force, this time by the scene's own presentation as well as its rich associations with literary works that tell of art's power to improve on nature. *The Tempest*, through Prospero's extensive use of the theatrical, is an extensive discussion of the whole range of *ars humanitas*. However, this time both language and dramatic art are presented in a predominantly negative light, with art ineffective and language frequently treacherous. *Henry VIII* continues to probe the unreliability of language, dramatising its failure to faithfully transmit the truth, and by this, also questions whether theatrical art has the ability to re-enact past events. Finally, *The Two Noble Kinsmen* takes the discussion of language and art in a new direction. Where formerly attention is focused on their effect on the listener and the viewer, this play examines their influence on the speaker and the performer. Late Shakespeare, thus it would seem, was still capable of—and making efforts towards—new departures.

A further indication of Shakespeare's active engagement with his art in his last period is the way in which topical subjects are incorporated into some of the plays. Most of his last plays are alive to contemporary events of popular interest. *Cymbeline* can be related to Prince Henry's investiture and James's political ambitions. *The Tempest* makes use of the accounts of the New World in the Bermuda Pamphlets. Both *Henry VIII* and *The Two Noble Kinsmen* are believed to reflect Prince Henry's premature death in 1612 and Princess Elizabeth's marriage to the Elector Palatine the following year and to have "shared in the mixed negative and positive emotions induced by this rapid succession of funeral and wedding" (McMullan, Introduction 64). But rather than simply referring to these incidents in a passing line or passage, or creating a safe analogy between fictional episodes and real-life events, the plays subject some of them to more creative use. This is most evident in *Cymbeline*, where, as we have seen, topical references, combined with an ambivalent authorial stand in the discussion, draws the audience in to form their own interpretation of political events as well as authorial opinions and intentions, thus enabling direct personal experience of the problematic process of report and interpretation from which the main- and sub-plots evolve. Like the carefully coordinated structures of the plays, such use of contemporary events seems to suggest intensive brainwork and masterly planning.

New development in late Shakespeare was also possibly partly stimulated by his collaborations with playwrights who had a different set of "specific capabilities" (Vickers 145). Wilkins's publications prior to his co-authorship of *Pericles* (*Three Miseries of Barbary* and *The Travels of Three English Brothers*) indicate that he had a "special interest in Mediterranean histories" (Honigmann, qtd. in Vickers 143), while Fletcher, who "belonged to the social class that frequented the more exclusive indoor theatres", "was a leading figure in the evolution of tragicomedy" (Vickers 145) and had, moreover, a knack for penning grandiose speeches and effective separate scenes. Of course, one cannot know for certain the detailed considerations which precipitated these collaborations, whether Shakespeare actively sought to collaborate or whether it was "forced" on him by the company, and whether it was his sudden interest in certain subjects that resulted in the choice of collaborators or the collaborators who triggered such interests. But there does seem to be a pattern of new development ushered in by collaboration in his last period. *Pericles*, co-authored with Wilkins, heralded a period of concentrated interest in "themes drawn from Greek and post-classical romance" (143-4). Collaboration with Fletcher on *Henry VIII* saw a shift from such themes to recent Tudor history, while *The Two Noble Kinsmen* is, in a way, essentially a rebellion against literary authority, both of established canons and of Shakespeare's own romance format.

Shakespeare's last plays are thus the result of his continued professional approach to his work and his sustained artistic development. Late Shakespeare was still trying to maximise artistic effect with available company resources, transforming his previous achievements, striving for new developments, thinking about and trying out the possibilities of language and art, making use of contemporary topics of interest or importance, and absorbing influences from other literary sources. Since continual change as a result of internal development lies at the centre of his working routine throughout his career, the last plays are duly different from his works at the other stages of his career, in the same way that the cumulative effect of such continual development distinguishes the mature comedies from his earliest works, the great tragedies from the problem plays, and so on. Moreover, as his sustained professionalism also means that he would have been responsive to external changes, and as the company's structure and composition as well as his own relationship with it did undergo a significant change around 1608, the plays produced towards the end of his career show a sharper divide from those written in the other periods, and thus a greater degree of homogeneity among themselves.

An examination of Shakespeare's last plays yields ample signs of new development which suggest that his "lateness" was, in short, marked by dramaturgical innovation, stylistic adjustment, and sustained professional strength. Late Shakespeare, like young Shakespeare and mature Shakespeare, was still aiming for and capable of "something new" (Vickers 500). If one is to sum up his lateness in a single sentence, nothing seems more appropriate—despite the feminine pronoun and possessive determiner—than to quote his own comment on Cleopatra, that triumphant master of language and theatricality whose creation heralds the coming of Shakespeare's last plays:

> Age cannot wither her, nor custom stale
> Her infinite variety. (*Antony* 2.2.240-1)

WORKS CITED

Ackroyd, Peter. *Shakespeare: The Biography.* 2005. London: Vintage Books, 2006. Print.

Aristotle. *Poetics.* Trans. S. H. Butcher. Project Gutenberg, 2008. Web. 25 Dec. 2012.

Barber, C. L. and Richard Wheeler. *The Whole Journey: Shakespeare's Power of Development.* Berkeley: University of California Press, 1986. Print.

Barber, Richard. *The Knight and Chivalry.* 2nd ed. Ipswich: The Boydell Press, 1974. Print.

Barton, Anne. "'Enter Mariners Wet': Realism in Shakespeare's Last Plays." *Essays, Mainly Shakespearean.* By Anne Barton. Cambridge: Cambridge University Press, 1994. 182-203. Print.

—. Introduction. *The Tempest.* By William Shakespeare. Ed. Anne Barton (Anne Righter). London: Penguin Books, 1968. 7-51. Print.

—. "Leontes and the Spider: Language and Speaker in Shakespeare's Last Plays." *Shakespeare's Styles: Essays in Honour of Kenneth Muir.* Eds. Philip Edwards, Ingo-Stina Ewbank and G. K. Hunter. Cambridge: Cambridge University Press, 1980. 131-50. Print.

—. *Shakespeare and the Idea of the Play.* London: Chatto and Windus, 1964. Print.

—. "Shakespeare and the Limits of Language." *Shakespeare Survey* 24 (1971): 19-30. Print.

Bate, Jonathan. General Introduction. Bate and Rasmussen, 14-63. Print.

—, ed. *The Romantics on Shakespeare.* 1992. London: Penguin Books, 1997. Print.

—. *Soul of the Age: The Life, Mind and World of William Shakespeare.* London: Penguin Books, 2009. Print.

—. "*The Tragedy of Cymbeline.*" Bate and Rasmussen, 2240-4. Print.

—. "Writ by Shakespeare: The Intrinsic Power of the Countess Scene in *Edward III.*" *Times Literary Supplement* 17 Jan. 1997: 3. Print.

Bate, Jonathan and Eric Rasmussen, eds. *The RSC Shakespeare: The Complete Works.* Oxford: Macmillan Publishers Limited, 2007. Print.

Beer, Gillian. *The Romance.* London: Methuen & Co. Ltd., 1970. Print.

Bellette, A. F. "Truth and Utterance in *The Winter's Tale.*" *Shakespeare Survey* 31 (1978): 65-75. Print.

Benson, Larry D. "*The Knight's Tale.*" *The Riverside Chaucer.* 3rd ed. Ed. Larry D. Benson. Oxford: Oxford University Press, 2008. 6-7. Print.

Bentley, G. E. "Shakespeare and the Blackfriars Theatre." *Shakespeare Survey* 1 (1948): 38-50. Print.

Bergeron, David M. "Creating Entertainment for Prince Henry's Creation (1610)." *Comparative Drama* 42 (2008): 433-49. Print.

—. "*Cymbeline*: Shakespeare's Last Roman Play." *Shakespeare Quarterly* 31 (1980): 31-41. Print.

Berry, Edward I. "*Henry VIII* and the Dynamics of Spectacle." *Shakespeare Studies* 12 (1979): 229-46. Print.

Bethell, S. L. *The Winter's Tale: A Study.* London: Staples Press Limited, 1944. Print.

The Bible, Authorized King James Version. Oxford: Oxford University Press, 2008. Print.

Bliss, Lee. "The Wheel of Fortune and the Maiden Phoenix of Shakespeare's *King Henry the Eighth.*" *ELH* 42 (1975): 1-25. Print.

Bloom, Harold. Introduction. Bloom, *Tempest*, xi-xiii. Print.

—. *Shakespeare: The Invention of the Human.* London: Fourth Estate, 1999. Print.

—, ed. *The Tempest* (Bloom's Shakespeare Through the Ages). New York: Infobase Publishing, 2008. Print.

—. "Who Else Is There?". Foreword. *Shakespeare and Me.* Ed. Susannah Carson. London: Oneworld Publications, 2014. vii-xiii. Print.

Bosman, Anston. "Seeing Tears: Truth and Sense in *All Is True.*" *Shakespeare Quarterly* 50 (1999): 459-76. Print.

Breggren, Paula S. "'For What We Lack / We Laugh': Incompletion and *The Two Noble Kinsmen.*" *Modern Language Studies* 14 (1984): 3-17. Print.

Bristol, Michael D. "In Search of the Bear: Spatiotemporal Form and the Heterogeneity of Economics in *The Winter's Tale.*" *Shakespeare Quarterly* 42 (1991): 145-67. Print.

Bullough, Geoffrey. *Narraive and Dramatic Sources of Shakespeare.* Vol. 8. London: Routledge & Kegan Paul, 1975. 8 vols. Print.

Butler, Martin. Introduction. *Cymbeline.* By William Shakespeare. Ed. Martin Butler. 2005. Cambridge: Cambridge University Press, 2012. 1-74. Print.

Chambers, E. K. *William Shakespeare: A Study of Facts and Problems.* Vol. 2. 1930. Reprint. Oxford: Clarendon Press, 1951. 2 vols. Print.

Charney, Maurice. "Shakespeare—and Others." *Shakespeare Quarterly* 30 (1979): 325-42. Print.

Chaucer, Geoffrey. *The Knight's Tale*. *The Riverside Chaucer*. 3rd ed. Ed. Larry D. Benson. Oxford: Oxford University Press, 2008. 37-66. Print.

Clark, Sandra. "Shakespeare's Final Phase: *The Two Noble Kinsmen* in its Context." Power and Loughnane, 124-38. Print.

Coghill, Neville. "Six Points of Stage-Craft in *The Winter's Tale*." *Shakespeare Survey* 11 (1958): 31-41. Print.

Cohen, Walter. "*The Two Noble Kinsmen*." Greenblatt et al., 3203-11. Print.

"Communicate, v." Def. II 6b. *The Oxford English Dictionary*. Third edition, 2009; online version September 2012. Web. 11 Dec. 2012.

"Condition, n." Def. 11b. *The Oxford English Dictionary*. Second edition, 1989; online version December 2011. Web. 4 Mar. 2012.

Cooper, Helen. *The English Romance in Time: Transforming Motifs from Geoffrey of Monmouth to the Death of Shakespeare*. Oxford: Oxford University Press, 2004. Print.

Crider, Scott F. "Weeping in the Upper World: The Orphic Frame in 5.3 of *The Winter's Tale* and the Archive of Poetry." *Studies in Literary Imagination* 32 (1999): 153-72. Print.

Croft, Pauline. "The Parliamentary Installation of Henry, Prince of Wales." *Historical Research* 65 (1992): 177-93. Print.

Crumley, J. Clinton. "Questioning History in *Cymbeline*." *Studies in English Literature, 1500-1900* 41 (2001): 297-315. Print.

Dawson, Anthony B. "*Tempest* in a Teapot." *"Bad" Shakespeare: Revaluations of the Shakespeare Canon*. Ed. Maurice Charney. London and Toronto: Associated University Presses, 1988. 61-73. Print.

Dean, Paul. "Dramatic Mode and Historical Vision in *Henry VIII*." *Shakespeare Quarterly* 37 (1986): 175-89. Print.

DelVecchio, Doreen and Antony Hammond. Introduction. *Pericles*. By William Shakespeare. Eds. Doreen DelVecchio and Antony Hammond. Cambridge: Cambridge University Press, 1999. 1-78. Print.

Donaldson, E. Talbot. *The Swan at the Well: Shakespeare Reading Chaucer*. New Haven and London: Yale University Press, 1985. Print.

Dowden, Edward. *Shakspere: A Critical Study of His Mind and Art*. London, 1883. Print.

"Easy, adj., adv., and n." Def. 12a. *The Oxford English Dictionary*. Second edition, 1989; online version June 2012. Web. 27 Aug. 2012.

Edwards, Philip. "Shakespeare's Romances: 1900-1957." *Shakespeare Survey* 11 (1958): 1-18. Print.

Egan, Robert. "This Rough Magic: Perspectives of Art and Morality in *The Tempest*." *Shakespeare Quarterly* 23 (1972): 171-82. Print.

Evans, Ifor. *The Language of Shakespeare's Plays*. London: Methuen & Co. Ltd., 1952. Print.

Everett, Barbara. "Reade Him, Therefore." *Times Literary Supplement* 17 Aug. 2007: 12-15. Print.

Frye, Northrop. *A Natural Perspective: The Development of Shakespearean Comedy and Romance.* New York and London: Columbia University Press, 1965. Print.

—. "Recognition in *The Winter's Tale.*" *Essays on Shakespeare and Elizabethan Drama in Honour of Hardin Craig.* Ed. Richard Holsey. London: Routledge & Kegan Paul Ltd., 1963. 235-46. Print.

—. "Romance as Masque." *Shakespeare's Romance Reconsidered.* Eds. Carol McGinnis Kay and Henry E. Jacobs. Lincoln and London: The University of Nebraska Press, 1978. 11-39. Print.

Garner, Stanton B. "*The Tempest*: Language and Society." *Shakespeare Survey* 32 (1979): 177-87. Print.

Glazov-Corrigan, Elena. "Speech Acts, Generic Differences, and the Curious Case of *Cymbeline.*" *Studies in English Literature, 1500-1900* 34 (1994): 379-99. Print.

Goddard, Harold C. "The Tempest." Bloom, *Tempest*, 172-87. Print.

Gossett, Suzanne. Introduction. The Arden Shakespeare (Third Series) *Pericles.* By William Shakespeare and George Wilkins. Ed. Suzanne Gossett. London: Methuen Drama, A&C Black Publishers Ltd., 2004. 1-163. Print.

Greenblatt, Stephen. "*Romeo and Juliet.*" Greenblatt et al., 897-903. Print.

—. "*The Tempest.*" Stephen Greenblatt et al., 3055-63. Print.

—. "Textual Note." *Romeo and Juliet.* By William Shakespeare. Greenblatt et al., 903. Print.

Greenblatt, Stephen et al., eds. *The Norton Shakespeare.* 2nd ed. London and New York: W. W. Norton & Company, Inc., 2008. Print.

Halio, Jay L. Introduction. *Henry VIII.* By William Shakespeare and John Fletcher. Ed. Jay L. Halio. Oxford: Oxford University Press, 1999. 1-61. Print.

Hazlitt, William. "The Tempest." Bloom, *Tempest*, 83-9. Print.

Herman, Peter C. "'Is this Winning?': Prince Henry's Death and the Problem of Chivalry in *The Two Noble Kinsmen.*" *South Atlantic Review* 62 (1997): 1-31. Print.

Hillman, Richard. "Shakespeare's Romantic Innocents and the Misappropriation of the Romance Past: The Case of *The Two Noble Kinsmen.*" *Shakespeare Survey* 43 (1991): 69-79. Print.

Hirst, David L. *Tragicomedy.* London and New York: Methuen, 1984. Print.

Honigmann, E. A. J. "Tiger Shakespeare, Gentle Shakespeare." *The Modern Language Review* 107 (2012): 699-711. Print.

Houston, John Porter. *Shakespearean Sentences: A Study in Style and Syntax*. Baton Rouge and London: Louisiana State University Press, 1988. Print.

Howard, Jean E. "*Cymbeline*." Greenblatt et al., 2963-72. Print.

Hoy, Cyrus. "The Language of Fletcherian Tragicomedy." *Mirror up to Shakespeare: Essays in Honour of G. R. Hibbard*. Ed. J. C. Gray. Toronto, Buffalo and London: University of Toronto Press, 1984. 99-113. Print.

Jackson, MacDonald P. *Defining Shakespeare:* Pericles *as Test Case*. Oxford: Oxford University Press, 2003. Print.

James I, King of England. *An apologie for the oath of allegiance first set foorth without a name, and now acknowledged by the authour, the Right High and Mightie Prince, Iames, by the grace of God, King of Great Britaine, France and Ireland, defender of the faith, &c. ; together with a premonition of His Maiesties, to all most mightie monarchs, kings, free princes and states of Christendome*. London, 1609. Text Creation Partnership Digital Edition. *Early English Books Online*. Web. 8 Jul. 2012.

—. "A Speach to Both the Hovses of Parliament, Delivered in the Great Chamber at White-Hall, the Last Day of March 1607." *King James VI and I: Political Writings*. Ed. Johann P. Sommerville. Cambridge: Cambridge University Press, 1994. 159-78. Print.

James, Henry. "Introduction to *The Tempest*." Bloom, *Tempest*, 121-32. Print.

Johnson, Samuel. *Johnson on Shakespeare: Essays and Notes Selected and Set Forth with an Introduction by Walter Raleigh*. London: Henry Frowde, 1908. Print.

Jones, Emrys. "Stuart *Cymbeline*." Rev. of *The New Shakespeare:* Cymbeline. Ed. J. C. Maxwell. *Essays in Criticism* 11 (1961): 84-99. Print.

Jonson, Ben. *Bartholomew Fair*. Ed. Edward B. Partridge. London: Edward Arnold, 1964. Print.

Kahn, Coppélia. *Roman Shakespeare: Warriors, Wounds and Women*. London: Routledge, 1997. Print.

Keen, Maurice. *Chivalry*. New Haven and London: Yale University Press, 1984. Print.

Kenney, E. J. "Explanatory Notes." Ovid, 381-466. Print.

Kermode, Frank. Introduction. The Arden Shakespeare (Second Series) *The Tempest*. By William Shakespeare. Ed. Frank Kermode. 1954. Surrey: Thomas Nelson & Sons Ltd., 1998. xi-xciii. Print.

—. *Shakespeare's Language*. New York: Farrar, Straus and Giroux, 2000. Print.

Kezar, Dennis. "Law/Form/History: Shakespeare's Verdict in *All Is True*." *Modern Language Quarterly* 63 (2002): 1-30. Print.

King, Ros. *Cymbeline: Constructions of Britain*. Aldershot: Ashgate, 2005. Print.

Knapp, James A. "Visual and Ethical Truth in *The Winter's Tale*." *Shakespeare Quarterly* 55 (2004): 253-78. Print.

Knight, G. Wilson. *The Crown of Life*. London: Methuen & Co. Ltd., 1947. Print.

Kott, Jan. *The Bottom Translation: Marlowe and Shakespeare and the Carnival Tradition*. Trans. Daniela Miedzyrzecka and Lillian Vallee. Evanston, Illinois: Northwestern University Press, 1987. Print.

—. *Shakespeare Our Contemporary*. Trans. Boleslaw Taborski. New York and London: W. W. Norton & Company Inc., 1974. Print.

Lawrence, William Witherle. *Shakespeare's Problem Comedies*. 2nd ed. 1969. Harmondsworth: Penguin Books Ltd., 1985. Print.

Leggatt, Alexander. *Shakespeare's Political Drama: The History Plays and the Roman Plays*. London and New York: Routledge, 1988. Print.

Lief, Madelon and Nicholas F. Radel. "Linguistic Subversion and the Artifice of Rhetoric in *The Two Noble Kinsmen*." *Shakespeare Quarterly* 38 (1987): 405-25. Print.

Mackail, J. M. *Lectures on Poetry*. London: Longmans, Green and Co., 1911. Print.

Magnusson, A. Lynne. "The Collapse of Shakespeare's High Style in *The Two Noble Kinsmen*." *English Studies in Canada* 13 (1987): 375-90. Print.

Mardock, James and Eric Rasmussen. "What Does Textual Evidence Reveal about the Author?". *Shakespeare Beyond Doubt: Evidence, Argument, Controversy*. Eds. Paul Edmonson and Stanley Wells. Cambridge: Cambridge University Press, 2013.111-20. Print.

Maus, Katharine Eisaman. "*Coriolanus*." Greenblatt et al., 2793-800. Print.

Maxwell, J. C. Introduction. *King Henry the Eighth*. By William Shakespeare and John Fletcher. Ed. J. C. Maxwell. Cambridge: Cambridge University Press, 1962. ix-xxxvii. Print.

McDonald, Russ. "Poetry and Plot in *The Winter's Tale*." *Shakespeare Quarterly* 36 (1985): 315-29. Print.

—. "Reading *The Tempest*." *Shakespeare Survey* 43 (1991): 15-28. Print.

—. *Shakespeare and the Arts of Language*. Oxford: Oxford University Press, 2001. Print.

—. *Shakespeare's Late Style.* Cambridge: Cambridge University Press, 2008. Print.

McMullan, Gordon. Introduction. The Arden Shakespeare (Third Series) *King Henry VIII (All Is True).* By William Shakespeare and John Fletcher. Ed. Gordon McMullan. London: Methuen Drama, 2000. 1-199. Print.

—. *Shakespeare and the Idea of Late Writing: Authorship in the Proximity of Death.* Cambridge: Cambridge University Press, 2007. Print.

—. "What Is a 'Late Play'?". *The Cambridge Companion to Shakespeare's Last Plays.* Ed. Catherine M. S. Alexander. Cambridge: Cambridge University Press, 2009. 5-27. Print.

Mikalachki, Jodi. "The Masculine Romance of Roman Britain: *Cymbeline* and Early Modern English Nationalism." *Shakespeare Quarterly* 46 (1995): 301-22. Print.

Mowat, Barbara A. *The Dramaturgy of Shakespeare's Romances.* 1976. Athens: The University of Georgia Press, 2011. Print.

Nicholl, Charles. *The Lodger: Shakespeare on Silver Street.* London and New York: Allen Lane, 2007. Print.

Nuttall, A. D. *Shakespeare the Thinker.* New Haven and London: Yale University Press, 2007. Print.

—. *William Shakespeare:* The Winter's Tale. London: Edward Arnold, 1966. Print.

Orwell, George. "Politics and the English Language." *The Collected Essays, Journalism and Letters of George Orwell.* Vol. 4. Eds. Sonia Orwell and Ian Angus. London: Penguin Books, 1968. 156-70. 4 vols. Print.

Ovid. *Metamorphoses.* Trans. A. D. Melville. 1986. Oxford: Oxford University Press, 2008. Print.

Pafford, J. H. P. "Appendix I: Miscellaneous Longer Notes." The Arden Shakspeare (Second Series) *The Winter's Tale.* Ed. J. H. P. Pafford. London: Methuen & Co. Ltd., 1963. 163-72. Print.

—. Introduction. The Arden Shakespeare (Second Series) *The Winter's Tale.* By William Shakespeare. Ed. J. H. P. Pafford. London: Metheun & Co. Ltd., 1963. xv-lxxxix. Print.

Pepys, Samuel. *The Diary of Samuel Pepys* (Excerpt). Bloom, *Tempest*, 45. Print.

Pitcher, John. Introduction. The Arden Shakespeare (Third Series) *The Winter's Tale.* By William Shakespeare. Ed. John Pitcher. London: Arden Shakespeare, Bloomsbury Publishing Plc., 2010. 1-135. Print.

"Portage, n.1." Def. 1 and 2a. *The Oxford English Dictionary.* Third edition, 2006; online version December 2011. Web. 21 Feb. 2012.

Potter, Lois. Introduction. The Arden Shakespeare (Third Series) *The Two Noble Kinsmen*. By John Fletcher and William Shakespeare. Ed. Lois Potter. London: Methuen Drama, 1997. 1-129. Print.

—. *The Life of William Shakespeare: A Critical Biography*. Oxford: Wiley-Blackwell, 2012. Print.

Power, Andrew J. "Late Shakespeare, Late Players." Power and Loughnane, 172-86. Print.

Power, Andrew J. and Rory Loughnane, eds. *Late Shakespeare, 1608-1613*. Cambridge: Cambridge University Press, 2013. Print.

Prior, Roger. "The Life of George Wilkins." *Shakespeare Survey* 25 (1972): 137-52. Print.

Rowe, Nicolas. *Some Account of the Life of Mr. William Shakespeare* (Excerpt). Bloom, *Tempest*, 57. Print.

Sahel, Pierre. "The Strangeness of a Dramatic Style: Rumour in *Henry VIII*." *Shakespeare Survey* 38 (1985): 145-151. Print.

Said, Edward. *On Late Style*. London: Bloomsbury, 2006. Print.

Schoenbaum, Samuel. *William Shakespeare: A Compact Documentary Life*. Oxford: Clarendon Press, 1977. Print.

Schreiber-McGee, F. "'The View of Earthly Glory': Visual Strategies and the Issue of Royal Prerogative in *Henry VIII*." *Shakespeare Studies* 20 (1988): 191-200. Print.

Shakespeare, William. *Antony and Cleopatra*. Greenblatt et al., 2643-721. Print.

—. The Arden Shakespeare (Second Series) *Cymbeline*. Ed. J. M. Nosworthy. 1995. London: Cengage Learning, 2007. Print.

—. The New Cambridge Shakespeare *Cymbeline*. Ed. Martin Butler. 2005. Cambridge: Cambridge University Press, 2012. Print.

—. *Cymbeline*. Greenblatt et al., 2947-3054. Print.

—. *King Lear* (A Conflated Text). Greenblatt et al., 2493-567. Print.

—. *The Life of Henry the Fifth*. Greenblatt et al., 1481-548. Print.

—. *The Most Excellent and Lamentable Tragedie, of Romeo and Iuliet. Newly Corrected, Augmented, and Amended: as It Hath Bene Sundry Times Publiquely Acted, by the Right Honourable the Lord Chamberlaine His Seruants*. London, 1599. *Early English Books Online*. Web. 1 Jun. 2014.

—. *A Midsummer Night's Dream*. Greenblatt et al., 849-96. Print.

—. *Much Ado About Nothing*. Greenblatt et al., 1416-70. Print.

—. *The Tempest*. Greenblatt et al., 3064-115. Print.

—. *Titus Andronicus*. Greenblatt et al., 408-63. Print.

—. *The Tragedy of Coriolanus*. Greenblatt et al., 2802-80. Print.

—. *The Tragedy of Hamlet, Prince of Denmark.* Greenblatt et al., 1696-784. Print.
—. *The Tragedy of King Richard the Third.* Greenblatt et al., 547-628. Print.
—. *The Tragedy of Macbeth.* Greenblatt et al., 2579-632. Print.
—. *Troilus and Cressida.* Greenblatt et al., 1859-935. Print.
—. *The True Tragedy of Richard Duke of York and the Good King Henry the Sixth (3 Henry VI).* Greenblatt et al., 326-97. Print.
—. *The Winter's Tale.* Greenblatt et al., 2892-961. Print.
Shakespeare, William, and George Wilkins. The Arden Shakespeare (Third Series) *Pericles.* Ed. Suzanne Gossett. London: Methuen Drama, 2004. Print.
Shakespeare, William, and John Fletcher. *All Is True (Henry VIII).* Greenblatt et al., 3129-201. Print.
—. The Arden Shakespeare (Third Series) *King Henry VIII.* Ed. Gordon McMullan. London: Methuen Drama, 2000. Print.
—. *The Two Noble Kinsmen.* Greenblatt et al., 3213-86. Print.
Shannon, Laurie J. "Emilia's Argument: Friendship and 'Human Title' in *The Two Noble Kinsmen.*" *ELH* 64 (1997): 657-82. Print.
Shapiro, James. *Contested Will: Who Wrote Shakespeare?* London: Faber and Faber, 2011. Print.
Sherman, Anita Gilman. *Scepticism and Memory in Shakespeare and Donne.* New York: Palgrave Macmillan, 2007. Print.
Sidney, Philip. *The Defence of Poesy.* In *The Library of the Old English Prose Writers.* Ed. Alexander Young. Vol. 2. Cambridge, 1831. 3-88. 9 vols. Print.
Siemon, James Edward. "Noble Virtue in *Cymbeline.*" *Shakespeare Survey* 29 (1971): 51-61. Print.
Smith, Jonathan. "The Language of Leontes." *Shakespeare Quarterly* 19 (1968): 317-27. Print.
Snyder, Susan and Deborah T. Curren-Aquino. Introduction. *The Winter's Tale.* By William Shakespeare. Eds. Susan Snyder and Deborah T. Curren-Aquino. 2007. Reprint. Cambridge: Cambridge University Press, 2012. 1-72. Print.
Spencer, Theodore. "*The Two Noble Kinsmen.*" *Modern Philology* 36 (1939): 255-76. Print.
Strachey, Lytton. "Shakespeare's Final Period." *Books and Characters.* London: 1922. Web. 31 May 2013.
Sutherland, John. *A Little History of Literature.* New Haven and London: Yale University Press, 2013. Print.

"Tale, n." Def. 5a. *The Oxford English Dictionary.* Second edition, 1989; online version September 2012. Web. 3 Dec. 2012.

Tanner, Tony. *Prefaces to Shakespeare.* Cambridge, Massachusetts and London, England: The Belknap Press of Harvard University Press, 2010. Print.

Teramura, Mira. "The Anxiety of *Auctoritas*: Chaucer and *The Two Noble Kinsmen.*" *Shakespeare Quarterly* 63 (2012): 544-76. Print.

Thomas, Keith. "Age and Authority in Early Modern England." *Proceedings of the British Academy* 62 (1976): 205-48. Print.

Thompson, Ann. *Shakespeare's Chaucer: A Study in Literary Origins.* Liverpool: Liverpool University Press, 1978. Print.

Tinkler, F. C. "*Cymbeline.*" *Scrutiny* 7 (1938): 5-20. Print.

Tompkins, J. M. S. "Why Pericles?" *The Review of English Studies* New Series 3 (1952): 315-24. Print.

Traversi, Derek. *Shakespeare: The Last Phase.* London: Hollis & Carter, 1954. Print.

"Trifle, n." Def. 1. *The Oxford English Dictionary.* Second edition, 1989; online version September 2012. Web. 4 Dec. 2012.

Van Doran, Mark. "The Tempest." Bloom, *Tempest*, 138-45. Print.

Van Es, Bart. *Shakespeare in Company.* Oxford: Oxford University Press, 2013. Print.

Vickers, Brian. *Shakespeare, Co-Author: A Historical Study of Five Collaborative Plays.* Oxford: Oxford University Press, 2002. Print.

Waith, Eugene M. *The Pattern of Tragicomedy in Beaumont and Fletcher.* New Haven: Yale University Press, 1952. Print.

Warren, Roger. Introduction. *Cymbeline.* By William Shakespeare. Ed. Roger Warren. Oxford: Clarendon Press, 1998. 1-77. Print.

"Welcome, n.1, adj., and int." Def. A. *The Oxford English Dictionary.* Second edition, 1989; online version December 2011. Web. 22 Feb. 2012.

Wells, Stanley. "Shakespeare and Romance." *Later Shakespeare.* Eds. John Russell Brown and Bernard Harris. London: Edward Arnold, 1966. 48-79. Print.

Welsh, Andrew. "Heritage in *Pericles.*" *Shakespeare's Late Plays: Essays in Honour of Charles Crow.* Eds. Richard C. Tobias and Paul G. Zolbrod. Athens: Ohio University Press, 1974. 89-113. Print.

Whitenack, Judith A. "Don Quixote and the Romances of Chivalry Once Again: Converted *Paganos* and Enamoured *Magas.*" *Cervantes: Bulletin of the Cervantes Society of America* 13 (1993): 61-91. Print.

Wilkins, George. *The Miseries of Enforced Marriage* (The Malone Society Reprints). Oxford: Oxford University Press, 1963. Print.

Wilson, Elkin Calhoun. *Prince Henry and English Literature*. Ithaca & New York: Cornell University Press, 1946. Print.

Wright, George T. *Shakespeare's Metrical Art*. Berkeley, Los Angeles and Oxford: The University of California Press, 1988. Print.

INDEX